Field Manual for the Archaeology of Ritual, Religion, and Magic

Field Manual for the Archaeology of Ritual, Religion, and Magic

C. Riley Augé

berghahn
NEW YORK · OXFORD
www.berghahnbooks.com

First published in 2022 by
Berghahn Books
www.berghahnbooks.com

Library of Congress Cataloging-in-Publication Data

A C.I.P. cataloging record is available from the Library of Congress
Library of Congress Cataloging in Publication Control Number: 2022016086

British Library Cataloguing in Publication Data

A catalogue record for this book is available from the British Library

ISBN 978-1-80073-503-3 hardback
ISBN 978-1-80073-504-0 ebook

https://doi.org/10.3167/9781800735033

Contents

Figures

Tables

Introduction

The biggest obstacle concerning religion, ritual, and magic encountered by archaeologists or other professionals involved in excavation, survey, or historical renovation or preservation projects is the lack of comprehensive knowledge about the material signatures of ritualistic, religious, or magical practices. The *Field Manual for the Archaeology of Ritual, Religion, and Magic* provides not only specific examples of the material culture associated with a wide range of ritualistic, religious, and magical practices, but it also includes instructions and models for recording at all sites to include data that may, with further analysis, indicate such practices.

The information presented in this book is meant to be both a resource for particular ritualistic, religious, and magical forms of material culture as well as a springboard for understanding and recognizing the ubiquitous and often embedded nature of people's beliefs in the material culture of their daily lives. The format is designed for users to find information quickly from lists, charts, tables, guides, and forms rather than from long sections of narrative text. It is also designed so that relevant sections can be easily cross-referenced to accommodate research of particular artifact and site types, attributes, or ethnic associations that can then be extended into ethnological comparative studies. While primarily designed for archaeologists, it is also a valuable resource for other professionals and avocational workers such as building renovators, historic preservationists, and construction workers who often encounter intentionally concealed objects (ICOs) and markings that constitute ritualistic or magical material culture. This book aids anyone discovering ICOs or other ritual and magic indicators in the identification of such finds and provides a mechanism for their documentation.

Skimming through the Table of Contents one can quickly see the range of topics covered in this manual. Each chapter is divided into specific categories of ritualistic, religious, or magical material culture, sites, associations, and references. Each chapter begins with a brief summary of the particular topic and important points for the researcher to consider. Additionally, extensive resource and reference listings provide directions for researchers to find further information on any given aspect of ritual, religion, and magic relevant to archaeological investigation and interpretation. Chapter 9 "Forms and Templates" provides archaeologists with a variety of recordation forms that may be used as is or modified for their particular sites and/or projects.

The manual, while not professing to contain every instance, material, or form of ritualistic, religious, or magical practice, should provide researchers with a broad and detailed understanding of the manifestation of these practices in order to more confidently recognize, record, and interpret such elements in the archaeological record.

THE BASICS: WHAT EVERYONE SHOULD KNOW

Before delving into greater details and specific categories, this brief primer highlights the basic concepts one should know about the material culture of ritual, religion, and magic. It is followed by the top eleven "Most Common Ritualistic, Religious, and Magical Tropes" used in expressions of these beliefs and practices and "Common Attributes of Ritualistic, Religious, and Magical Material Culture."

- All cultural/ethnic groups use material culture to express their beliefs.
- In contexts of culture contact through trade, migration, conquest, colonialization, or religious conversion, expressions of belief may be appropriated or hybridized from one of the groups by individuals or communities of the other group.
- Not all unknown, enigmatic, or supposedly anomalous objects are ritualistic.
- Not all rituals contain religious, spiritual, or supernatural association or meaning.
- There are several types of ritual: religious, magical, political, judicial, military, social, personal, educational, entertainment, etc.
- An object's ritualistic, sacred, or magical power or designation is often context specific.
- For many cultures, ritualistic, religious, and/or magical belief and praxis is inseparably interwoven with everyday thoughts, tasks, and behavior.
- While there are distinct separations between sacred and profane or secular spaces in some situations, this is not always the case.
- The objects and symbols used in ritual, religion, and magic are usually part of larger systems of associated meanings rather than existing as isolated items.
- Ritualistic or magical objects are often found in groups of associated items.
- Evidence of religious or magical belief may manifest as an absence of material culture or through apparently mundane everyday lifestyles and choices.
- Magical objects can be virtually anything.
- The key sacred or powerful aspect of a religious, ritualistic, or magical object may not be the form or subject of the object itself but rather some particular attribute (e.g., its color, material, shine, etc.) of the object.

- Sensory experience is an important aspect of religious, ritualistic, and magical practice and is often intentionally materially created or manipulated for maximum effect.
- Ritual is performative, which means that beyond utilized objects, there may also be archaeological signatures of performance spaces and activities.
- Objects, fossils, and structures from ancient eras are often reinterpreted by more recent people and incorporated into their religious, ritualistic, or magical practices.
- Evidence of magical belief and practice may lie outside the assumed boundaries of an archaeological site (e.g., culturally modified trees or rocks in the woods or mirror shards in a stream beyond a village boundary).
- All religious practice has some material element(s): objects, structures, or spaces.
- Religious belief or notions of the sacred often include entire landscapes of interrelated sites, features, and sensory elements.
- In many cases it is difficult or impossible to identity or confirm sacred sites based on archaeological evidence alone; context and additional strands of information are required for corroboration.
- Anthropomorphism is a key aspect of most ritual, magical, or spiritual beliefs and is expressed through material objects.
- Some religious, ritualistic, or magical practices have gendered aspects that must be understood in their respective cultural contexts.
- Some objects may be simultaneously or alternately magical and quotidian.
- Plants are likely the most varied and widely used materials in ritual, religion, and magic.

MOST COMMON RITUALISTIC, RELIGIOUS, AND MAGICAL TROPES

If time and resources do not allow for a thorough consideration of any potential ritualistic, religious, or magical material signatures at the site under excavation, but you want to at least be cognizant of the most likely objects, spaces, or practices that may occur at any site regardless of time period, geographic place, or culture, then these are what you should be on the lookout for.

1. Foundation and Abandonment Sacrifices

The practice of offering sacrifices at the time of a building's construction or renovation stretches across the world and through the millennia. Foundation sacrifices were common in religious, political, and residential buildings. The purpose of these offerings was manifold: to appease the spirits of the place and propitiate their goodwill; to ensure the structure's future integrity; and to protect the inhabitants from evil and misfortune. These objects could be embedded in the fabric of the structure's walls or foundation stones: placed in cellars or subfloor spaces; situated under the floorboards; buried under door sills or threshold stones; entombed under hearth stones; or placed in post holes. The earliest foundation sacrifices involved human and/or animal victims. Later, representative substitutions sufficed in the form of figurines, coins, images, horns, skulls, eggs, written measurements of a person's shadow (or the rod or tape used in the measuring), clothing items, books, and written inscriptions. Other common foundation sacrifices consisted of sharp objects (often metal) like weapons, agricultural tools, scissors, or knives. At the time of abandonment, similar offerings were made and included in the fill matrices. Related to abandonment sacrifices is the practice of termination ritual wherein buildings, features, or burials are intentionally destroyed, defaced, overbuilt, or desecrated by an incoming conquering society.

2. Threshold and Boundary Treatments

The most common placement for magical or religious objects or elements is at some threshold space or along boundaries of designated areas. These treatments can be for protection; to demarcate sacred zones or designate the portals between human and spirit realms; to define tribal or cultural boundaries; to elicit divine blessings for fertility of crops/livestock or people; or to indicate areas of spiritual danger. Thresholds and boundaries can be human-made features (e.g., doorways, windows, gates, chimney holes and hearths, roofs, corners, fences, field perimeters, etc.) or natural features (e.g., caves, springs, rivers, mountains and buttes, gaps and divides, forests, etc.).

3. Eggs

Eggs, natural or made from alternative materials, are probably the most ubiquitous and universal of all ritualistic, religious, and/or magical objects. They are used in virtually every context and for every ritualistic, religious, and/or magical purpose. They incorporate the three most often associated ritual colors (white, red, and black), and they often have related divine or magical numeration (e.g., three, six, nine). Eggs are used in rites and practices of protection, maleficium, divination, offering, sacrifice, fertility, and cosmological representation. They are often placed under thresholds, over doors and windows, in walls and under floors, hanging from rafters or ceilings, buried in fields, placed in trees, placed in or on graves. The color of the eggs or the hens who lay them is significant. The most frequently expressed egg colors are white, red, black, green, or multicolored designs. It is often dictated that ritually or magically used eggs have to come from black or white hens. Eggs are found in many contexts, including: mortuary features, religious structures, agricultural fields, livestock shelters, domiciles, water sites, and ceremonial sites. Eggs used ritualistically can occur as natural eggs, fashioned from wood, wax, glass, porcelain, clay, stone, jade, or papier mâché, or depicted as images in paintings, carvings, and needlework.

4. Elementals (Air, Water, Earth, Fire)

The four primary components of the natural world play important roles in all belief systems. Some systems emphasize particular elementals (e.g., Zoroastrianism is characterized by its focus on fire and water). Others integrate all the elementals throughout their rituals and practices. The elementals often are believed to function as vehicles of fertility, purification, or communication with the spirit world. They can be incorporated into ritualistic, religious, and magical practice in their natural forms or they can be represented through symbols or symbolic materials. Ritual or sacred space is often situated near water sources and/or where other elemental forces are accentuated. (See Chapter 6 "Ritualistic, Sacred, and Magical Landscapes" for specific examples).

5. Spatiality

Virtually all religious, ritual, and magical beliefs and applications have some spatial association. This spatial construct may include definite boundaries: a demarcation of sacred and profane spaces and/or areas of perceived danger or spiritual power. The space may be small and confined or extend over a vast landscape (e.g., pilgrimage routes). The spatial construct can be highly complex and incorporate ideas of right/left, up/down; front/back; in/out; above/under; and male/female with other notions of accessibility, authority, and space. The space may represent a miniaturized version of the cosmos and contain measurements, orientations, and structural arrangements mimicking or auspiciously aligning with the structure and power of the spiritual world. Some archaeological evidence of this special spatiality may be nothing more than the pounded ground or tracts left from activities like circumambulations or pilgrimage routes or traces of moveable features used to delineate spaces used for particular ritualistic, religious, or magical practices. Spatiality is also an important aspect of proximity, arrangement, and orientation of associated objects. In some instances, the spatiality component manifests through the non-endemic occurrence of natural materials like stone, fossils, shells, and plants. These objects, referred to as manuports, have been intentionally transported by humans from their naturally occurring location as talismans, amulets, or spiritually powerful objects that retain a connection with their original location, often over vast distances.

6. Intentionally Concealed Objects (ICOs)

In both religious and magical practices, powerful or sacred objects are intentionally hidden within the structural fabric of a building, buried, or submerged in water. These objects may be votive offerings, sacrifices, or magically protective agents. In the case of the latter, they usually occur in and around hearths and chimneys, door and window thresholds, walls and floors, roofs and rafters, and cellar spaces, but may also be found in tree crevices, under stones, or buried under paths and crossroads. Building renovators and other workmen are the most likely to encounter ICOs, but archaeological excavation can also reveal these hidden magical objects. Both religious and magical markings can occur in places dimly lit or visually inaccessible (e.g., high above the line of vision or underneath areas not normally viewed); while not technically hidden, they are intentionally concealed due to their obscured placement. ICOs can manifest in a variety of forms: sharp objects (often metal) like weapons, agricultural tools, scissors, or knives; desiccated/mummified animals (cats, rats and mice, chickens, frogs, etc.); animal skulls and skeletons; worn out footwear and clothing; perforated or broken objects like coins and swords; curse tablets; and precious objects like coins and jewelry. Additionally, they can be symbols and markings incised, painted, or burned into a hidden or visually inaccessible area.

7. Binding

The notion that tying up or binding by some means (bands, chains, cords, knots, ribbons, rope, shackles, stakes, string, strips of cloth, tape, etc.) has a direct spiritual or metaphysical power is seen in many cultures. The binding may be literal with materials used to physically restrain or tie an object, individual, or animal or a part thereof (e.g., knots tied in horses' manes or tails) or it may be expressed through sympathetic associations such as tying knots in a cord to render someone sterile or creating intricate patterns in needlework to trap malign forces. This binding may also be represented or enacted through weaving, braiding, lacing, or twisting. Moreover, binding applies to the encircling of objects, features, or buildings with chalk, chains, cords, rope, etc. This encircling is related to ideas of a spiritually or magically protective circle that both protects the encompassed element from preternatural forces and designates it as under the control and influence of those doing the circling/binding. Binding elements are found in a wide range of rituals including those associated with love, marriage, sexuality, fertility, birth, death, healing, sacrifice, cursing, blessing, divination, discovery of witches, trapping evil, and fear of revenants, among many others.

8. Repetition

Ritual practices are virtually never a "one-off" affair. Their efficacy is often dependent on numerous iterations, and those iterations are frequently patterned repetitions. Commonly, the patterns are based on numerology with repetitions occurring according to particular ascribed numbers such as three, seven, or nine. The repetition patterns can manifest in several ways: the ritual may be enacted a specific number of times; key objects or symbols may occur in repeated numbers or patterns; the ritual may need to be repeated over a series of days or at different times during the day; a series of individuals may repeat the ritual; or particular symbols may be repeated across a range of surfaces, objects, and contexts.

9. Bodily Fluids

The fluids contained in or secreted from the human or animal body frequently play important roles in religious, ritualistic, and magical practices. The different fluids (e.g., blood, menstrual blood, milk, phlegm, saliva, semen, tears, urine) are attributed particular properties and symbolic meanings related to their colors, odors, functions, or means of production. These substances can be used in both beneficent and maleficent rituals. Because they are all aspects of living bodies, they represent life or the life force in various ways; this powerful connection to the well-being of individuals makes these elements preferred and potent components in sympathetic magic and other rituals.

10. Reversal

Many cultural traditions perceive the spirit-world to be a reversed or mirror image of the earthly world of the living. Objects intended for the spirit-world or accompanying the dead to this realm may be indicated by their backward, upside-down, or reversed positioning. This is demonstrated by backwards writing on votive and curse tablets, torcs worn in reverse direction on corpses, and pots placed upside-down in burials or offering sites, or weapons and tools placed or depicted on the opposite side of their usual use.

11. Masking

Virtually all cultural groups at some point in their histories have utilized masks in various ritual enactments including religious, healing, initiation, military/

battle, mortuary, political, trance, seasonal/agricultural, hunting/fishing, and storytelling, among others. Masks were not always meant to be worn, but were also carried in processions, displayed on walls, buried in graves, sacrificed as votives and offerings, made in miniature to be carried or worn as pendants, and attached to statuary, buildings, poles, or furniture. Masks worn on the head/face could be partial, covering only a section of the face; frontal to cover the whole face; helmet-like covering the entire head; or hat-like sitting on top of the head and leaving the wearer's face exposed. They depict humans, deities, demons, animals, and spirits. The materials used to construct masks include metal (gold, silver, copper, bronze, iron), clay, wood, linen, plant fiber, cartonnage, turtle shell, jade, animal hides, skulls, leather, feathers, antlers/horns, shells, plaster, ivory, wax, and stone.

COMMON ATTRIBUTES OF RITUALISTIC, RELIGIOUS, AND MAGICAL MATERIAL CULTURE

The key sacred or powerful aspect of a religious, ritualistic, or magical object may not be the form or subject of the object itself, but rather some particular attribute (e.g., its color, material, shine, etc.) of the object. It is possible for multiple and various objects to be used as offerings, sacrifices, amulets, or other religious, ritualistic, or magical purposes. To understand their uses in these contexts requires a more detailed analysis of their shared attributes.

Colors, whether applied or as natural attributes, are either symbolically or inherently agents of spiritual or magical power. Some colors (like red and blue) are virtually universal in their association with protection against malign forces.

Hollow, concave, rounded, sickle-shaped objects generally represent female creative power, whereas **long, tapered** objects generally represent phallic, male creative power.

Intentionally "killed" objects are those items bent, burnt, perforated, torn, broken, cut, dented, melted, or smashed intentionally at the time of deposition or inclusion in a ritualistic context. By their "death," these objects enter the spiritual realm to accompany the dead to the afterlife or to work their power in the world of the spirits.

Iron and other metals (like brass, copper, silver, and gold) are commonly believed to inherently possess the power to repel evil.

Loud sounds are understood in many cultures to scare away evil spirits. To this end, many ritual practices include creating loud sounds through beating on drums, gongs, or other noise producing materials or through other means like fireworks, explosions, and gunfire.

Numbers, in many belief systems, possess inherent powers. Association with a particular number may be the defining element of spiritual or magical force attributed to an object. Three is the most common ritualistic, religious, or magical number, which is expressed in various triplicate representations or as multiples (six, nine, twelve, etc.) Other numbers also have particular meanings and associations; for example, the five-point star on the base of a rowan berry is what marks the rowan tree as apotropaic as the star is seen as a representation of the Pentangle of Solomon.

Objects comprised of multiple spiritual attributes are believed to be particularly effective or powerful as each element contributes its essence to combine with the potent essences of the other attributes.

Sharp objects (knives, weapons, agricultural tools, thorns, pins/needles, glass shards, etc.) pierce the veil between spiritual and mundane planes as well as act metaphysically to injure/destroy negative spiritual entities.

Shimmer and all its related aspects (shine, glare, glimmer, sheen, flash, sparkle, glitter, glaze, luster, flicker, iridescence, etc.) characterize the substances that absorb, emit, reflect, or refract light. This shiny quality manifests through a wide range of materials and objects: mirrors, sequins, glass, pearls, polished metal, shells, stone, tinfoil, water, textiles (silk, velvet, and satin), fire, metallic thread, gemstones, mercury, phosphorus, peacock and other feathers, butterfly and insect wings, etc.). Shimmer may symbolize or embody spiritual forces, but it may also be used to channel, control, diffract, trap, or deflect them.

Spotted (and all its variations: speckled, mottled, brindled, dappled, piebald, etc.) animals, feathers, and clothing often represented or referenced spirit-world beings. This may be related to how these coloration patterns are types of camouflage that, under different lighting conditions, can make animals and objects seem to shape shift, disappear and reappear, or waver, implying an instability or transparency of form.

CHAPTER I

Defining Ritual, Religion, and Magic

DEFINITIONS

The terms *ritual*, *religion*, and *magic* defy simplistic or definite explanation. Depending on the perspective, worldview, or theoretical focus of those attempting to define these concepts, the definitions can greatly vary in scope, detail, and emphasis. For the purposes of this manual, ritual, religion, and magic are understood as systemized practices whose symbolic and/or material forms express an underlying belief in the connection and power between the elements involved (e.g., material properties, texts, gestures, and temporal and spatial associations) and the efficacy of the desired outcome of the performance. This broad inclusionary understanding allows for consideration of those beliefs and practices that involve supernatural or spiritual elements as well as secular social or political rituals.

Rituals are structured performances with explicitly or tacitly agreed upon elements (e.g., actions, words, symbols, objects, colors, sensory experience, participants, time, and space, etc.) that create perceptions of or iterate social cohesion; enact cultural, religious, or personal identity; provide a framework and outlet for coping with life's difficulties; or marking life's milestones through rites of passage or celebration. While often associated with religious or magical beliefs, secular social or political rituals (e.g., sports, education, and military) may or may not involve elements of religion or magic.

The term *religion* usually refers to a formal belief system shared by an extended group of people. This can be restricted to one cultural group or subgroup or be as vast and far-reaching as belief systems like Christianity or Islam spanning the world in various permutations. Religions generally include a divine, spiritual, or sacred essence embodied in one or more deities who possess transhuman power and are associated in various ways with cosmic creation, human salvation and/or after-death existence, as well as influencing all aspects of daily human life. Religious practice is often highly ritualistic. In varying degrees, it may incorporate elements that can be classified as magical.

Magic, like religion, presupposes some cosmic force beyond human existence. This force may be governed by divine or demonic beings or exist inherently within particular objects, materials, or places. In all regards, it is believed to be accessible to humans and usable by them to influence various aspects of the world—mundane and spiritual. While rituals may not necessarily incorporate any magically based belief or behavior, magical practice always involves ritualized observances. It is through the ritualized proscription of objects, behaviors, gestures, and words that magic is believed to be activated.

Rituals and religious or magical practice may indicate individual beliefs and behaviors or that of larger groups from communities to transglobal organizations. A ritualistic, religious, or magical performance entails varying combinations of words, symbols, objects, gestures, and acts believed by the participant(s) to work in communion by virtue of some metaphysical relationship between those components and a naturally inherent force or power. In the case of magic, for example, this power might be the belief in sympathetic associations, in other words, that objects bearing any similarity to each other can affect each other. In formal religious services, it is divine power that is tapped and channeled through ritual performances. However, petitioning or invoking this same divine power frequently also underlies magical medicinal remedies and apotropaic charms and amulets. The proper performance of secular rituals implies a successful continuation of social structures, values, and ideals. Rituals, then, provide a multidimensional conduit through which symbolic messages and metaphysical power can flow for the participants' individual and communal benefit. The spatial, temporal, and material rules defining any particular ritual, religious practice, or magical enactment are culture and context specific.

To recognize and understand those ritualistic, religious, or magical beliefs and practices that involve a spiritual or supernatural element, it is important to realize that any belief in the supernatural constitutes a worldview that accepts the unverifiable existence of beings, forces, and influences inhabiting an invisible metaphysical realm. This realm coexists and interacts with the empirical human world in various ways, but is specifically engaged through performance of ritual, religious, and/or magical beliefs.

Religious practices usually include some ritualistic components with material or otherwise distinguishable characteristics like the embedded use of divinely attributed numbers, colors, directions, or actions that leave a trace. Magical concepts may or may not be implicated within the religious belief system and praxis; however, there will always be some manifestation of an influential, interactive relationship between humans and nonhuman forces or powers. These powers may be animistic, animatistic, or theistic, or some other conceptualization of nonhuman sentient beings or energies.

Using these broad definitions of ritual, religion, and magic, archaeologists and other researchers should understand these components of spirituality or other ritualistic behaviors are present in some form in virtually every landscape and built archaeological site. This manual will assist with the recognition and revelation of those components. As a primer, the following breakdown of the basic categories of spiritual forces provides insight into how, where, when, and why particular objects, materials, or sites outlined in the remainder of this manual were and are used as religious, ritualistic, and/or magical elements.

MAGICAL AGENCY

Magical materials, their usage, and expression differ culturally, but many traditions seem to share similar conceptualizations of magical agency. One common idea holds that evil (whatever shape it takes) can either be diverted, confused, or trapped by objects that engage its sensibilities. These objects usually capture evil's attention through complex designs, bright colors (especially red and blue), shiny or reflective surfaces, diverting or loud sounds, or imitative images (like eye beads to deflect the evil eye).

Another widespread aspect of magical belief concerns the connection between objects and victims/practitioners and their source of power. Sympathetic magic, first formalized by Edward Tylor as early as 1871 as "the association of ideas" and further developed and expounded by James Frazer in 1890 and Marcel Mauss in 1902, premised the belief that like affects like (*similus simluli*); however, their subsequent consideration of sympathetic magic revealed that it finds various expressions throughout the world. In some cases the sympathy may reside in a physical resemblance or symbolic similarity between two objects, in which case an object that looks like or is perceived to express shared qualities with another has the ability to affect the other. This can manifest in three ways: like produces like, like acts upon like, or like cures like. The object of similarity need not be concrete; abstract images or names may be sufficient. In other situations, the sympathetic notion, termed "contiguity," posits that any part of the whole represents its totality and thus any manipulation of the parts (like hair, nail clippings, etc.) will result in a like manipulation of the whole. Contiguity also refers to the apparently causal relationship between events and objects that occur either simultaneously or sequentially in the same time or space. Related to contiguity, sympathetic contagion espouses the belief that anything a person or animal has had contact with retains a direct connection with that person or animal and can be used in the same way as actual bodily parts. The final form of sympathetic magic—sometimes termed "antipathetic"—sees a correspondence between opposites. Although conceptualized as a distinct aspect of magical belief, theoretically antipathy is the underlying relationship in like cures like because the same element or quality produces the opposite effect. Today psychological studies are proving that even if people deny holding any magical beliefs, they still reveal deep-seated notions of sympathetic, contagious, and contiguous associations between humans, objects, and contamination or danger.

CHAPTER 2

Classification and Typology

CREATING CLASSIFICATION SYSTEMS

In order to meaningfully classify and record religious, ritualistic, or magical artifacts, it is necessary to understand the complex nature of this special form of material culture. These data, if not identified and classified appropriately, risk being lost within artifact classification/cataloging systems that divide artifacts according to material type, form, or pragmatic function. Objects recovered from obvious sacred and/or religious contexts are less susceptible to this risk, but even in these contexts significant elements can be overlooked or misinterpreted. In other contexts, many, if not most, artifacts evincing religious, ritualistic, or magical belief and practice are comprised of mundane materials and forms and may go unremarked or unidentified as anything but quotidian or aesthetic material culture (for further discussion of this issue see Augé 2013, 2020; Gazin-Schwartz 2001). Regardless of the context, there are several important aspects of all ritualistic, religious, and magical behaviors and associated objects that must be considered when classifying, typologizing, and recording this material:

- Where do they occur?
- What associated objects and/or attributes are involved?
- What material(s) is (are) used?
- How do they correlate to the broader landscape?
- How do they represent or objectify cosmological concepts?
- Are they related to seasonal or calendric periods or events?
- Are they related to crisis situations and contexts?
- Are they associated with occupations?
- Are they sex/gender specific or sex/gender related?
- Are they associated with formal religious contexts and authorities?
- Are they associated with informal, domestic, or other nonformal contexts and practitioners?
- Do they operate simultaneously or alternatively as both mundane and supermundane objects?
- In what ways are sensory elements involved?

- What hidden or embedded components need to be considered?
- In what ways might ideas of sacred numerology be implicated in the objects themselves or their deposition, orientation, arrangement, or association?

TWO CRITERION MODELS FOR IDENTIFICATION

To assist in answering these questions and, thus, in the proper identification and recordation of ritualistic, religious, and magical material culture, two criterion models have been developed. The first, created by Colin Renfrew and Paul Bahn (2004: 416–17), focuses on formal ritual and religious contexts. Originally developed for prehistoric sites, it equally applies to similar formal historic sites.

Table 2.1. Renfrew and Bahn's criteria for identifying ritual in archaeological contexts. *Source*: Renfrew and Bahn (2004: 416–17). Reproduced with the permission of the authors and publisher.

Focusing of Attention
1. Ritual may take place in a spot with special, natural associations (cave, grove of trees, spring, mountain top).
2. Alternatively, ritual may take place in a special building set apart for sacred functions.
3. The structure and equipment used for the ritual may employ attention-focusing devices, reflected in the architecture, special fixtures (e.g., altars, benches, hearths), and movable equipment (e.g., lamps, gongs and bells, ritual vessels, censers, altar cloths, and all the paraphernalia of ritual).
4. The sacred area is likely to be rich in repeated symbols (this is known as "redundancy").
Boundary Zone between this World and the Next
5. Ritual may involve both conspicuous public display (and expenditure), and hidden exclusive mysteries, whose practice will be reflected in the architecture.
6. Concepts of cleanliness and pollution may be reflected in the facilities (e.g., pools or basins of water) and maintenance of the sacred area.
Presence of the Deity
7. The association with a deity or deities may be reflected in the use of a cult image, or a representation of the deity in abstract form (e.g., the Christian Chi-Rho symbol).
8. The ritualistic symbols will often relate iconographically to the deities worshipped and to their associated myth. Animal symbolism (of real or mythical animals) may often be used, with particular animals relating to specific deities or powers.
9. The ritualistic symbols may relate to those seen also in funerary ritual and in other rites of passage.

Participation and Offering
10. Worship will involve prayer and special movements—gestures of adoration—and these may be reflected in the art or iconography of decorations or images.
11. The ritual may employ various devices for inducing religious experience (e.g., dance, music, drugs, and the infliction of pain).
12. The sacrifice of animals or humans may be practiced.
13. Food and drink may be brought and possibly consumed as offerings or burned/poured away.
14. Other material objects may be brought and offered (votives). The act of offering may entail breakage and hiding or discard.
15. Great investment of wealth may be reflected both in the equipment used and in the offerings made.
16. Great investment of wealth and resources may be reflected in the structure itself and its facilities.

The second model, created by the author (revised from Augé 2020: 286–87), emphasizes magical rather than religious, and mundane rather than formal practice; although, many of the criteria delineated in this model may occur in formal religious or ritual contexts as well.

Table 2.2. Criteria for identifying magic in archaeological contexts. *Source:* revised from Augé (2020: 286–87). Reproduced with the permission of the publisher.

Spatial Orientation
1. Objects or symbols often occur at boundaries perceived as permeable to danger or evil forces (e.g., doors, windows, hearths, roofs, corners, cellars, walls, fences, property boundaries, and crossroads).
2, Objects or symbols may occur in areas of close proximity to potential victims (e.g., near beds, cradles, stables/barns).
3. Placement of magical objects or symbols may correspond to the right/up/forward/male/sacred or left/down/behind/female/profane constructs or similar cultural associations.
4. Objects may be intentionally concealed (e.g., buried, walled-in, in hidden niches) or deliberately overt (e.g., attached to doors/windows, carved or painted on architectural features). May be hyperobtrusive—so obvious, no one notices.
5. Objects or symbols are often situated in household or personal space, occurring in mundane settings amidst everyday activities.
6. Orientation often corresponds with cosmologically associated directions or contains symbols to represent this directionality.
7. Elements of the landscape may work together as an integrated magical setting (e.g., plants, water, cardinal directions, caves, forests, mountains, stones, scentscapes, and soundscapes).
8. Concentrations of symbols and specially assembled and/or oriented materials in a particular structure may indicate the presence of a specialized practitioner.

(continued)

Table 2.2. Continued

Materiality
9. Objects are usually utilitarian, possibly worn beyond use or intentionally "killed" (e.g., bent, broken, folded, pierced, cut, etc.) to act in or upon the spirit world.
10. Objects may be of natural materials deemed extraordinary (e.g., holed stones) or cosmically powerful (e.g., iron, particular plants).
11. Written charms or symbols may combine verifiable religious names, words, and images with invented ones.
12. Objects or symbols may include colors as correlates to natural features (e.g., blue=water), substances (e.g., red=blood), states (e.g., black=death, spirit realm), or directions (e.g., black=left/down, white=right/up).
13. Objects and symbols may be combined into assemblages that include numerical and symbolic components with human/animal elements and natural inanimate materials.
14. Objects may include human or animal elements (e.g., fingernails, hair, urine, tails, ears, talons, skulls, carcasses).
15. Shininess or other reflective qualities of natural and human-made objects are commonly deemed effective wards against dangerous forces.

Ideological Concepts
16. The objects or symbols may express a sympathetic correlation with the dangers/ harm they are meant to affect or the people, animals, or property they are meant to protect or harm.
17. Symbol imagery and the number of objects will likely relate to cosmological number associations.
18. Images, symbols, orientation, and numerology will likely be repeated across several domains (e.g., architectural, funerary, sartorial, decorative, and landscape).

ANGLO-AMERICAN CLASSIFICATION MODELS

Beyond the criteria laid out in Tables 2.1 and 2.2, what archaeologists and other professionals in the field want and need to know concerns the actual material objects or signatures of religious, ritualistic, or magical belief and practice. They need typologies and classification models. Typologies of all the various forms and iterations of religious, ritual, or magical material culture from around the world have not been formally constructed. This manual is a start to this effort, but it is important work that archaeologists can significantly contribute to by meticulously recording their findings of such data. The following two tables (Tables 2.3 and 2.4) are extracts from more detailed classification models from Augé (2020: 175, 177) using data from sixteenth to nineteenth-century Anglo-European traditions to illustrate how to construct useful classification models of religious, ritualistic, and/or magical material culture. They consider such categories as functional groups, artifact classes and representative artifacts for those classes, artifact forms and materials, and depositional locations for those artifacts.

Typologies and classification models can take various forms and represent a range of detail and organization depending upon the "splitting" or "lumping" proclivities of the compiler. The degree of finely detailed type categories may be dictated by the needs of the particular research questions under consideration.

Table 2.3. Anglo-European apotropaic magical material culture classification model. © C. Riley Augé.

Functional Group	Artifact Class	Representative Artifacts
Agricultural	Animal hardware Farming equipment	horseshoes, horseshoe nails, horse-brasses hoes, plows, axes, sickles/scythes
Domestic	Food Food, preparation Food, consumption Food, storage Furnishings/Decorative Heating/Lighting Sewing/Needlecraft Textiles	salt cauldrons, kettles, knives, sieves plates, bowls, utensils barrels, stoneware jugs, glass bottles chairs, chests, beds, cradles, mirrors, patterns and symbols, artistic work candles, lamps needles, pins, knitting needles, scissors, thread household linens, rags, felt hearts

Table 2.4. Anglo-European apotropaic magical material culture manifestations and locations. © C. Riley Augé.

Class	Form and/or Material	Location
Bottles	glass phials, Bellarmine (Bartmann) stoneware jugs, globular wine bottles, beer and soda bottles; usually, but not always, containing pins, needles, iron nails, thorns, felt hearts, hair, fingernail clippings, urine, holy water, bones	in or under hearths; under door sills; buried along boundary lines and walls; under floors; in cellar or foundation walls; usually buried inverted
Clothing/Textile	shoes, gloves, jackets, vests, hats, cloth scraps, ribbons, swaddling clothes	in secret compartments in hearth and chimney, roof, walls, around doors, under floors; swaddling clothes, cloth scraps, and ribbons tied to trees and shrubs usually near spring or well

TYPOLOGIES OF MAGICAL OBJECTS

Creating typologies is also a useful undertaking for the identification and analysis of particular objects used in ritual, religious, or magical practices. The tables below are example typologies for three of the most common magical objects found in seventeenth to early twentieth century Anglo-European contexts from England, Europe, America, and Australia: witch bottles (Table 2.5), concealed cats (Table 2.6), and concealed footwear (Table 2.7).

The following ICO footwear typology (Table 2.7) is a depositional typology rather than a footwear classification. There are twenty-four possible types of footwear: for each Adult Female, Adult Male, Adult Undetermined, Child Female, Child Male, and Child Undetermined there are Dress Shoes, Work Shoes, Dress Boots, and Work Boots. It is important to note the left, right, or straight last of concealed shoes. M. Chris Manning's (2012) shoe typology is an example of a "lumped" or collapsed group organization. The following is an example of a "split" or expanded group typology.

Table 2.5. Witch bottle typology (of known archaeological examples). Drawings by C. Riley Augé. © C. Riley Augé.

Type	Period/ Place	Form	Material	Attributes/ Associations	Disposition
1. Bellarmine (Bartmann)	15–17th centuries, originally produced in Frechen, Germany, later also produced in England	round-bellied, long-necked jug with one handle opposite a bearded face design on neck and a seal (official or decorative) on body below face image	stoneware, brown or gray	usually, but not always, containing a combination of items including: pins, needles, iron nails or tacks, thorns, felt or leather hearts, hair, fingernail clippings, urine, holy water, bones, shells, lithics, salt, sulfur, written charms	in or under hearths; under door sills; buried along boundary lines and walls; under floors; in cellar or foundation walls; usually buried inverted
2. Onion bottle	late 17th–early 18th centuries Dutch, English	squat, round bodied bottle; free-blown so often irregular in body and/or neck symmetry	dark green glass	usually, but not always, containing a combination of items including: pins, needles, iron nails or tacks, thorns, felt or leather hearts, hair, fingernail clippings, urine, holy water, bones, shells, lithics, salt, sulfur, written charms	in or under hearths; under door sills; buried along boundary lines and walls; under floors; in cellar or foundation walls; usually buried inverted

3. Case bottle	late 17th century Dutch, English	square-sided bottles to fit neatly into wooden cases for transport	dark green glass	usually, but not always, containing a combination of items including: pins, needles, iron nails or tacks, thorns, felt or leather hearts, hair, fingernail clippings, urine, holy water, bones, shells, lithics, salt, sulfur, written charms	in or under hearths; under door sills; buried along boundary lines and walls; under floors; in cellar or foundation walls; usually buried inverted
4. Wine bottle	mid-18th century Dutch, English	long-necked, squarish bodied bottle	dark green glass	usually, but not always, containing a combination of items including: pins, needles, iron nails or tacks, thorns, felt or leather hearts, hair, fingernail clippings, urine, holy water, bones, shells, lithics, salt, sulfur, written charms	in or under hearths; under door sills; buried along boundary lines and walls; under floors; in cellar or foundation walls; usually buried inverted
5. Medicinal phial or bottle	late 17th–early 20th centuries, English, North American	small, narrow-bodied, free blown bottle or manufactured	light green or colorless glass	usually containing pins or in association with pins, other sharp objects; some have pins stuck into the outside of cork stopper	in wattle and daub walls above door lintels; under or beside walls in churches and cathedrals; buried inverted along structure and property boundaries
6. Sauterne bottle	early 19th century, English, French, North American	free blown, tall-bodied, slightly steep shoulder, pronounced kick-up, pontil scar	aquamarine glass	usually, but not always, containing a combination of items including: pins, needles, iron nails or tacks, thorns, felt or leather hearts, hair, fingernail clippings, urine, holy water, bones, shells, lithics, salt, sulfur, written charms	in or under hearths; under door sills; buried along boundary lines and walls; under floors; in cellar or foundation walls; usually buried inverted

Table 2.6. Concealed cat typology (of known archaeological examples). © C. Riley Augé.

Type	Attributes	Disposition
A – Predator and Prey	Cat is intentionally posed with or accompanied by rats, mice, or birds	subfloor or foundation spaces, often in particularly constructed concealment niches, concealed in walls, roofs, rafters, thresholds, hearths; domestic structures, churches, civic buildings
B1 – Solitary Foundation Deposit	Single cats	subfloor or foundation spaces, often in particularly constructed concealment niches; domestic structures, churches, civic buildings
B2 – Solitary	Single cats, may be associated with shoes, sharp objects, flora, dolls, books	concealed in walls, roofs, rafters, thresholds, hearths; domestic structures, churches, civic buildings
C1 – Multiple Foundation Deposit	Multiple cats	subfloor or foundation spaces, often in particularly constructed concealment niches; domestic structures, churches, civic buildings
C2 – Multiple	Multiple cats, may be associated with shoes, sharp objects, flora, dolls, books	concealed in walls, roofs, rafters, thresholds, hearths; domestic structures, churches, civic buildings
D1 – Manipulated	Single or multiple cats with severed paw or leg (often left paw)	subfloor or foundation spaces, often in particularly constructed concealment niches, concealed in walls, roofs, rafters, thresholds, hearths; domestic structures, churches, civic buildings
D2 – Manipulated	Multiple cats arranged in a cross or other formation	subfloor or foundation spaces, often in particularly constructed concealment niches, concealed in walls, roofs, rafters, thresholds, hearths; domestic structures, churches, civic buildings
E – Skeletal	Cat skull or skeleton	subfloor or foundation spaces, concealed in walls, roofs, rafters, thresholds, hearths; domestic structures, churches, civic buildings

Table 2.7. Concealed footwear typology. © C. Riley Augé.

I-Single Shoe/Boot	II-Matched Pair	III-Multiple Shoes and/ or Boots
I-a Solitary deposit, unmanipulated*	II-a Single pair, unmanipulated	**III-a Solitary deposit**
I-b Solitary deposit, manipulated	II-b Single pair, manipulated	III-a1 Mixed adult
I-c Associated deposit, unmanipulated	II-c Single pair with associated deposit, unmanipulated	III-a2 Mixed adult, one gender
I-d Associated deposit, manipulated	II-d Single pair with associated deposit, manipulated	III-a3 Mixed adult, one shoe type
	II-e Multiple pairs, unmanipulated	III-a4 Mixed adult, one gender and shoe type
	II-f Multiple pairs, manipulated	III-a5 Mixed adult and child
	II-g Multiple pairs, with associated deposit, unmanipulated	III-a6 Mixed child
	II-h Multiple pairs, with associated deposit, manipulated	III-a7 Mixed child, one gender
		III-a8 Mixed child, one shoe type
		III-a9 Mixed child, one gender and shoe type
		III-b Associated deposit
		III-b1 Mixed adult
		III-b2 Mixed adult, one gender
		III-b3 Mixed adult, one shoe type
		III-b4 Mixed adult, one gender and shoe type
		III-b5 Mixed adult and child
		III-b6 Mixed child
		III-b7 Mixed child, one gender
		III-b8 Mixed child, one shoe type
		III-b9 Mixed child, one gender and shoe type

(*continued*)

Table 2.7. Continued

Associated Deposits:	Deposition Locations:	Other Distinctions:
Objects deposited in association with footwear can be practically anything, but most often include items such as: Books (Bibles, hymnals, etc.) Paper (with names, newspaper articles) Other clothing items (hats, socks, etc.) Animals/bones (cats, chickens, eggs, etc.) Tobacco pipes Lamps Flowers and seeds/nuts Sharp implements Horse-related objects Household objects (glass, ceramics) Bottles Toys/Dolls, doll eyes Holed stones	**Accessibility**—Deposits may be in locations only accessible at the time of deposition or they may be in places where accessibility is ongoing to allow for maintenance or additions to the deposit. **Placement**—Often near chimney/hearth in domestic structures; in domestic, public, and religious buildings also found under floors, in walls, rafters, and foundations, around windows and doors, and at a point where structural additions or repairs have occurred.	**Single or Diachronic Events**—Deposits may be a one-time occurrence or be an ongoing event with footwear and/or associated materials being added over time. **Last**—Shoes may be left, right, or straight lasted. Depending on the condition of the footwear, lastedness may not be distinguishable.

Note: *Manipulation refers to cutting in half, slashing, piercing, hanging, or otherwise deliberately "killing" the shoe/boot.

GENDER AND ASCRIBING USAGE

Gender is a complex, culturally relative construction. It is often so entangled with biological sex that it is sometimes difficult to remember that gender is culturally constituted and not a simple dualistic attribution. It is important not to project assumptions of a binary, two-gender structure on past cultures. While many cultures recognize three or more gender categories within society, these third or fourth genders, "changing ones," or ungendered groups (e.g., children, eunuchs, or postmenopausal women) may be seen as special individuals and perceived as spiritual intermediaries, healers, or seers. These individuals may have particular roles in political, religious, or magical rituals.

Besides recognizing multiple gender categories and any special correlations these may have with ritual praxis, archaeologists also need to consider more mundane aspects of gender. To determine who may have used particular devices and materials requires close analysis of the site's greater context—historical, social, ideological, and cultural. This is especially important if one is attempting to tease out gendered attributions. In some contexts there are clear distinctions between male and female behaviors and associated materials; in other cases these distinctions blur, and it becomes necessary to look at underlying motivations as well as gendered tasks, activity spheres, and material accessibility. The following two tables (Tables 2.8 and 2.9) provide examples from a seventeenth-century study (Augé 2020) illustrating one approach to analyzing women's and men's variations in motivations and manifestations of magical usage. Similar analytical graphic organizers may be helpful in the interpretation of ritual, religious, and/or magical materials found in other contexts.

The key to creating classification or typological schemes for ritualistic, religious, and magical material culture is to be as inclusive as possible, providing sections for complex associations, relationships, and contexts.

Table 2.8. Correlation of women's stressful situations and the overarching fears they represent with the associated placements, forms, and functions of apotropaic strategies. © C. Riley Augé.

Situation	Placement	Form	Function	Fear/Stressor
Butter making	1) in churn or attached to churn bottom 2) attribute of churn	1) pierced or crooked coin; horseshoe; needles and pins 2) churn made of rowan wood	1–2) prevent butter from bewitchment	gender competency; inability to provide for family; inability to protect house, yard, and foodstuffs
Childbirth/ Pregnancy	1) under bed 2) hung over doors, windows, and beds 3) worn around neck 4) under pillow, on windowsill 5) on threshold	1) knife or scissors 2) flora, holed stones 3) diamond 4–5) knife	1) cut pain and ease labor 2–4) ward off incubi 5) protect infant at birth from evil forces	death in childbirth; gender competency; sexual assault

Table 2.9. Correlation of men's stressful situations and the overarching fears they represent with the associated placements, forms, and functions of apotropaic strategies. © C. Riley Augé.

Situation	Placement	Form	Function	Fear/Stressor
Building construction	1) built into chimney/hearth 2) marked on hearths, window/door sills, ceilings, furniture 3) built into walls, roofs, or foundations	1) salt-glazed bricks; clay; niche for apotropaia; geometric shapes 2) symbols, geometric shapes, words 3) witch bottles, worn shoes, dead cats, animal skulls, metal objects—horseshoes, spoons, knives, fish spears, pikes	1–3) prevent witches and other evil spirits/beings from entering the house and undermining its integrity	sociopolitical failure, lack of public authority and respect; gender competency; financial failure
Livestock endangered	1) burned in hearth 2) buried, whole, feet up away from other livestock 3) buried under threshold of barn/stable 4) burned whole, live animals away from house	1) tails, ears, hearts 2) whole animal carcass 3) dogs, cows 4) horses, cows, sheep, chickens, swine	1) to unbewitch animal 2–3) prevent bewitchment/ illness from transferring to other animals 4) to stop bewitchment	crop failure/ loss of livestock; financial failure; inability to provide for family; inability to protect property

CHAPTER 3

Ritual, Religion, and Magic Functions and Devices

The following lists provide researchers with the reasoning and purpose behind ritualistic and magical behaviors. Understanding the intentions and expectations behind the actions and associated objects may assist in locating, recognizing, or interpreting the signatures of these behaviors and their material artifacts.

DIVINATION

Basic Functions or Uses of Magic

- Determine most auspicious time for building
- Determine most auspicious time for military actions
- Determine most auspicious time for weddings or other special ceremonies
- Determine outcome of an undertaking
- Divine the presence of game animals
- Foretell the future
- Identify a criminal
- Identify a witch
- Identify future spouse
- Reveal the truth

Common Devices and Materials

- Anthropomorphic figurines and dolls
- Astrological charts
- Bird and animal entrails and parts
- Bones
- Books
- Bowls (brass, ceramic, copper, glass)
- Calendars
- Cards
- Chimney hooks
- Coins
- Colored beans
- Crystal balls
- Crystals and gems
- Dice

- Eggs
- Flour, grains, and fruit
- Gongs
- Human sacrifice parts
- Key and Bible
- Keys
- Mahjong tiles
- Mirrors
- Molten metal
- Needles
- Pearls
- Pendulums
- Plants
- Psychotropic plants/toxins
- Rings
- Salt
- Scrying bowls and mirrors
- Shears and Sieve
- Shells
- Shoes
- Shoulder blades
- Spindles
- Spinning wheels
- Statues
- Sticks (e.g., bamboo, yarrow)
- Stones
- Swords, knives, and other sharp objects
- Tea leaves and coffee grounds
- Water
- Wax
- Witch bottles

Types of Divination with Material Components

- Acultomancy/aculomancy—by needles and pins
- Agalmatonmancy—by statues
- Aichmomancy—by sharp objects
- Ailuromancy—by cats
- Alectormancy/alectromancy—by rooster sacrifice
- Alectryomancy/alectoromancy—by rooster divination
- Aleuromancy—by flour
- Alomancy/halomancy—by salt
- Alphiomancy—by barley
- Amathomancy—by sand
- Anthomancy—by flowers
- Anthropomancy—by human sacrifice
- Archaeomancy—by sacred relics
- Areolation—by altars
- Aruspicina—by entrails
- Astragalomancy—by dice
- Axinomancy—by axe
- Batraquomancy/batrachomancy—by frogs
- Belomancy/bolomancy—by arrows
- Bibliomancy—by the Bible
- Botanomancy—by burning sage or figs
- Canomancy—by dogs
- Carromancy—by melting wax
- Catoptromancy—by mirrors
- Cephaleonomancy—by boiling a donkey's head
- Chalcomancy—by striking gongs or copper bowls
- Cartomancy—by cards
- Choriomancy—by pig bladders
- Cleidomancy—by keys
- Conchomancy—by shells
- Cosquinomancy/coscinomancy—by hanging sieves
- Cottabomancy—by wine in brass bowl
- Cromnyomancy—by onion sprouts
- Cyathomancy—by cups
- Cyclomancy—by wheels
- Dactyliomancy—by finger rings

- Daphnomancy—by burning laurel wreaths
- Dendromancy—by trees (yews, oaks, mistletoe)
- Extispicy—by the remains of sacrificed animals
- Favomancy—by beans
- Fructomancy—by fruit
- Gastromancy—by crystal ball
- Geomancy—by earth
- Hakata—by dice or bones
- Hieromancy/hieroscopy—by studying a sacrifice's entrails
- Hyomancy—by wild hogs
- Ifá—geomancy patterns through palm nuts, opele, cowrie shells
- Kau cim—by bamboo
- Knissomancy—by incense
- Lecanomancy—by bowl of water
- Lithomancy—by stones or gems
- Lychnomancy—by candles
- Macharomancy—by swords or knives
- Mahjong—by Mahjong tiles
- Margaritomancy—by pearls
- Molybdomancy—by molten metal
- Numismatomancy—by coins
- Onychomancy/onymancy—by finger and toenails
- Oomancy—by eggs
- Osteomancy/ossomancy—by bones
- Orinithomancy—by birds
- Pallomancy—by pendulums
- Papyromancy—by folding paper, especially money
- Phyllomancy—by leaves
- Poe divination—by throwing stones on floor (Taoist temple practice)
- Rhabdomancy—by rods, sticks, or wands
- Scapulimancy—by bovine or caprid shoulder blades
- Scarpomancy—by old shoes
- Scatomancy—by excrement
- Slinneanachd—by animal shoulder blades
- Sphondulomancy—by spindles
- Stichomancy—by books
- Stigonomancy—by burning writing onto bark
- Tasseography—by tea leaves

FERTILITY

Basic Functions or Uses of Magic

- Ensure agricultural and pastoral fertility and abundance
- Ensure health and abundance of wild animals and plants
- Facilitate easy birthing
- Promote human fertility
- Protect unborn fetuses from physical and spiritual harm

Common Devices and Materials

- Anthropomorphic figurines with exaggerated or emphasized genitalia
- Body parts of animals seen as prolific (e.g., rabbits/hares)

- Eggs
- Figurines, carvings, or images of spirits associated with the plant world (foliate heads, tree spirit figures, grain/grass woven masks and figures, scarecrows/harvest figures)
- Figurines or images of animals associated with abundance (e.g., fish, rabbits/hares)
- Figurines or images of animals associated with rebirth or cosmic creation (snakes, turtles)
- Genitalia-shaped objects (made from clay, metal, stone, wood)
- Honey
- Images of animals (depicted in multiples) for successful hunting
- Objects made from first or last harvests of grains to sacrifice as offerings for next season's good harvest (often woven with grain sheaves)
- Symbolic imagery of plants or animals specifically used as metaphors for sexuality/fertility (e.g., daisies, rams)
- Symbolic images or objects representing the full or crescent moon (e.g., bull horns)
- Symbolic objects representing the female womb (chalices, bowls, mortars)
- Symbolic objects representing the male phallus (arrows, clubs, obelisks, pestles, spears, and other pointed objects)
- Whips (woven willow, leather thongs)

HEALING

Basic Functions or Uses of Magic

- Controlling the weather (relieve drought, flooding, etc. to heal the land)
- Cure animal afflictions
- Cure human ailments
- Eliminate agricultural infestations
- Eliminate pestilence
- Enhance agricultural fertility
- Enhance human fertility
- Prevent spread of animal diseases
- Prevention of human ailments
- Transference of human ailments
- Unbewitching animals
- Unbewitching people

Common Devices and Materials

- Animals and animal parts
- Anthropomorphic figurines and dolls
- Binding materials (rope, string, thread, tape)
- Candles
- Clothing of afflicted
- Cooking pots
- Eggs
- Ex-voto afflicted body part shapes (ceramic, clay, metal, wax, wood)
- Hazel rods
- Holy water
- Incense and censors

- Images of holy personages
- Metal pins and nails, chimney hooks
- Mortar and pestles
- Musical instruments (bells, drums, flutes, rattles)
- Pieces of hangman's rope
- Plants
- Rags/cloth
- Ribbons
- Shells
- Statues of deities or saints eroded, smoothed by the afflicted rubbing it for healing
- Stones and gems
- Symbols and numbers
- Thread
- Wooden chips or slivers from benches, doors, altars, or other sacred structures or furniture
- Wooden chips or slivers from execution structures (crucifixion timbers, gallows, scaffolds)
- Written charms, sacred textual passages, and prayers

LOVE AND MARRIAGE

Basic Functions or Uses of Magic

- Affect or impede sexual arousal
- Alter one's appearance to seem more desirable or beautiful to the object of desire
- Bind a lover or spouse to oneself
- Capture the desire or love of a chosen one
- Guarantee marital success
- Protect couple during wedding rites
- Protect and bless newlyweds crossing the threshold of their new home
- Protect loved ones on journeys
- Reveal one's future spouse
- Transfer a desired one's affection from another to oneself

Common Devices and Materials

- Badges (made of lead and depicting sexual/erotic motifs)
- Besoms (brooms)
- Brooches (silver, lead, gold; hearts, circles—often inscribed)
- Containers of bodily fluids (blood, semen, urine, menstrual blood)
- Fingernails
- Hearth chains
- Images (pictures, poppets)
- Locks of hair
- Mirrors
- Padlocks
- Philters
- Plants and floral images (e.g., daisies, roses)
- Poppets (anthropomorphic figures from clay, cloth, cord, dough, sticks, straw, wax, or wood)
- Rings (often made of lead)
- Shoes (usually worn out)
- Sheela-Na-Gig stone carvings

MALEFICIUM

Basic Functions or Uses of Magic

- Acquire power, wealth, influence, or knowledge
- Become invisible in order to commit crime
- Control victims
- Kill or harm livestock
- Kill or harm people
- Revenge upon another
- Summon demons or devils

Common Devices and Materials

- Animals and animal parts (black cocks, lizards, frogs/toads, snakes, squirrels, mice, birds)
- Blood
- Eggs
- Fingernail clippings
- Grave dirt
- Hand or finger of hanged criminal
- Hearts (human and animal)
- Human bones (especially finger bones)
- Human fat
- Lock of hair
- Miniature coffins (usually made of alder, birch, or lead)
- Piece of hangman's rope
- Poppets (anthropomorphic figures from clay, cloth, cord, dough, sticks, straw, wax, or wood)
- Rags/cloth tied in knots or twisted
- Semen
- Sharp objects (pins, knives, thorns, nails)
- Stones
- Symbols
- Urine
- Weapons (shields, spears, bows, guns, blowguns, holsters, sheaths)
- Written curses, spells

MORTUARY (see also "Mortuary" section in Chapter 5)

Basic Functions or Uses of Magic

- Appease spirits of the dead
- Mortuary materials used in protective charms or maleficium
- Prevent deceased from returning from the realm of the dead
- Protect deceased from evil spirits
- Protect living from the deceased
- Provide deceased with protection and guidance on journey to afterlife

Common Devices and Materials

- Animals and animal parts
- Anthropomorphic figurines and dolls
- Beads
- Bottles
- Bricks or stones (in corpse mouth; arranged in/around/on grave or grave marker)
- Candles
- Charcoal
- Cinnabar (also called vermillion—mercury sulphide ore)
- Coins
- Dishes (plates, bowls)
- Eggs
- Food
- Grave markers
- Jade
- Jewelry
- Mercury (also called quicksilver)
- Metal objects (made from brass, bronze, copper, gold, iron, and silver)
- Ocher
- Perforated metal discs
- Plants
- Prone, disarticulated, or impaled corpse
- Salt
- Sharp objects (stakes, scythes, knives, projectile points, spears, swords)
- Shells
- Soot
- Stones
- Symbols (on grave markers, funerary vessels, and objects; funerary clothing and textiles)
- Textile production tools (spindles, whorls, etc.)
- Weapons
- Weight or sharp object on corpse's throat/upper chest
- Wooden rods/wands (hazel, poplar, and willow)

PROPITIATION/IMMOLATION

Basic Functions or Uses of Magic

- Appease ancestors or spirits of the dead
- Assure fertility for crops
- Assure good weather (sufficient rainfall, return of the sun, etc.)
- Assure productive hunting or fishing expeditions
- Assure safe travels
- Gain power or influence
- Receive special knowledge
- Restore health of individuals, community, or livestock

Common Devices and Materials

- Altar or sacrificial stone
- Animals (goats, sheep, cattle, oxen, birds, horses, dogs, bears, foxes, deer)
- Animal figures
- Anthropomorphic figurines
- Aromatic wood
- Bent, broken, or folded objects
- Blood
- Burnt objects
- Eggs (marble, porcelain, wax, wood)
- Humans
- Incense
- Food (eggs, fruit, grain, milk, honey, beer, wine, meat)
- Metal objects (weapons, chimney hooks, coins, jewelry)
- Plants (flowers, herbs)
- Shells
- Tobacco
- Written charms, prayers, promises

PROTECTION AGAINST

Basic Functions or Uses of Magic

- Animals
- Bad luck
- Building/structural failure
- Cannibals
- Death
- Demons
- Devils
- Disease
- Drowning
- Economic failure
- Enemies
- The evil eye
- Evil forces
- Evil spirits
- Fairies
- Fire
- Ghosts, wraiths, revenants, poltergeists
- Gods, goddesses, and lesser deities
- Incubi and succubae
- Injury
- Intruders
- Law enforcement
- Lithobolia attacks
- Natural disasters (e.g., floods, earthquakes, volcanic eruptions, tsunamis, droughts, hurricanes, tornados)
- Misfortune
- Sea creatures
- Spirits of the dead
- Storms (thunder, lightning)
- Thieves
- Vampires, werewolves, or other monstrous creatures
- Witches

Common Devices and Materials

- Animals and animal parts (birds, cattle, cats, chickens, dogs, fish, frogs, horses, pigs, wolves; heads, hides, horns, teeth, hearts, claws, skulls, bones, feathers)
- Animal gear (bridles, harnesses, reins, yokes)
- Anthropomorphic figurines and dolls
- Bottles
- Bowls and plates
- Brooms
- Candles
- Cauls (often contained in a locket, jeweled case, box, or other container)
- Charcoal
- Clothing and accessories (hats, belts, scarves, aprons, etc., often with magical colors, designs, objects attached)
- Coins (bent, folded, or perforated)
- Colors
- Cooking pots
- Crosses
- Doors
- Door hardware (knockers, hinges, latches, openers)
- Eggs
- Footwear (shoes or boots worn/ damaged; usually left lasted; often children's)
- Fossils
- Garlic
- Gemstones
- Grain
- Hearts (human, animal, red cloth, heart-shaped objects, heart designs)
- Holy water
- Imagery (painted, incised, drawn, carved, embroidered, molded)
  » Animals and birds (often anthropomorphized)
  » Beggars
  » Body parts (eyes, feet, hands, legs)
  » Churns and churners
  » Deformities (burn or disease scarred, dwarfism, extreme ugliness, gigantism, hunchbacks, lameness—especially crippled legs, physically misshaped)
  » Entertainers (acrobats, animal-human hybrids, animal trainers, anthropomorphic animals, dancers, fools, jugglers, magicians, musicians)
  » Heads (demons/devils, foliate, grotesques, human, monsters)
  » Hybrids (animal-animal, animal-plant, human-animal, human-plant)
  » Knots and interlaced designs
  » Masks
  » Scatological
  » Sexual (genitalia, copulation)
  » Violence (battle, devouring, fighting, injuring, killing, maiming, wrestling)
  » Wildmen
- Incense
- Iron objects (horseshoes, nails, chimney hooks, construction hardware, blades, agricultural hardware, weapons, crosses)

- Jewelry (earrings, bracelets, necklaces, rings, often with magical gemstones)
- Keys and locks
- Knot work
- Metal discs with imagery (bracteates, jettons, tokens)
- Metal objects (made from brass, bronze, copper, gold, iron, and silver)
- Milk
- Millet
- Miniature coffins (usually made of alder, birch, or lead)
- Mustard seeds
- Musical, noisy objects (wind chimes, bells, gongs, drums, perforated coins, shells, metal plates, discs, bones, thimbles, cones, or beads)
- Numbers
- Ocher
- Papal bullae
- Piece of hangman's rope
- Pilgrim badges
- Plants
- Poppets (anthropomorphic figures from clay, cloth, cord, dough, sticks, straw, wax, or wood)
- Prayer beads (rosaries and paternosters)
- Quartz
- Rags/cloth (tied in bushes/trees, near sacred bodies of water or landscape features)
- Rice (grains and flour)
- Salt
- Sand
- Scapulars
- Scrolls
- Sharp objects (agricultural tools, ceramic shards, glass, knives, needles and pins, nails, scissors, sharpened bones, stakes, thorns, weapons)
- Shells
- Shiny, reflective objects (bottles, glass, iridescent feathers, metallic thread, mirrors, polished metal, polished stone, water)
- Statuary or figurines of symbolic animals or figures (wood, bone, clay, metal, stone, paper, straw, leather, textile, ivory)
- Stones
- Symbols (carved, written, burned, wrought, molded, drawn, painted)
- Tar
- Tattoos
- Textiles (worn, placed on altars, statuary, or other ritualized objects and spaces)
- Thread/yarn (usually red or blue: tied to animals, carried on person, sewn into linens, clothing, and other textiles)
- Water
- Weapons (bayonets, blowguns, bows, clubs, gun parts, guns, holsters, knives, projectile points, sheaths, shields, spears)
- Wine

SUCCESS

Basic Functions or Uses of Magic

- Assure fertility and adequate sun and rain for crops
- Assure productive hunting or fishing expeditions
- Assure the finding of and the abundance of wild food resources
- Ensure finding and happily retaining love
- Ensure victory in battle/war
- Influence financial/economic prosperity
- Provide an enhanced level of efficacy in daily occupations and undertakings
- Provide the winning edge in competitions
- Remove obstacles to the achievement of goals

Common Devices and Materials

- Achievement
  » Amulet bags of assorted items (e.g., bones, crystals, feathers, ocher, plant material, red thread, sharp objects)
  » Amulet jewelry (charms, pendants, pins, rings)
  » Colors of garments or objects associated with productivity (e.g., blue, gold, red)
  » Figurines of deities or spiritual animals
  » Gemstones
  » Hangman's rope to use for taming/breaking horses
  » Holed stones
  » Plant materials (acorns, luck-associated plants like four-leaf clover, psychotropic drugs for enhancing one's abilities for achievement)
- Battle/War (for more, see "Conflict" section of Chapter 5)
  » Amulet jewelry (badges, lockets, lucky symbols, pins, magical objects, religious icons and symbols)
  » Animal parts and images representing totems
  » Banners and flags with insignias
  » Enemy's possessions (clothing, hair, weapons, etc.)
  » Figures and figurines (animal, deity, or human forms made of ceramic, cloth, metal, wood, etc.)
  » Protective images and symbols painted on war vehicles
  » Red ocher on weapons and horses
  » Structures for ritual purification before battle (fasting and meditation sites, sweat lodges, temples and chapels)
  » Tinkle cones or other noise makers attached to battle gear
  » Weapons decorated with religious or apotropaic images, objects, or symbols
  » Written religious, magical, or good luck texts or printed images

- Competition
  - » Amulet jewelry
  - » Mascot figurines or images
  - » Special (not mundane) equipment or tools used only in the competition
  - » Team or group uniform, banners and flags, and/or colors
- Financial/Economic
  - » Apotropaic symbols (flora/fauna, geometric, or religious) embedded in or attached to doors, floors, hearths, roofs, walls, and windows
  - » Beckoning cats (Manoki Neko)
  - » Guardian statues or figurines flanking entrance
  - » Hangman's rope as talisman for success in gambling
  - » Small shrines
  - » Wind chimes or mobiles usually incorporating propitious colors for protection and abundance
- Hunting
  - » Altars for propitiation to prey animals
  - » Amuletic jewelry (earrings, nose piercings, necklaces, pendants)
  often made of animal claws, teeth, bone, or hair
  - » Animal bones and parts
  - » Bone and antler mounds
  - » Costumes created from animal hides, horns, antlers, and bones
  - » Designated areas for the ritual transformation into/out of prey animal
  - » Headdresses with animal components
  - » Images of prey animals (painted, carved, etc.)
  - » Robes, hoods, etc., made from animal hides
  - » Statuary or figurines of symbolic animals or figures (wood, bone, clay, metal, stone, paper, straw, leather, textile, ivory)
  - » Watercraft used for hunting (carved or painted with symbols and animal imagery)
  - » Weapons for hunting (carved, painted, covered with ocher, or made from sacred/powerful materials)

TREASURE HUNTING

Basic Functions or Uses of Magic

- Locate buried or hidden treasure
- Locate lost property
- Locate stolen property

Common Devices and Materials

- Divining rods
- Plants
- Stones/gems

CHAPTER 4

Ritual, Religion, and Magic by Ethnicity and Religion

This chapter provides lists of commonly found objects and materials used in specific ethnic and religious traditions (formal and popular) including magical practices. The lists should not be taken as conclusive, as each region or religious belief system is vast and necessarily includes many cultural groups and belief variations. Additionally, within each specific tradition individuals will use whatever substitutions they deem satisfactory if prescribed materials are not accessible. In contexts of mixed cultural traditions, it is also possible for one cultural group to appropriate or hybridize elements from another. Researchers have certainly not identified all objects or materials used in ritualistic, religious, or magical practices. For site-specific material culture see Chapter 5 "Ritual, Religion, and Magic at Particular Site Types."

Cultural Regions/Ethnicities

AFRICAN/AFRICAN AMERICAN

- Animal bones and teeth (e.g., alligator feet and teeth; raccoon penis bone)
- Animal skins
- Baskets
- Bats
- Blacksmithing (anvil, forge, hammer, fire, water)
- Beaded belts
- Beads (usually blue)
- Bells
- Binding material (red thread, yarn, string, strapping, tape)
- Bodily fluids (blood, semen, urine)
- Bottles (usually blue or green)
- Butter (and other animal fats)
- Carved animal figures
- Carved human/spirit figures (often made from a specific wood)
- Chalk
- Circles and wheels
- Colored bottles

- Consumer goods or labels as substitutes for ritualistic ideas
- Containers (bags, often red flannel; bottles, often blue or green)
- Cosmogram cross design
- Dolls
- Eggs
- Eye images
- Feather plume headdress
- Feathers
- Flywhisks
- Fingernail clippings
- Grave dirt
- Haint blue paint (usually on ceiling of porches)
- "Hands" (a charm bundle usually wrapped in red flannel with grave dirt, human finger bones)
- Holed stones
- Horn vessels (cups, bowls)
- Human bones (usually finger bones)
- Iron and iron agricultural tools
- Latticework (trellises, diamond-pattern fences and arbors, similar pattern on pots)
- Lion mane headdress
- Lock of hair
- Masks
- Mirrors and colored, mirrored spheres
- Nagelfiguren (wooden statues pierced with nails)
- Nkondi/nkisi
- Ocher
- Perforated coins or discs
- Pins or knives
- Plants
- Plates and bowls
- Red cloth
- Rock art
- Shells (e.g., conch, cowrie, turbo mollusk)
- Stones (e.g., quartz)
- Symbols (animal, anthropomorphic or therianthropic, geometric, naturalistic)
- Tree imagery
- Tubular wooden rattles (sometimes pierced with iron nails)
- Washing powder

●—●—●

ANCIENT WORLD (e.g., BABYLONIAN, EGYPTIAN, MESOPOTAMIAN, SUMERIAN)

- Amuletic figures of deities and sacred animals (made of glazed earthenware, gemstones, and precious metals)
- Amuletic jewelry (bangles, girdles, necklaces, pendants) usually of precious metals and gems
- Animal-headed canopic jars
- Astrological animals, calendars, and symbols
- Cowrie shells (natural and wrought in gold)
- Curse figures and vessels (curses inscribed on clay pots and figurines then ceremonially smashed)

- Cylinder-seals
- Elaborate burials for elites with provisions for the afterlife
- Ex-votos
- Figurines, imagery, and statuary of deities and rulers
- Gemstones (inscribed/engraved with animals, deities, symbols, or text)
- Headrests carved or painted with magical text, symbols, and protection spells
- Incense and censors
- Inscribed cylinders of gold or silver buried under four corners of new building
- Labyrinths and mazes
- Magical and sacred plants
- Magico-religious texts
- Masks
- Monumental statuary of deities and rulers
- Monumental structures (burial chambers, palaces, pyramids, temples)
- Mummification tools, vessels, paraphernalia, and preparation chambers
- Mummified humans and animals
- Musical instruments (cymbals, drums, harps, ivory and bone clappers, lutes, sistra)
- Nested coffins and sarcophagi (often painted with image of the deceased)
- Rhyta and other ritual drinking and feasting vessels
- Royal headdresses and regalia (e.g., Egyptian *Was* or *Heq* scepter)
- Sacred and magical symbols (e.g., ankh, *djed* pillars, hair sidelocks, sun and moon images, *wedjat*)
- Structures and residences exclusively for priestly caste
- Therianthropic figurines, images, and statuary
- Theriomorphic figurines, images, and statuary of deities in their animal guises
- Undecorated rock-cut cave tombs
- Wands (usually curved objects made from hippopotamus ivory and inscribed with magical text, symbols, and protective spells)
- Wax poppets with bits of intended victim's hair or nail clippings attached
- *Wedjat* (Eye of Horus)

ARCTIC/SUBARCTIC/PACIFIC NORTHWEST

- Animal bones
- Baskets
- Bone pins with human heads
- Carved animal figures (wood, bone, ivory [teeth/tusks], clay, soapstone)
- Carved dance sticks
- Carved human/spirit figures and heads (wood, bone, ivory [teeth/tusks], clay, soapstone)
- Carved weapons with symbols or anthropomorphic imagery (bone harpoon heads)
- Colors red, black, and white

- Dolls
- Drums (caribou hide, wood, cloth)
- Finger masks (wood, fur)
- Funerary costume for deceased (embroidered, patterned, decorated in predominantly black and white)
- Gut parkas (seal, sea lion, walrus)
- Hats with animal carving decorations, feathers, beads, embroidery
- Inuksuit (singular, *Inuksuk*) (stone place-marking and memorial structures)
- Ivory pipes
- Masks (often animal-shaped with a human face carved in body; animal or celestial images: made of wood or seal/caribou skin and painted with soot, minerals, berry juice, or blood; decorated with feathers, teeth, tassels, beads, attached figures)
- Miniature boats, canoes, kayaks (wood, bark, animal skins)
- Miniature paddles and spearheads
- Necklaces of various amulet figures
- Pack yokes (carved and painted with attached caribou teeth or other symbols)
- Puppets, *puguqs*, marionettes
- Seal and walrus bladders
- Shaman belts (with bells, knotted cloth, whalebone amulets, etc.)
- Shaman figures (often Theriomorphic)
- Slate mirrors with anthropomorphic attributes
- Slate plaques with incised anthropomorphic designs
- Storage boxes (whale- and seal-shaped)
- Symbols (animal, spirit, geometric; on harpoon heads, knives, ice scratchers, storage boxes, baskets, drag floats, drums, water tubs, arrow straighteners, etc.)
- Totem poles
- Trees used as hiding places for shamanic dolls (usually spruce)
- Tupilaq (grotesque spirit figurines used by shamans; wood, stone, bone)
- Whale ear bones
- Whale floats (some with quartz crystal eyes)
- Wooden spinning top with feathers

ASIAN

- Altar cloths
- Anthropomorphic and therianthropic statutes, figurines, and carvings of deities and spirits
- Bamboo sticks
- Banner poles (carved, incised, or plain)
- Banners and flags
- Beads and holed discs (often of jade)
- Beckoning cat (Maneki Neko)
- Bells and gongs
- Braided knotwork

- Brass, holed discs (sometimes with zodiacal figures/designs, auspicious animals, or written characters)
- Brocade amulet pouch (with bells, usually red and white tassels, knot, and paper insert)
- Brooms
- Byobu (usually six-paneled screens)
- Canopies
- Carp figures and images
- Colors (usually gold, red, white, green)
- Dolls (grass, straw, paper)
- Eggs
- Embroidered designs (clothing and accessories, household and religious textiles)
- Garlands
- Gold coins, bars, and pods
- Incense and censors
- Jade
- Masks
- Mercury
- Netsuke and Ojime (carved figural objects comprising part of men's traditional dress; made of ivory, wood, lacquer, clay/porcelain, rhinoceros horn, boar tusk, or cane)
- Paper images and origami shapes
- Paper "money" for sacrificial burning
- Prayer flags
- Rock art
- Shadow puppets
- Statuary or figurines of guardian figures (e.g., kitchen gods above or near stoves)
- Statuary or figurines of symbolic animals or figures (stone, clay, palm, paper) often at entrances
- Tattoos and tattooing tools
- Teahouses and teaware (Japan)
- Temples and shrines
- Tree imagery
- Triangle amulets
- Woven ropes
- Yarrow sticks

AUSTRALIAN/SOUTH PACIFIC

- Animal bone mounds (especially dugong)
- Animal bones and body parts
- Bao ancestral stone (human spirit transformed at death into a stone and kept in a communal shrine)
- Bull-roarer
- Carved "canoe god" figures
- Carved deity figures
- Dugong ear bones and skulls
- Drums (sometimes carved into magical animal shapes)
- Fish-shaped boats
- Maban (shell through which a person can listen and speak to the spirits)
- Masks
- Ngelmu books (Javanese books of magical formulae)
- Outrigger canoes

- Rock art
- Tattoos and tattooing tools
- Tjurunga (also spelled Churinga; usually oblong polished stone or wood objects used in sacred ceremonies)
- Wayang (leather or wooden shadow puppets)

EUROPEAN/AMERICAN

- Animals and animal parts (usually cats or chickens, but also dogs, fish, horse and cow skulls, mice, owls and other birds, pigs, rats, sheep and goats, squirrels, toads and frogs, wolves)
- Beads
- Bent or broken pins, knives, and swords
- Blue paint (Southern European; usually covering doors, gates, and around windows)
- Books (Bibles, grimoires, alchemical, metaphysical)
- Bottles
- Bracteates
- Candles and candlesticks
- Carved, burned, or painted symbols and initials (alchemical, astrological, botanical, geometric, metaphysical, religious, or representative of a magical object, e.g., gridiron)
- Carved, painted, or embedded geometric designs (hexafoils, circles, pentangles, spirals, triangles, wheels)
- Cauldrons and cooking pots
- Cauls (often contained in a locket, jeweled case, box, or other container)
- Clockwise spiraled or twisted designs and textiles equated with "good" vs. counterclockwise designs equated with "evil" or deviance; may also be gender associated: clockwise/male; counterclockwise/female
- Coins (e.g., bearing image of ruler, divine person, or sacred animal; altered: bent, perforated)
- Colored prayer rags tied to bushes/ trees usually at sacred water sites (springs, wells, rivers)
- Colors (usually white, black, red, and blue)
- Crosses
- Eggs
- Embroidered clothing and accessories (aprons, hats, scarves, shawls, shirts, skirts, etc.)
- Eye images
- Fossils
- Garlic
- Gemstones
- Hand images
- Hangman's rope
- Hearts (animal, cloth, and designs)
- Holed stones
- Horseshoes
- Incense and censors
- Inscribed objects with religious reference (e.g., IHS, IHC, INRI, AGLA, Ave Maria)
- Jettons

- Keys and locks
- Knotted rags, cords, or thread
- Masks
- Miniature replica iron weapons (daggers, pole axes, spears, swords)
- Mirrors
- Noisemakers (bells, drums, gridirons, rattles, whistles, wind chimes)
- Numbers (usually three, five, seven, and their multiples)
- Papal bullae
- Plants (see "Glossary of Ritualistic, Religious, and Magical Plants")
- Plates (usually containing salt)
- Poppets (dolls, human figures made of cord, wax, wood, rags, straw, or clay)
- Prayer beads (rosaries and paternosters)
- Reflective metal or stone objects
- Religious clothing/vestments
- Religious jewelry (brooches, necklaces, rings, and pins)
- Religious statues and figurines
- Religious structures (shrines, churches, temples, altars, chapels, synagogues)
- Religious textiles (altar cloths, tapestries, banners, cushions, draperies)
- Salt
- Scapulars
- Sharp/pointed metal implements (scythes, pikes, knives, scissors, nails, pins, hoes, etc.)
- Shimmering objects and materials
- Stones
- Surgical instruments for sacrifice
- Tar
- Tokens
- Tree imagery
- Worn or damaged clothing or footwear
- Woven fences (Eastern European)

LATIN AMERICAN/MESOAMERICAN

- Altars
- Animal bones and body parts
- Ball courts
- Baskets (burial and ritual offering)
- Burial urns
- Cacao
- Carved animal figures
- Carved human/spirit figures
- Ceramic vessels for offerings and sacrifices
- Colors—especially green, black, red, white, and gold
- Hand images
- Human remains
- Human skeletal imagery (emphasis on the head)
- Imagery depicting ritual (e.g., ballgame, coronation, feasting, sacrifice)
- Incense and censors
- Instruments for bloodletting and sacrifice (e.g., cactus spines, flint or obsidian blades and lancets; shark's teeth, stingray spines or obsidian replicas)
- Manatee ear bones
- Masks

- Mercury (liquid "quicksilver" or cinnabar—mercury sulfide ore—also called vermillion)
- Monumental statuary
- Mosaics (usually of turquoise and/or jade; body adornments, figurines, masks, and tablets)
- Political structures of monumental size (palaces)
- Psychotropic plants/toxins
- Rain sticks made from dead cactus tubes
- Religious statues and figurines
- Religious structures of monumental size (step-pyramids, temples, tombs)
- Sacrificial tables
- Shells (amuletic adornments; funerary beds; ritual drinking vessels)
- Skulls and skeleton figures
- Stelae, obelisks
- Stools (carved wooden Shaman seats; also miniature ceramic models)
- Stones (jade, obsidian, turquoise, etc.)
- Terraglyphs
- Tree imagery
- Tubular wooden rattles
- Tzompuntli (rack for displaying heads of sacrificial victims)

MEDITERRANEAN/CLASSICAL

- Figurines and statuary of deities
- Gemstones carved with imagery of deities, animals, mythological creatures, and text
- Human skulls modified or perforated to hang from or be attached to buildings/structures
- Incense and censors
- Jewelry (bracelets, rings, ear and nose rings, necklaces and pendants)
- Lead curse tablets
- Magical symbols and texts
- Masks
- Miniature replica iron weapons (spears, swords)
- Religious and civic structures of monumental size (temples, political ceremonial buildings)
- Therianthropic images, figurines, and statues

MIDDLE EASTERN/INDIAN

- Animal designs (embroidered, woven, dyed, painted)
- Animal figurines
- Beads
- Colors
- Eggs
- Embroidered clothing and accessories

- Evil eye beads
- Gemstones
- Genitalia imagery
- Hand images
- Henna plants and preparation vessels
- Henna tattooing tools
- Incense and censors
- Jewelry (bracelets, rings, ear and nose rings, necklaces and pendants)
- Kolams
- Masks
- Metal objects (brass, bronze, copper, iron, gold, and silver)
- Mirrors (polished metal or glass)
- Mustard seeds
- Numbers
- Qur'an
- Qur'anic inscriptions (in tile or calligraphy)
- Religious structures of monumental size (mosques, temples)
- Symbols (animal, geometric, flora)
- Textiles (prayer cloths/aprons, prayer rugs, tassels and pompoms, threshold hangings, wraps)
- Tree imagery

NATIVE AMERICAN

- Animal parts (antlers and horns, bird bones, claws, deer legs, hides, hooves, skulls, talons, teeth)
- Baskets
- Beads (bone, glass, metal, seed, shell, stone, wood)
- Beads, glass (predominately blue and white, but also yellow, green, and red)
- Burial platforms or scaffolds
- Cairns
- Carved animal figures (bone, clay, hoof, stone, wood, and sometimes with other objects like projectile points, beads, or shells attached)
- Carved human/spirit figures
- Ceremonial containers carved or molded in animal or human forms
- Circles
- Colors (usually white, black, red, yellow, and blue)
- Colored prayer cloths tied to bushes/trees
- Fasting beds
- Feathers
- Fetish necklaces of shells, beads, and carved figures
- Holed shells
- Holed stones
- Incense and censors
- Kivas
- Masks
- Medicine bundles
- Medicine wheels
- Metal buttons
- Metal firearm side plates
- Musical instruments (drums, flutes, rattles, whistles)
- Naturally formed stones or wood that resemble humans or animals

- Numbers (usually three, four, five, or seven)
- Ocher
- Painted animal figures
- Painted/decorated dog travois
- Painted geometric figures
- Painted human/spirit figures
- Petroglyphs
- Peyote
- Peyote rattle
- Pictographs
- Pipes
- Rock shelter/cliff burials

- Sage
- Stones (e.g., quartz, turquois, jade)
- Stone effigies
- Sundance lodges
- Sweat lodges
- Sweet grass
- Tattooing tools
- Terraglyphs
- Tinkle or jingle cones
- Tobacco
- Tree imagery
- Vermillion (also called cinnabar—mercury sulphide ore)

SCANDINAVIAN

- Animal carcasses, antlers/horns, bones (e.g., bears, boar, dogs, deer, elk, frogs, horses, sheep/goats)
- Belts hung with amulets
- Cauldrons
- Coins
- Drinking horns
- Drums and drum hammers
- Figurines (anthropomorphic, theriomorphic, and therianthropic deities, magic-wielders, spirits, etc.)
- Heads and head symbolism
- Hogback burial/memorial stones
- Imagery (carved, embroidered, woven, wrought of deities, dragons and other mythical beasts, "face-mask motifs," sacred animals, sorcerers, spirit beings, warriors, "weapon-dancers," etc.)
- Incense and censors (usually fir or juniper)

- Iron tools (adzes, agricultural, axes, chain links, wheel hub mounts)
- Ithyphallic figurines and objects (made of metal or wood)
- Jewelry (brooches, gemstones, pendants, rings, etc.)
- Keys
- Masks
- Miniature boats and ships
- Miniature chair/throne objects (often of precious metal)
- Picture stones
- Pouches of assorted amulets and charms (e.g., animal bones, feathers, owl pellets, tusks, etc.)
- Psychotropic plants
- Rock art
- Rune carvings on leather, wood, or stone
- Runestones
- Sacrificial vessels (buckets, cauldrons)

- Ship or boat burials
- Staff rings (iron or silver rings hung with miniature staffs, weapons, sickles, fire-steels as amulets—occurring in groups of three or more; may be multiples of single type [e.g., staffs] or

combinations of types [e.g., staffs, hammers, and sickles])
- Staffs (iron and wood)
- Weapons (full-sized and miniature replicas of axes, daggers, hammers, spearheads, swords)
- Whetstones

Religion

Religions are highly complex, variable, and dynamic, often borrowing or integrating objects or practices from other belief systems and changing through time. Many religions share similar, if not identical, material elements, but possibly with different meanings and uses; likewise, there can be a wide range of variation within one religion's sects and subsects. It is, therefore, impossible and naïve to simply provide a checklist of elements that comprehensively and unequivocally identifies a particular religion. It is also true that some religious traditions do use distinctive material elements. The following lists are meant to identify common elements associated with the major religious traditions. As always this is just a starting point for more in-depth research on your particular sites.

It must also be kept in mind that the scarcity of religious material evidence does not necessarily indicate a secular site. While some religious systems and practices are extremely ostentatious or at least overt, others are intentionally austere. This austerity may, in fact, be the signature of religious belief and practice. Clues to this absence of evidence as indicators of religious enactment include:

- Absence of or minimal use of alcohol consumption
- Absence of or minimal use of tobacco products
- Adherence to old, basic technologies even when newer technologies are affordable
- Basic foodways (basic meat cuts, non-exotic foods, plain ceramics, wooden vessels and utensils, etc.)
- Basic housing (caves, huts, stone cells, etc.)
- Few decorative objects
- Few possessions (especially if family is known to be affluent)
- Plain (often dark colored) clothing
- Plain or minimally decorated furnishings

BUDDHISM

- Altar cloths
- Amulet pendants (often ceramic) depicting Buddha or associated symbols
- Banner poles or staffs (carved, incised, or plain)
- Banners and flags
- Beads (bracelets and anklets)
- Bells
- Bodhi tree (images or plants)
- Braided knotwork
- Buddha and bodhisattva figurines, heads, statues
- Buddha relics
- Deity statues
- Dragon headed banner poles
- Canopies
- Carp images and figures (some woven out of palm leaves)
- Ch'an t'ang (special mediation chamber—Zen)
- Colors (saffron, red, white)
- Dragon/serpent gate and stairway guardian statues/figures
- Eight-spoke Wheel of Law
- Eye-bead
- Floral garlands and leis
- Gardens of sand, rocks, bridges, minimal flora
- Gates and gateways into temple complexes
- Gold coins, bars, and pods
- Gongs
- Griha (sanctuary hall for object of worship: Bodhi tree, Buddha, stupa, etc.)
- Incense and censors
- Lanterns
- Lotus flower
- Mandalas (made with colored grains of sand)
- Masks
- Murals depicting religious events and stories
- Prayer flags
- Prayers printed on paper (often contained in prayer wheels)
- Prayer wheels (metal)
- Religious clothing (saffron-colored monks' robes)
- Rock-cut cave sanctuaries and monasteries
- Saffron-colored sashes
- Shrines (miniature house and field temples)
- Singing bowls
- Statuary or figurines of symbolic animals or figures (stone, clay, palm, paper) often at entrances
- Stupas
- Symbols (bat, empty throne, foot-print, umbrella, wheel)
- Tassels
- Teachings printed on dried palm leaf strips or stone tablets
- Temples and monasteries
- Tingsha (small cymbals)
- Toran
- Tree imagery
- Vessels (various materials) for water at shrines or for washing Buddha images
- Vihara (monastery)
- Walls enclosing temple complexes
- Wooden pillars carved with Buddhist prayer

CANDOMBLÉ

- Animal sacrifices (goats, pigs, sheep, chickens)
- Cowrie shells
- Dandá (*Cyperus rotundus*, magical plant)
- Dendê (African palm oil *Elaeis guineenis*)
- Figa
- Magical plants
- Necklaces of colored glass, crystal, or ceramic beads
- Obí (Seed of African kola *Cola acuminate*)
- Otá (Sacred rock kept in ceramic pot in shrine)
- Pano-da-costa (colorful ceremonial cloth)
- Patuá (small cloth amulet bundle: sacred objects, devotional messages, and plant parts)
- Peji (small, individual shrines with offerings and sacred objects)
- Peregun (*Dracaena fragrans*; used in ceremonies)
- Rue (*Ruta graveolens*) and Ewe amin (*Lygodium volubile Sw*) (protection against evil eye)
- Terreiro (temple)
- Tobacco

CHRISTIANITY

- Acoustic jars (earthenware jars under choir stalls or in chancel and nave walls)
- Alms boxes
- Altars (stationary and portable)
- Aspergillum (holy water sprinklers)
- Aspersorium (situla) (bucket for holy water used in conjunction with aspergillum)
- Baptismal fonts
- Bells
- Bibles
- Blue domes on Greek Orthodox churches
- Boundary shrines
- Burials usually oriented east-west, with head in the west; in shared burials of married couples, the wife is usually on the left side of the husband
- Candles and candlesticks
- Chests to store communion vessels
- Church institutions (asylums, hospitals, schools)
- Clothing (hats, robes, vestments)
- Collection plates
- Colors (red, white, and blue lights; liturgical colors: white, red, violet, green, black)
- Communion food (wine, bread, wafers)
- Communion vessels (chalices, cups, ewers, plates)
- Consecration crosses (twelve painted on the walls inside and outside at consecration points)

- Crosses and crucifixes
- Eggs
- Flagellation devices (barbed or knotted whips/scourges, cat-o-nine tails, chains)
- Gemstones
- Graves oriented east-west with head in the west, feet in the east
- Holy communities (abbeys, monasteries, nunneries)
- Holy relics (cloth; human bones, hair, skin, and teeth; burial soil; nails; wood)
- Holy water and holy water fonts
- Hymnals
- Iconostasis (screen separating congregation from clergy in Orthodox church)
- Images (animals, carvings, cherubim, gargoyles, grotesques, misericords, paintings, stained glass of divine figures and events)
- Incense and censors
- Inscribed panels with scripture (wood, stone)
- Jewelry (broaches, pendants, pins, rings, rosaries)
- Labyrinths
- Monograms (IHC, IHS, INRI, XP, XPC)
- Orientation of church building generally west to east with altar at east end
- Pews
- Prayer beads (rosaries and paternosters)
- Prayer books
- Pyx (vessel to hold Eucharist bread)
- Reliquaries/chasse
- Reredoses (alabaster, painted wood panels, or stone backing for altar)
- Roods
- Rood screens
- Sacred architecture (chapels, churches, shrines)
- Scapulars
- Sepulchers
- Sexton's wheels
- Stained glass windows
- Statues and figurines of Jesus, the Virgin Mary, Saints, and Apostles
- Staves (churchwarden and banner)
- Symbols (Chi Ro, cross, double V, fish, hexafoil, pentangle)
- Textiles (altar cloths, banners, cushions, draperies, tapestries)
- Tomb effigies
- Tree imagery

CONFUCIANISM

- Carved wooden ancestor spirit tablets (comprise the household shrine altar)
- Clothing (vestments, robes, headwear)
- Colors: white, red, orange, gold
- Dragons
- Figurines and statues
- Fireworks
- Food offerings
- Giant deity effigies
- Household ancestor shrines

- Hsing tan (temple podium)
- Incense sticks and coils, and incense burners
- Number five
- Paper money and artifacts burned at burials
- Phoenix images
- Stone guardian mortuary figures
- Temples and altars
- Yin and Yang symbol
- Willow branches

DAOISM

- Clothing (vestments, robes, hats)
- Coins used for divination
- Colors: white, blue, yellow, red, orange, gold, black
- Daode jing (or Tao Te Ching), principal teachings of Daoism
- Figurines and statues of deities
- Fireworks
- Five "poisons": centipede, scorpion, snake, toad, lizard; designs on clothing and amulets
- Gendered spatial positioning: Men=East (Yang)/Women=West (Yin)
- Giant god effigies
- Incense sticks and coils, and incense burners
- Lanterns
- Number five
- Paper money and artifacts burned at burials
- Pilgrimage routes
- Sacred natural sites: caves, mountains, springs
- Symbolic paper artifacts and money
- Yin and Yang symbol

HINDUISM

- Aspergillum
- Bhoga-mandir (sacrificial pavilion)
- Colors: saffron, blue, green, yellow, white
- Dhwaja-stambia (square pillar depicting trisula—symbol of Siva)
- Embroidered, woven, or dyed designs-animals, nature, geometric (clothing and accessories, household and religious textiles)
- Figurines and statues of deities
- Fire altars
- Gemstones
- Genitalia imagery, especially vulvas and phalluses
- Ghanadvara (solid door through which temple deity manifests)
- Giant god effigies (often brightly colored)
- Gulal (brightly colored powder used at Holi, the Festival of Colors)
- Henna plants and preparation vessels
- Henna tattooing tools

- Incense and censors
- Kala (apotropaic monster head over doors and in temple niches)
- Kolams
- Mandalas
- Masks
- Mirrors
- Numbers three and seven
- Ritual water tanks and reservoirs
- Rock-cut cave sanctuaries
- Sacred trees: Bel and Butea frondosa
- Sacrificial pits (often lined with logs and marked by post holes for canopies)
- Shadow puppets
- Shiva lingam stone (also called Narmadeshwar Egg or Narmada Bana Lingam)
- Symbols (animals, eyes, footprints, geometric shapes, lotus, paisley, spirals, swastika, trees, trisula, vines, wheels)
- Temples and altars (sometimes in caves or carved into cliffs)
- Torans
- Tree imagery
- Walls enclosing temple complexes

ISLAM

- Aboveground graves
- Alms collection boxes
- Burials usually on right side with head oriented to and facing Mecca; sometimes this body position was supported by bricks or facilitated by a narrow grave shaft. Body usually shrouded but not coffined.
- Colors: green, blue
- Cresent moon symbols (often mounted on top of mosques and pointing toward Mecca)
- Evidence of religious-based dietary restrictions (e.g., absence of alcohol vessels or production, dogs, or pork; use of specific slaughtering or butchering patterns)
- Eye-beads
- Henna plants and preparation vessels
- Henna tattooing tools
- Household layout structured to separate public from private spaces, seclude women, and provide male communal space (angled doors and windows above street level restrict view into interior; female/private family space farthest away from street; guests only access front of house and have separate guest quarters or facilities)
- Mirrors (polished metal or glass)
- Mosques
- Muslim settlements traditionally had distinctive elements and layout (*medina*-outer walled precinct with *rabat* suburbs, and inner walled *casbah* citadel for ruler's residence and mosque; cemeteries usually lay exterior to the outer wall. Not all features are present in every Muslim settlement.)

- Prayer rugs
- Qur'an
- Qur'ani inscriptions (in tile or calligraphy)

- Six-pointed star motif
- Tree imagery

JAINISM

- Cloth mouth and nose-covering masks
- Cosmic wheel
- Figurines and statues of tirthan-karas (early teachers of the faith)
- Home shrines and altars
- Jain Prateek Chihna symbol

- Mandalas
- Offerings laid out in large mandala geometric formations
- Rock-cut cave sanctuaries
- Saffron
- Temples and monasteries

JUDAISM

- Amulets
  » Written charms (Biblical names; incantation; Biblical quotes; magical symbols—especially the pentagram and hexagram, straight and curved lines tipped with circles, squares, spirals, and other geometric forms, magic number squares)
  » Objects (fox tails and teeth, red coral necklaces, red thread, herbs and aromatic roots, phal-lic-shaped stones, holed stones, caul, piece of *Afikomen* Passover bread, *heh* inscribed metal plate, animal parts, rings and medal-lions, gemstones)
- Aron Kodesh (Torah ark decorated cupboard to hold Torah scrolls in the synagogue)

- Beth-knesset (house of assembly and prayer)
- Candles (votives, pairs for Shabbat and other sacred occasions)
- Colors: red, blue, white
- Eruv (fence or line to delineate Shabbat travel distance)
- Evidence of religious-based dietary restrictions (e.g., absence of pork; Kosher butchering practices)
- Genizah (cemetery, coffin, or special storeroom for retired/worn out sacred texts) .
- Incense altar
- Incense and censors
- Incense shovel or vase
- *Kabbalah* (Theosophical text)
- Kiddush cup (goblet used a part of blessing made over wine or grape juice)

- Megillot scrolls and cases (outer case metallic; inner bag for tefillin or tallit)
- Menorah (seven-branched candelabrum)
- Mezuzah (small case containing holy text attached to doorposts of houses)
- Name-magic (invoking names of angels or demons from religious texts)
- Netilat yadayim (two-handled hand washing cup)
- Numbers
- Red string bracelet
- Seder plate
- Sefer Torah (Torah scroll)
- Shards of Kiddush wedding cup
- Sherds of plate from engagement party
- Shewbread table
- Shofar (ritual instrument usually made from a ram's horn)
- Siddur (Jewish prayer)
- Silver ritual objects
- Spice box and spices
- Star of David (six-pointed star comprised of two intersecting triangles)
- Symbols (plant, figural, and geo-metric images; Menorah; incense shovel or vase; Shewbread table; Torah shrine; Ark of the Scrolls)
- Synagogues
- Tallit gadal (prayer shawl)
- Tallit katan (prayer apron)
- Tebam (reader's platform)
- Tefillin box and straps (black boxes containing holy text worn by men on head and left arm)
- Tree imagery
- Tzedahkah (collection box)
- Water vessel located at cemetery entrance/exit for washing hands
- Yadayim (singular, Yad) (Torah pointer with a small silver hand tip)

MORMONISM

- Bee and beehive symbolism
- Book of Mormon
- Divining rods
- Irrigation systems as vehicle to transform land into sacred landscape
- Moroni raising a trumpet figure (on top of temples)
- Seer stones
- Temple garments (special under-garments of rough material)
- Temples

RASTAFARIANISM

- Colors: red, green, black, and yellow
- Dreadlocks
- Ethiopian flag

- Holy Piby (the "Blackman's Bible")
- Kebra Negast (Ethiopian epic)
- Lion symbol
- Marijuana (ganja) use in rituals
- Star of David

• • •

SANTERÍA-REGLA DE OCHA (and OTHER AFRO-CARIBBEAN RELIGIONS: ESPIRITISMO, OBEAH, MYAL, QUIMBOIS)

- Agogós (metal chimes)
- Ajá (palm frond whisk)
- Animal sacrifices and blood (goats; pigeons; white, yellow, or black chickens, doves, and canaries; roosters; opossums; monkeys; sheep; oxen; deer; bulls; turtles; pigs; rabbits; quails; horses; guinea hens; black dogs; snakes; ducks; fish; calves; owls)
- Batáa (set of three sacred drums)
- Canastilleros (cabinet to house soperas)
- Candles
- Chalice (iron with little rooster finial)
- Coconuts
- Colors associated specifically with orisha (saint): red, white, gold, black, green, blue, yellow, purple
- Cowrie shells
- Eleguá (graven head of Lord of the Crossroads with cowrie shell eyes, ears, and mouth; usually of ceramic or cement placed behind entrance door)
- Elekes (beaded necklaces of different colors and shapes)
- Ewe (ritual plants)
- Foods and animals associated specifically with orisha (saint)
- Gourds
- Igbodu (altar)
- Ilé (house church)
- Iron bow and arrow
- Iron tools (swords, shovels, hammers, chains, machetes, horseshoes, railroad spikes, iron pot)
- Iruka (horsetail switch)
- Macuto (magical pouch with plants and name of "target" inside)
- Miniature keys
- Muñequitas (spirit guide dolls; muñecas de trapo—handmade cloth dolls)
- Nganga (spiritual cauldron)
- Numbers associated specifically with each orisha (saint)
- Opele (divination chain of shells, coconut pieces, and round pieces of leather)
- Otanes (sacred stones)
- Plants associated specifically with each orisha (saint)
- Resguardos (amulets made of seeds, shells, or plants)
- Sopera, iron cauldron, wooden batea, and earthenware urn (vessels to house otanes; painted in colors associated with particular saints)
- Statues of saints
- Three thrones (royal blue, white, red satin draped)
- Tobacco
- Velador (cabinet to store Eleguá and associated cauldron)

SHINTO

- Banners and banner poles
- Clothing (vestments, robes, headwear)
- Colors: red, blue, yellow, white, purple
- Ema (votive tablet hung in shrine)
- Fuda (protective amulet—wooden plaque with inscription usually hung in homes)
- Masakaki (poles to which banners are attached outside temples)
- Masks
- Mirrors
- Omamori (protective amulet—a small textile bag containing paper prayer—carried on person)
- Processional routes
- Shiminawa (large woven ropes)
- Statuary and figurines (animals, deities, spirits, and demons; often theriomorphs)
- Swords
- Temples and shrines
- Torii (ceremonial gateway, usually painted vermilion)

SIKHISM

- Altar cloths
- Altars
- Chaur, chauri, or chanwar (wooden or metal handled switch made of yak or horse's tail)
- Colors: white, blue, gold, saffron (red discouraged)
- Gurdwara (place of worship)
- Guru Granth Sahib (holy book)
- Gutka (religious handbook)
- Iconography of Guru Nanak and ten human Gurus
- Kaccha (cotton undergarment)
- Kangha (wooden comb)
- Kara (iron or steel bracelet)
- Khalsa (main symbol of Sikhism that includes khanda)
- Khanda (symbol with circle, double-edged sword, and two-curved swords)
- Kirpan (a short, curved sword)
- Nishan sahib (pennant bearing Khanda emblem)
- Palki (cushioned, canopied stand for the Guru Granth Sahib)
- Rumalas (brightly colored velvet or satin coverings for the Guru Granth Sahib)
- Temples
- Turban

VODOU

- Altars
- Anthropomorphic figures
- Asson (rattle made of calabash gourds and snake vertebra)
- Cowrie shells (*Cyprea Moneta*)
- Eleke (also called collier; various colored beaded necklace of initiates)
- Flags (embroidered and decorated with flashy elements)
- Gris-gris (small pouch, usually red, filled with herbs and other plants
- Hounfor (ritual house)
- Ikin (palm nuts for divination casting)
- Lambi (conch shell horn)
- Ngánga (burlap bag or an iron kettle to hold spirits of the dead)
- Obi (coconut husks or kola nuts for divination)
- Ogan (flattened bell)
- Opele (divination tool consisting of a chain of eight palm nut halves attached to swivels)
- Peristyle (open-sided building adjacent to hounfor altar room)
- Poteau-Legba (also Poteau-mitan; brightly painted center post of Peristyle, surrounded by altar step)
- Shakeree (also shekeré or acheré, musical instrument: yellow gourd draped in shell or bead netting)
- Supera (also awo or awo pot; porcelain soup tureen to hold or feed vodou spirits)

ZOROASTRIANISM

- Agiary (fire temple)
- Avesta (holy book)
- Baresman or barsom (bundle of twigs held by priest during worship)
- Dakhma (place of exposure for the dead or a grave)
- Disposal of dead by sky-burial exposure on high platforms or plateaus called "Towers of Silence"
- Fire braziers/urns
- Fravashi (circle with flanking wings symbol, sometimes with human figure)
- Funerary tower
- Haoma or hom (plant crushed for its juice at main act of worship; probably ephedra)
- Imagery carved in stone of deity (Ahura Mazda), priest figures, and winged guardians (fravashis)
- Incense and censors
- Kusti (woven cord worn as girdle)
- Numbers three and seven
- Rock-cut cave sanctuaries
- Shirt (pure white with small purse sewn into throat; kusti is worn over this shirt)

- Stone mortar
- Temples
- Tree imagery

- Zand (translation copy of Avesta with commentary)

Ritual and Magical Practitioners

The above objects are general lists, making no distinction between specialist and lay practitioners. The following list is provided as a guide to help identify potential specialists. This list is not ethnically or culturally specific nor does it refer to religious leaders from large, formalized religions. The practitioners here are known by various titles and perform various suites of rituals. They are known as healers; medicine men/women; conjurers; cunning folk; seers; shamans; or oracles. Their ritual and magical materials may include:

- Animal costumes
- Animal parts (antlers/horns, bones, claws, feathers, hair/fur; heads, hearts, skins, teeth)
- Beads (often blue or white glass, bone, ivory, or shell)
- Bells
- Binding material (rope, sinew, string, thongs, thread)
- Blades (brass, gold, obsidian, silver, etc.)
- Bodily markings or adornments
- Crystals and gemstones
- Depiction in rock art
- Designated dwelling (may be different in form or materials from other residences; may be situated apart from others or specially oriented; may be situated in association with water, special trees, or other natural elements; may be marked by special symbols and objects or threshold delineators)
- Dolls

- Evidence of alternative gender identity (common in Shamanic traditions)
  » Clothing (mixed male/female items or transvestism)
  » Grave goods that are often associated with opposite gender
  » Reversal of left (female)/ right (male) depictions or orientations
- Fans
- Figurines (anthropomorphic, theriomorphic, or therianthropic) (bone, ceramic, clay, ivory, metal, stone, straw, wood). May be intentionally broken or self-exploding
- Headdresses
- Holed stones
- Incense and censors
- Instruments for bloodletting and sacrifice (e.g., cactus spines, flint, obsidian, or metal blades and lancets; shark's teeth, stingray spines or obsidian replicas)

- Marionettes and puppets
- Masks
- Metal boxes (small caskets suspended from chains)
- Metal ornaments
- Musical instruments (drums and drumsticks, flutes, gongs, rattles, tambourines, whistles)
- Osteophones (large animal bones used as percussion instruments)
- Perforated coins or metal discs
- Piercing objects (awls, needles, pins, thorns)
- Pigments
- Plant materials (including psychotropic substances)
- Pouches or bundles
- Shells (e.g., conch, cowrie, turbo mollusk)
- Special clothing (robes, shawls, tunics, hoods, etc.)
- Spoons (perforated or marked with symbols or images)
- Staffs
- Stools or chairs
- Swords
- Symbolic markings
- Tattoos and tattooing kits (blades, bone needles, cactus spines, quills)
- Texts with mystical content, imagery, and symbols
- Tobacco pipes
- Vessels for ritual beverages, libations, foods, offerings

CHAPTER 5

Ritual, Religion, and Magic at Particular Site Types

This chapter will look at the types of material culture that may be found at sites where ritual, religious, or magical practices occur. The sites are divided into the following groups:

- Ceremonial (feasting, food procurement, fraternal, initiation, military, political)
- Conflict (battlefields, fortifications, jails/prisons, prisoner camps/ detention centers; punishment/judgment sites)
- Monumental (burials, cultural markers, guardian statuary, memorials)
- Mortuary (burials, cemeteries, cenotaphs)
- Mundane/Secular (commercial, domestic, institutional, occupational, public)
- Sacred (pilgrimage, religious features, religious structures, sacrifice)
- Underwater (inundated sites, shipwrecks)

CEREMONIAL

Ceremonial rituals, whether secular or sacred, are group affairs. They usually have a dedicated space that can accommodate the participants and may also have other embedded ritualistic components like orientation, viewshed, soundscape, and lighting that contribute meaning and sensorial experience to the events marking them as significant and supramundane. Ceremonies are generally highly performative and may leave traces of dances, processionals, and enactments as well as audience spaces. It is common for ceremonies to extend over significant periods of time and for distant groups to congregate for the event; therefore, ceremonial sites likely contain evidence for these temporary increases in population.

Feasting and Ritual Food Vessels and Features

- Baskets and plates for food offerings
- Chalices
- Communal drinking vessels (multiple handles)
- Cups (may have special form, decoration, or material to designate cup as a ritual vessel)
- Intentionally "killed" drinking, eating, or libation vessels on, around, or at threshold of ritual site
- Jugs
- Long-spouted jugs
- Oversized cooking pots
- Oversized roasting spits and cooking pits
- Plates/platters and bowls (ceramic, metal)
- Rhyta/rhyton (horn-shaped drinking vessel often with animal head or body—metal, stone, ceramic)
- Shell vessels
- Stone relief vessels

Other Feast-Associated Material Culture

- Altar or structure for reverencing animal(s) or plant(s) featured at feast
- Designated furniture (platforms, seating, tables, thrones)
- Designated space (courtyards, feast halls)
- Distinctive faunal remains (different and/or exotic animals; different cuts of meat; larger quantities)
- Distinctive floral remains (different and/or more exotic plants; larger quantities)
- Large refuse pits to accommodate the increased volume of feasting detritus
- Musical instruments (drums, flutes, gongs, harps, horns, rattles, trumpets)

Food Procurement

- Dedicated structures or spaces for rituals for participants undergoing temporary transformation into/ back from prey animal
- Musical instruments (bells, cymbals, drums, gongs, rattles)
- Open area for ritualized hunt enactment
- Open area for ritualized rain or sun dances or ceremonies
- Pottery, glass, wood, or metal vessels for purification or offering
- (alcoholic drinks, anointing oils, blood, incense, plant or animal sacrifices, paints, psychotropic drugs, water)
- Purification features (fire, water)
- Ritual clothing/costumes made from animal or plant elements representing the prey or foodstuff desired
- Rock art (caves, cliff faces, rock shelters) depicting hunting/fishing scenes

- Sacred mound of accumulated animal prey bones (may be specific elements: skulls, ear bones)
- Sacrificial features and tools (altars, stone platforms)

- Sympathetic figures (animals or plants) representing the animal or plant spirits
- Temple or shrine for agricultural, hunting/fishing, or elemental spirits/deities

Fraternal (Freemasons, Elks, Woodsmen, etc.)

- Dedicated buildings usually displaying embedded symbolism of the organization
- Embedded numerological measurements and geometric configurations (on both a micro scale, e.g., grave markers, and a macro scale, e.g., urban landscape)

- Ritual regalia (clothing, daggers, drinking vessels, metal insignia pins, signet rings, swords)
- Symbols (inscriptions, marquetry, mosaics, paintings, tiles, etc. in/on buildings, funerary markers, memorials)

Initiation

- Isolated or dedicated structures to house initiates
- Musical instruments (bells, cymbals, drums, gongs, rattles)
- Open area for dancing or ritualized combat
- Pottery, glass, wood, or metal vessels for purification or other initiation substances (alcoholic drinks, anointing oils, blood,

incense, paints, psychotropic drugs, tattooing inks, water)
- Purification features (fire, water)
- Sacrificial features and tools (altars, stone platforms)
- Subterranean (caves, tunnels) ritual spaces
- Tattooing, mutilation, piercing, or scarification tools

Military

- Banners and flags with poles
- Burials with military/warrior regalia, equipment, or weapons
- Carved walls, posts, processional features depicting military victories
- Cemeteries
- Designated areas for spectators and participants in rank or award conferring rituals

- Display of war booty (precious objects from foreign areas)
- Open area for marching, choreographed parade, inspection, or ritualized combat
- Posts or post-holes for military banners/flags/emblems
- Triumphal arches

- Victory stones (type of oracle to predict/ensure victory in battle)
- War memorial structures

Political

- Appropriation of previous ruler's structures and objects, reused in such a way to express the conqueror's might and legitimacy
- Banners and flags with poles
- Coronation and sacrificial scaffolds
- Coronation stones, stelae, Menhirs, etc. used to determine legitimate rulership
- Dance platforms
- Dedicated structures to house foreign dignitaries
- Defacement of previous ruler's imagery
- Deliberate destruction of conquered society's religious and significant sociopolitical ceramics and other material culture
- Deliberate destruction (termination ritual) of conquered society's political and religious structures and possibly overbuilt with conqueror's own structures
- Designated vantage point for political personages to address audience or be viewed by audience (usually elevated and strategically defensible)
- Escutcheons and escutcheon pins
- Extensive or exclusive use of gold and/or silver for objects and decoration
- Feast associated areas
- Intentional desecration of conquered society's burials and destruction of burial goods
- Open area or processional corridor for parading of political personages
- Posts or post-holes for political banners/flags/emblems
- Ritualized sacrifice and burial of previous ruling family, often entombed in/under new ruler's structures/temples
- Screens (panels with symbols and imagery and wrought in precious materials)

CONFLICT

Places where combat has occurred or that are related to antagonistic behaviors often have ritualized aspects. Sometimes these sites have direct correlations to religious beliefs or sacred sites. In other cases, the implementation of magical amulets for protection in such situations may be visible at either a cultural or individual level. Evidence of religious and/or magical belief manifests in several ways in these contexts.

Battlefield

- Animal claw necklaces
- Animal figurines or images (black cats and pigs were popular across Europe in World War I and World War II; totemic or sacred spirit animals are common across several cultures)
- Animal parts (bones, claws, feathers, talons, etc.)
- Banners and flags with poles
- Battlefield corpses with severed heads, feet, and/or hands
- Beads
- Bells and clinking, jingling noise makers
- Belts and bandoliers
- Black cat images, buttons, and badges
- Cactus spikes
- Catholic saints medals
- Chains and belts of strung coins
- Coin sewn into clothing
- Cotton shirts covered with magical circles, squares, and other symbols
- Cotton waist cords
- Crooked, bent, or perforated silver coins
- Crosses/crucifixes (commercially made or crudely fashioned out of virtually any material including bullets)
- Designs sewn onto uniforms
- Effigies
- Elephant with raised trunk, images and charms
- Enemy images and masks attached to weapons
- Enemy's clothing and/or possessions
- Figa red coral charm
- Fumsup mascots
- Graffiti of religious or magical images, symbols, or texts in shelters and trenches
- Hand of Fatima and other hand images, charms, and badges
- Headdresses
- Helmets decorated with protective and/or divine imagery
- Horse gear decorated with protective/empowering colors, beads, designs, or materials
- Horseshoe images, charms, and badges
- Human hair or body parts (heads, bones)
- Hunched back figurine charm
- Lockets (containing photos or hair)
- Magical plants and their images or as charms
- Masks
- Medals
- Miniature cast metal figures of Joan of Arc and the Virgin Mary in little lead capsules
- Modified personal gear marked with religious or magical symbols (e.g., padlocks, canteens, cigarette lighters)
- Modified weapons or ammunition (marked with religious or magical symbols, made into amulets, or added to amulet pouches)
- Number thirteen charms (while associated with bad luck by British and American soldiers, it was considered a lucky number by the French)
- Padlocks

- Painted magical symbol or image on nose or tail of aircraft
- Paper charms with divine images or text
- Pig images and charms
- Pouches or bundles containing assorted materials (amulets)
- Prayer beads, rosaries, paternosters
- Protective images and symbols painted on war vehicles
- Rabbit's foot
- Religious icons or paintings
- Religious or amulaic jewelry (crosses, crucifixes, medallions, miniature weapons, pendants, pins/badges, rings)
- Rings made from coffin nails
- Robes and hats with attached amulets of bones, leather, metal, etc.
- Scabbards and holsters embroidered, beaded, or studded
- Shells
- Shields (constructed from or decorated with enemies' hair; materials, images, symbols, colors of power, etc.)
- Sites for pre-battle ritual dancing and mock battles
- Situated in proximity to sacred, spiritually powerful source (physical proximity or viewshed)
- Stones with protective associations
- Swastika badges, charms, keys, and pins
- Sweat lodges (usually situated on periphery of battle camp)
- Tattoos
- Touchwood charms
- Weapons or armor decorated with protective/empowering colors, beads, designs, or materials
- Wooden charms with inscriptions wrapped and sealed

Fortifications

- Banners and flags with poles
- Chapel, shrine, or meditation space
- Guardian statues or carvings at entrances and corners
- Inscriptions (charms, curses, prayers, symbols)
- Iron hardware (symbolic imagery on hinges, studding, etc.)
- Measurements and/or orientation associated with religious or cosmological modeling
- Open area for marching, choreographed parade, inspection, or ritualized combat
- Protective or divinely associated colors (e.g., white, blue, red)

Jails/Prisons

- Dedicated chapel/worship space or structure
- Inscriptions/graffiti (charms, curses, prayers, symbols)
- Modified personal gear marked with religious or magical symbols (e.g., padlocks, canteens, cigarette lighters)
- Open area for inspection

Prisoner Camps/Detention Centers

- Cemeteries (may include prisoner-generated burial or commemorative practices)
- Inscriptions/graffiti (charms, curses, prayers, symbols)
- Modified personal gear marked with religious or magical symbols (e.g., padlocks, canteens, cigarette lighters)
- Open area for marching, choreographed parade, or inspection
- Stones inscribed with religious or magical text

Punishment or Judgment Sites

- Crossroad execution sites (cages, gallows, etc.)
- Designated areas for stoning accused, convicted, or sacrificial victims
- Designated tree or grove for hangings
- Hilltop execution sites (crucifixions)
- Judicial ordeal features and objects (braziers for heating iron devices; beds of hot coals; vessels for hot water)
- Open-air assembly grounds marked by bridges, crossroads, mounds, or standing stones
- Oracle statues or stones
- Religious objects (holy texts, icons, relics, vestments, etc.) used to ascertain guilt and/or punishment
- Religious relics used for oath-taking at religious or civic locations
- Thrones, dais, or special chairs for the judge(s)/oracles/juries
- Water bodies (boggy fens, cenotes, ponds, etc.) for execution or sacrificial drowning
- Water bodies (cisterns, lakes, ponds, rivers, wells) for swimming tests or dunking to identify witches or the guilty

MONUMENTAL

The use of monumental structures and features often expressed the power and bigger-than-life stature of divine beings or demigod rulers. Extremely tall structures also implied a closer proximity to the heavenly realm. While some monumental structures and features were places of ritual gathering and ceremony, others were understood as spiritually dangerous or taboo.

Types of Monumental Structure and Features

- Cenotaphs
- Dolmens
- Heads
- Henges/circles
- Long barrows
- Menhirs
- Monoliths
- Obelisks
- Picture stones
- Pyramids
- Rune stones
- Statues (deities, guardian spirits, demons, divine rulers, etc.)
- Stelae
- Stupas
- Totem poles

Possible Characteristics

- Access or visibility controlled, restricted, or obstructed through additional structural or landscape elements
- Alignment with other ritualistic structures or landscape features
- Associated burials
- Associated offerings, caches, or hordes
- Astronomical alignments
- Decorated with images and/or text (carved, incised, pecked, painted)
- Embedded numerological significance of measurements or enumeration of features
- Oversized proportions
- Processional pathways/routes (possibly demarcated with additional features)
- Situated away from habitation sites
- Situated on the landscape for maximum visibility
- Situated, oriented, and aligned according to cosmological ideology
- Spatially designated as a sacred/ritual site
- Statues may be anthropomorphic or therianthropic and representing gods, rulers, ancestors, or guardian spirits
- Stone material may have been chosen for its color, texture, or sound-producing qualities

MORTUARY

Mortuary contexts and associated material culture can include tremendous variation that can be found as close to home as burials under the house floor to isolated sites of excarnation or inhumations on mountain tops. This section lists several potential sites of ritualistic, religious, or magical associations with a variety of mortuary contexts.

General

Regardless of the culture or belief system involved, most burial (inhumation) customs will include one or more of the following components:

- Basket
- Body wrapping (blankets, cere-cloths, cloth strips, plant materials, etc.)
- Coffins, caskets, and/or vaults
- Coffin/casket hardware
- Demarcation between burial area and mundane space (i.e., fence, wall, hedge, etc.)
- Facilities for offerings (food preparation, burning offerings, flowers and other plant offerings)
- Facilities for preparation (areas for washing, wrapping, or dressing corpse; desiccation pits; mummification rooms)
- Facilities for purification (anointing, praying, smudging, washing)
- Funerary jars/urns
- Grave markers identifying deceased
- Patterned orientation and/or alignment of burials
- Religious or magical grave marker symbols
- Shrouds (with or without shroud pins or buttons)

Cemetery Types

- Battlefield
- Catastrophe
- Church
- Ethnic
- Family
- Institutional
  » Asylum
  » Hospital
  » Orphanage
  » Poorhouse (almshouse)
  » Prison
- Lodge
- Military
- Monastic
- Paupers'
- Private
- Public
- Religious sect
- Royal
- Socioreligious deviant

Other Burial/Mortuary Sites

- Agricultural fields (e.g., rice paddies)
- Caves, rock shelters, or shafts
- Church interment (in crypts, floors, walls, or ossuaries)
- Cliff side sites
- Grain silos or pits
- House subfloors
- Ice field excarnation sites
- Mountain top excarnation sites
- Residential yards
- Suspended from trees
- Water bodies (cenote, ocean, river, well)

Other Mortuary Elements Indicating Ritual and Belief

- Ash residue from cremation (in urns/jars, on altars, on pyre platforms, or in burials)
- Burial contains more than one individual (intentionally manipulated and positioned; jumbled together; or only particular body parts [e.g., skulls] are included)
- Burial opened and corpse burned
- Corpse buried with amulets (beads, plants/food, coins, figurines, perforated discs, shells, ocher)
- Corpse buried with animal(s)
- Corpse buried with pebbles in its mouth
- Grave floor treatments: covered with chalk, charcoal, or shell
- Light (candle, lantern, oil lamp, lightbulb) or symbol of light placed on grave, and used in homes and sacred buildings in funerary rites
- Maiden's garlands (flora, textile, and decorative elements constructed into a memorial hanging hung in churches)
- Mummification (intentional process or natural desiccation)
- *Os resectum* (small body part— usually finger joint—to be retained after cremation and interred separately, usually in an inscribed vessel)
- Plate or bowl of salt in or on grave
- Processional paths or dancing circles in cemeteries
- Scratch marks on inside of coffin or on bricks in wall burials indicating live burial
- Segregation (based on age, gender, ethnicity, religion, social deviance, cause of death)
- Shoe on coffin lid
- Under floor, under thresholds, or in-wall burials

Atypical Burials (e.g., Deviant, Non-normative, Irregular)

Burials that deviate from the norm generally indicate the deceased was considered special in some way (positively or negatively) that set the individual apart and required differential burial treatment in accordance with that special status, identity, or ability. These atypical treatments often were associated with ideologies of the afterlife or spirit world and the appropriate rituals to assist the deceased's spiritual passage and/or avert any harmful consequences to the living.

- Burial contains more than one individual (intentionally manipulated and positioned; jumbled together; or only particular body parts [e.g., skulls] are included)
- Burial is not on alignment with other graves
- Burial trappings (e.g., coffin, grave goods) absent or distinctly different
- Corpse bound (ankles, neck, wrists)
- Corpse buried at crossroads
- Corpse buried face down (prone)
- Corpse buried outside the boundaries of burial ground
- Corpse buried with animal(s)
- Corpse buried with sharp blade or weight on neck
- Corpse buried with stone or brick in mouth

- Corpse impaled, beheaded, or disarticulated
- Corpse in sitting position
- Corpse or grave weighted down
- Corpse subjected to overkill
- Disposal different than norm (inhumation vs. cremation; in water vs. in the earth)
- Grave either significantly shallower or deeper than norm
- Mass graves (e.g., prisoners of war, sacrifices)
- Scratch marks on inside of coffin or on bricks in wall burials indicating live burial
- Segregated groups (criminals, unbaptized)

Grave Goods

Many human burials are accompanied by additional inclusions of material culture. Some of these are simply the deceased's clothing or surviving remnants of that attire (e.g., belt buckles, fragments of cloth, etc.), but often in burials of the past objects representing religious or magical beliefs completed the assemblage. These objects could signify a wide range of notions both about the person and his or her position and/or role in society in addition to ideas about the proper ritualistic protocols necessary for that person's journey to and placement in the afterlife. Even mundane remnants like the clothing or clothing fasteners mentioned above reveal an aspect of mortuary ritual that reflect the importance of social status, gender, and social role.

Most often archaeologists use grave goods to interpret one or more of the following about the corpse(s):

- Age or age group
- Degree of social normalcy or deviance (criminality, disability, foreignness, monstrosity, etc.)
- Gender and/or sex
- Occupation or social role
- Sacrifice victim
- Social class/position
- Social status
- Transition from one belief system to another

It would be impossible here to list every example of items used as grave goods, not to mention listing them according to their respective cultures, geographical regions, or time periods. The particular items constitute an immense scope, but the following list provides some of the general categories and most common specific artifacts used as grave goods across time and culture:

- Alcoholic substances and related containers (amphorae, buckets, cauldrons, drinking cups and horns, flagons, tankards, vats)
- Animal remains (claws, mummies, skeletons, skulls, teeth, etc.)
- Arrowheads and other projectile points
- Baskets

- Beads
- Bone needles
- Books (evidenced by surviving clasps, hasps, or hinges)
- Candles
- Censors
- Chains and manacles
- Charcoal
- Cinnabar
- Clothing
- Coins
- Crosses and crucifixes
- Dice
- Drinking and eating vessels (ceramic, glass, metal, wood)
- Drinking horns and mounts
- Eggs (carved or decorated in a variety of materials)
- Feathers
- Figurines and dolls (animal, anthropomorphic, and theriomorphic)
- Foodstuffs
- Fossils
- Furniture (full-sized or miniature models: beds, chairs, couches, footstools, thrones)
- Gaming pieces
- Grinding stones, vessels, and tools
- Grooming articles (combs, tweezers, etc.)
- Heart-shaped amulets, lockets, pendants, symbols
- Hematite
- Incense
- Jewelry (arm bands, bracelets, earrings, hair rings, head bands or circlets, necklaces, pendants, rings, torques)
- Keys and locks
- Liturgical objects/vessels or replicas (made of pewter or lead instead of silver or gold)
- Loom weights
- Masks (ceramic, copper, gold, silver, jade, shell, stone)
- Mirrors
- Musical instruments (drums, flutes, harps, horns, rattles, stringed instruments)
- Numerical patterns (within measurements, arrangements, or repetition of motifs and elements)
- Ocher
- Papal bullae
- Perforated discs
- Perforated spoons
- Pilgrimage badges, shells, staves, and tokens
- Plant offerings
- Pottery storage and offering vessels (bowls, jars, jugs, plates, pots, urns)
- Prayer beads (rosaries and paternosters)
- Precious metal (bronze, copper, gold, silver)
- Precious stones (amber, carnelian, jade, jet, lapis lazuli, turquoise, etc.)
- Quartz crystals
- Shell
- Spindle-whorls
- Statuary (deities, guardians, retainers, etc.)
- Tattooing kits
- Text (on bark, paper, stone, wood, etc.)
- Textiles
- Thimbles
- Tiles
- Tobacco pipes

- Vehicles (full-sized or miniature models: boats, carts, chariots, wagons, etc.)
- Wax
- Weapons (axes, knives, swords, etc.)
- Weights and scales
- Wooden rods
- Writing stylus

Tomb/Burial/Funerary Structures

- Barrow
- Burial or cremated remains niche
- Catacomb
- Chamber tomb
- Charnel house
- Cinerarium
- Cist graves (stone pit or cave burial)
- Cliff burial
- Columbarium
- Cremation pits
- Crematorium
- Crypt
- House tomb (usually rectangular)
- Kurgan
- Lanterne des morts (Graveyard lantern columns)
- Loculi tombs
- Mastaba
- Mausoleum
- Mound
- Ossuary
- Pyre
- Rock-cut tomb
- Rock shelter tomb
- Scaffold
- Sepulcher
- Shaft tomb
- Tholos/tholoi/beehive (usually circular)
- Tree burial
- Tumulus/tumuli
- Under floor chambers
- Vault

Burial Furniture

- Baskets
- Beds and couches
- Bundle
- Caskets
- Coffins
- Cylinders (lead, wood for cremation remains)
- Funerary jars/urns (glass, pottery)
- Larnakes (singular, larnax) (clay coffin)
- Logs
- Pithoi (singular, pithos) (funerary jar)
- Platforms
- Sarcophagi
- Ships and boats
- Stone or brick pillows and earmuffs
- Tree trunks

Burial Markers

- Animal horns
- Cenotaphs
- Ceramics (decorated vessels, figurines)

- Fenced enclosures (wooden, metal, stone)
- Glass (bottles, fishing floats)
- Gravehouse (ramada, shed)
- Grave rails
- Metal (crosses, plaques)
- Stone (blocks, posts, pillars, slabs, statues, boulders, cairns, carved forms)
- Wood (posts, crosses, planks, carved poles and pillars)

Burial Positions

- Fully extended
- Kneeling
- Left or right arm crossed over chest
- Left or right arm crossed over pelvis
- Left or right arm extended at side
- Left or right arm raised toward or over head
- Lying on left side
- Lying on right side
- Prone (face down)
- Semi-flexed (semi-fetal)
- Sitting
- Standing
- Supine (face up)
- Tightly flexed (tight fetal)

Burial Compositions

- Interment of full skeleton(s)
- Interment of partial skeleton(s)
- Interment mixture of full and partial remains
- Mass graves
- Multiple interment (contemporaneous or bodies added at later date(s))
- Single interment
- Single or multiple interment with animal(s)

Animal Burials

While mortuary contexts primarily relate to human corpses, animal burials can also indicate ritualistic practices. Many animals or animal parts are included in human graves or tombs, but some are given their own dedicated burials or entombment. The most common animals found buried or entombed include:

- Alligators
- Bears
- Birds
- Cats
- Cattle/oxen
- Chickens
- Dogs
- Fish
- Frogs/toads
- Horses
- Mice and rats
- Monkeys
- Pigs/wild boar
- Rabbits/hares
- Sheep and goats
- Wolves

Other attributes of ritualistic animal burials include:

- Arrangement in geometric array
- Arrangement in posed attitude
- Body manipulated (severed left foot, long bones or skull intentionally disarticulated, etc.)
- Bones arranged as an altar
- Buried along perimeter of battlefields, crop fields, sacred areas, or territories
- Buried at crossroads
- Buried on back, feet up
- Buried under structure (floor, hearth, threshold, or walled up)
- Cremated (possibly mixed with human remains)
- Includes grave goods
- Marked or painted with ocher
- Masked (possibly with image of different species)
- Mummified
- Numerical patterns (within measurements, arrangements, or repetition of motifs and elements)
- Orientation corresponding to religious cosmological ideas
- Placement in burial containers (baskets, coffins, wrappings, urns, etc.)
- Specific body parts (mandibles, scapulae, skulls, etc.)
- Specific body side parts (left or right)
- Specific sex and/or age of animal

MUNDANE/SECULAR

Everyday secular settings, despite such a neutral label, are still sites in which people enact their beliefs and rituals. These rituals include both those with no association to religious or spiritual beliefs and those directly related to ideas of the divine or supernatural. Wherever people live, work, or socialize, they will incorporate or embed material expressions of their rituals and beliefs. As noted in Chapter 4 "Religion," sometimes these beliefs are evidenced by an absence of particular material culture.

Domestic

- Ampullae from pilgrimage shrines (often found along crop field boundaries)
- Animal or human hearts pierced with nails, pins, or thorns in niches in the hearth
- Animal skulls or carcasses (livestock) buried around barns, stables, fields
- Animal skulls under the floor
- Antlers attached to doors, roofs, or walls
- Architectural elements resembling eyes (e.g., dormer windows)
- Assemblages of spiritual objects (crystals, beads, pottery, figurines, symbols, sharp and/or metal items, bones, perforated coins and stones, etc.) often under the floor

- Bottles, jugs, or vials (filled with urine, cloth hearts, pins, thorns, nails, fingernail/toenail parings, hair) buried under thresholds or hearthstones, found broken or concealed in hearths, buried at field corners or perimeters
- Bowls marked with protective texts or designs; often inverted and buried under thresholds, under floors, and in corners
- Burned or painted symbols, sigils, and names on ceilings
- Burn marks on rafters, joists, jambs, and sills
- Circles embedded in floors, hearth stones, and walls
- Colors of protection or religious association (e.g., red, blue, white, green) on exterior walls and porch ceilings or utilized in conjunction with painted symbol on house and barn exteriors
- Crosses on doors and door stones, hearths and hearthstones, roofs, and walls
- Door knockers, often of iron and in the shape of a protective symbol or animal
- Doors, windowsills, and gates painted an apotropaic color (usually red, blue, or white)
- Eggs
- Guardian statues or figurines flanking entrances and gates
- Holed stones
- Horseshoes
- House layout designed to embody and enforce religious gender ideas and taboos (e.g., secluded female areas; angled doorways; blocked external views into house interior)
- House layout indicating male/female (possibly right/left) division of space and cardinal orientation
- Inscribed cylinders of gold or silver buried under four corners of new building
- Keys and locks (sometimes inscribed with symbols or religious name references)
- Magical and religious symbols carved or scratched into and around windows, doors, hearths, ceilings, and rafters
- Magical and religious symbols carved or scratched on furniture and wooden boxes, and household utensils and vessels
- Metal (usually iron), sharp implements embedded in or buried around thresholds, hearths, foundations (e.g., farming tools, knives, swords, pikes, scissors, pot hooks, etc.)
- Mirror shards in wells, streams, or ditches
- Mobiles made of palm or other sacred plant material, usually incorporating bells, sacred colors, and animal or anthropomorphic figures; may also include representation of sacred numbers. Hanging over entrances and windows, or around perimeters of houses or shrines.
- Nails pounded on or around doors and windows (may have head painted red)
- Niche inside chimney often containing a spiritual midden of old shoes, dead cats or chickens, apotropaic plants, bent or broken sharp metal objects, etc.
- Niches built into walls for household shrines

- Perforated coins
- Prayer beads
- Protective designs, symbols, and images painted on house and outbuilding exteriors or on ground leading to threshold
- Protective plant products (e.g., onions, berries, roots, etc.) placed in hearths, cradles, beds, amulet pouches, etc.
- Protective plants planted at corners of house or property or under/ around doors, windows, and gates, or attached to walls and roofs
- Reflective, shiny objects (glass, glazed ceramics, metal) placed on/ around thresholds
- Salt around threshold areas or in vessels in corners
- Small shrine structures in domestic yards or fields
- Spiritual midden in the roof, walls, or under the floor
- Stove tiles embossed with protective designs or images
- Tar around doors and windows
- Underfloor burials
- Weathervanes depicting roosters, crosses, or other religious or magical imagery
- Wind chimes (beads, bottles, glass, metal bells, shells)
- Woven fences

Commercial

- Beckoning cats (Maneki Neko)
- Cylinder-seals
- Horse brasses
- Magical symbols embedded in fabric (interior or exterior) of building
- Product seals or stamps with religious or magical imagery/text
- Protective or auspicious colors to block or neutralize bad fortune and enhance prosperity
- Protective statues or figurines flanking entrance
- Small shrines
- Wind chimes

Institutional (Asylums, Alms Houses, Hospitals, Orphanages)

- Cemeteries
- Chapel, shrine, or meditation space
- Dedicated buildings usually displaying embedded symbolism of the organization
- Embedded numerological measurements and geometric configurations or orientations
- Magical or religious symbols embedded in or attached to fabric (interior or exterior) of building
- Transitional (admission or departure ritual) space

Public/Civic

- Access approaches defined to direct, restrict, or sensorially manipulate passage
- Access approaches often broad to accommodate populace, especially on ritual occasions
- Architectural components for manipulating sound (e.g., speaking tubes or channels or acoustics that amplify sound)
- Dedicated buildings usually displaying embedded symbolism of the organization
- Embedded numerological measurements and geometric configurations or orientations
- Foundation sacrifices in the fabric, foundation, or piling/post holes of bridges
- Large scale feasting areas
- Objects associated with seasonal festivities (e.g., badges with agricultural imagery such as plows, crops, and animals; charm chains and necklaces with bells and floral motifs; coins; foliate heads and imagery; May poles)
- Open areas for games, parades, processions, or other large scale ritual performances
- Platforms for oration (religious or political)
- Possibly aligned on landscape with religious structures to associate divine power with civic authority
- Public execution or sacrifice spaces and structures
- Public mortuary structures (e.g., cremation platforms)
- Situated in dedicated areas distinct from residential neighborhoods
- Situated so as to be visually prominent
- Stages or performance platforms for religious, political, or moralistic plays
- Statuary of humans, deities, or animals associated with the municipality
- Urban shrines dedicated to town or ruler

Occupational

- Designated clothing or colors indicating connection of occupation with notions of pollution, taboo, sanctity, or authority
- Designated colors (for clothing/uniforms, occupational premises, etc.)
- Drinking vessels for initiation into guilds
- Figurines or statuary of deities specific to occupations
- Jewelry (badges, brooches, charms, medals, pins, or rings with occupational specific images or symbols)
- Patron saints medals or badges specific to occupations
- Strands of knotted rope (sailors)
- Symbols painted on vehicles (e.g., "evil eye bead" on boat prows)
- Tools of trade decorated with totemic animals, symbols, or special words

SACRED

In contrast to mundane sites, sacred sites here refer to those explicitly recognized and designated as places related to spiritual or religious practices.

Pilgrimage

Pilgrimage is a serious healing or enlightening spiritual journey undertaken for a variety of reasons all of which are premised on the belief that the pilgrimage experience and destination are imbued with beneficial spiritual power.

Pilgrimage Destinations

- Formal religious buildings (churches, shrines, etc.)
- Sacred trees and groves
- Sacred water bodies (holy wells, lakes, rivers, springs)
- Sites associated with divine healing
- Sites associated with miracles
- Sites associated with religious personages (birthplaces, burial places, death places, places of enlightenment, etc.)
- Sites of important religious events
- Sites of tragic historical/cultural events

Additional Pilgrimage Sites

- Embarkation sites for pilgrims gathering before setting out on the pilgrimage
- Labyrinths embedded in religious buildings' floors act as surrogate pilgrimage routes
- Shrines, water sites, and sacred trees along the main pilgrimage route
- Sites along the route for acquiring pilgrimage appropriate clothing and badges
- Sites along the route for respite and sanctuary (hostelries and monastery guest houses)

Pilgrimage Material Culture

- Badges (made of ceramic, paper, or lead/tin)
- Bell-reliefs
- Bells
- Bracteates
- Candlesticks with biblical inscriptions
- Clothing (cloaks, tabards) bearing a cross insignia
- Clothing of a designated "pilgrim" color and form (e.g., white robe or tunic; sandals)
- Devices to simulate for pilgrims the life, journeys, and tribulations of a particular saint (e.g., boats for sea-voyage pilgrimages and boat-shaped oratories)

- Graffiti (on features and structures along pilgrimage routes and at destinations)
- Guidebooks
- Horns
- Padlocks
- Pathway markers to lead or direct pilgrims to the pilgrimage destination
- Rattles
- Relics (fragments of bone, cloth, nails, wood)
- Satchels or scrips
- Shells
- Staves
- Tokens
- Vials/ampullae (once containing water in which relics had been immersed)
- Votive figurines
- Whistles

Religious Architecture

Architectural structures erected to encompass and/or focus religious practices and the enactment of beliefs take many forms across the world. They can range from small and simple shrines to monumental and complex buildings like temples, mosques, and cathedrals. While each may be intended to embody and project a particular religious faith, often participants incorporate various iterations of traditional beliefs within the formal structures. Religious architecture may include one or more foundation sacrifices marking the erection or renovation of sacred buildings. They may also include abandonment sacrifices made at the time a building was intentionally deserted. It may be necessary to look beyond the obvious examples of religious material culture in these structures to identify indicators of alternative ritualistic and magical practice; for example, graffiti of magical or quasi-religious nature is a common element in many Christian churches.

Conversely, the discovery of particular religious material culture in spaces not "consecrated" may indicate that the object was used to transform that profane space into sacred space (e.g., portable Catholic altars). It was also commonplace for new religious groups to appropriate the sites of previous traditions, resulting in a succession or palimpsest of religious structures built upon the foundations or sites of earlier sacred places.

Religious structures are often situated in proximity to water (springs, wells, rivers) deemed to have a sacred character. Water plays a purifying role in many traditions and was necessary to cleanse (purify) both people and objects.

Wherever religious structures are situated, remember they were always an integral part of larger landscapes in which their locations had intention and meaning; in other words, they were not randomly placed nor disconnected from social and political systems.

The following lists provide examples of common ritualistic, religious, and/or magical material culture found in specific formal religious structures.

Abbeys (Monasteries, Nunneries, Convents, Priories, Beguinages, Hermitages, Hospitals)

- Bells or gongs
- Cemeteries
- Complex of various structures with specific functions to create a self-sufficient and relatively isolated community of religious devotees; may include: worship area (church, chapel, temple, shrine, martyrium), cloister and garth, chapter house, common house, choir, refectory, cellars, scriptorium, hospital, privies, baths, cells, separate lodgings for religious leader, guest house
- Dipinti
- Flagellation devices (barbed or knotted whips/scourges, cat-o-nine tails, chains)
- Gardens and orchards
- Gender segregated or defined areas (women often on the north side)
- Graffiti
- Imagery (frescos, paintings, mosaics, carvings, statuary) often of religious topics, but also of secular persons, mythological beings, and flora and fauna
- Incense and censors
- Inscriptions in stone and wood features
- Often remotely situated, but can also be found in fertile landscapes for crop and livestock production; also located close to pilgrimage routes or on cliffs visible to pilgrims
- Prayer beads (rosaries and paternosters)
- Reliquaries and relics
- Restricted access
- Ritual/liturgical vessels
- Statues of deities
- Walled enclosure
- Wax official seals

Churches

- Catholic
  » Altar of Repose (storage niche for the Host)
  » Altar rail
  » Altars
  » Anchorite cells
  » Aspergillum (Holy water sprinkler—gold, silver, or brass ball head with handle)
  » Aspersorium (matching bucket for aspergillum)
  » Aumbries (cupboards for sacred books and vessels)
  » Baptismal font
  » Bells (hand bells and belfry bells)
  » Buried/intentionally concealed ceramic pots and jugs
  » Candles and candlesticks
  » Cardinal orientation and alignment (east/west alignment; north=devil's door)
  » Catafalque
  » Cathedra (bishop's throne)
  » Censors and incense
  » Chancery
  » Chrismatory (vessel for chrism oil, usually silver or pewter)
  » Collection plates
  » Communion vessels
  » Confessional
  » Corbels

» Crucifix figures
» Crypts
» Dalle
» Dedication crosses
» Disposal pits for the burning of used sacred textiles
» Ewers
» Ex-votos
» Flagellation devices (barbed or knotted whips/scourges, cat-o-nine tails, chains)
» Frithstools (seat for individual claiming sanctuary)
» Gargoyles and grotesques
» Gender segregated or defined areas (women often on the north side)
» Hearses
» In-floor and crypt burials
» Liturgical comb
» Lych-gates
» Magical symbols and graffiti
» Misericords
» Monstrances (also called oster-sorium; ususally ornate gold or silver starburst design; com-posed of luna—removable vessel that contains the Host—and the thabor—the stand upon with the monstrance sits)
» Mosaic and painted ceilings, walls, and floors
» Murals on ceilings and walls of divine beings and religious events/stories
» Organs
» Pews and stalls
» Piscina (basin) and sacrarium (drain) for washing sacred objects
» Portable altars with inset marble or porphyrite stone and small reliquary chamber

» Prayer beads (rosaries and paternosters)
» Protective imagery and symbols (on baptismal fonts, bench ends, capitals, coffin/sarcophagi lids, corbels, doors, pillars, rood screens, roof bosses, stoups, tympanum, walls)
» Pyx (silver or ivory storage vessel for the consecrated host)
» Reliquaries and relics
» Rood screens
» Roof bosses
» Saint effigies
» Sedilia (stone seats for priest, deacon, and subdeacon)
» Sepulchers
» Silver spoons
» Stained glass windows
» Stoups
» Tomb effigies
» Virgin Mary statues

• Orthodox Christian
» Altars
» Amben (large pulpit or reading desk)
» Analgium (stand for choir books)
» Aspergillum (Easter Orthodox: ranistirion—standing tapered, lidded brass or silver vessel; Russian Orthodox: kropilo—whisk of hair, cloth, or plant fiber with wooden or metal handle)
» Bells
» Censors and incense
» Colors: white, green, purple, red, blue, gold; specific to liturgical calendar
» Communion vessels
» Egg chandeliers
» Gender segregated or defined areas (women often on the north side)

» Iconostasis (screen separating congregation from clergy)
» Mosaic and painted ceiling and wall iconography
» Pews and stalls
» Religious icons
» Reliquaries and relics
• Protestant
» Altars (some sects)
» Arched windows and vaulted roofs (Anglican)
» Aspergillum and aspersorium (Anglican)
» Baptismal fonts
» Bells
» Cardinal orientation and alignment (east/west alignment)
» Cedar liturgical furnishings
» Cherubim sculptures/carvings
» Collection plates
» Crucifix figures
» Inscribed scriptural panels (stone, wood)
» Lych-gates
» Magical symbols and graffiti
» Maiden's garlands
» Organs
» Pulpits
» Red door (Episcopalian)

Mosques

• Ablution area in courtyard or near entrance (fountain, pool, pot of water, tap)
• Colonnaded halls
• Colors (blue, green, white, yellow)
• Columns
• Courtyards (sahn)
• Dikka (platform from which Musezzin projected prayer responses)
• Domes
• Friezes
• Horseshoe and semicircular arches
• Mihrab (prayer niches situated on wall oriented to Mecca)
• Minarets
• Minbar (short flight of steps next to Mihrab used as a pulpit)
• Mosaic tiling
• Pishtaq (monumental gateway)
• Qur'an stands and chests
• Raised and screened enclosure for ruler or Imam
• Separated and/or screened area for women usually situated behind men's area
• Vaulted ceilings

Shrines (Receptacle, Building, or Altar to Contain Sacred Relics and/or to Make Devotions and Offerings)

• Aedicula (canopied niche for deity statue or object of reverence with flanking columns)
• Altars
• Colors (usually white, red, green, blue, gold)
• Ex-voto paintings of miracles
• Ex-votos
• Incense and censors
• Reliquaries
• Statues and figurines of deities
• Vessels for offerings
• Water source (fountain, pond, vessels of water)

Stupas

- Eight stupas, one for each aspect of Buddha
- Five types (varying in size according to function)
  - » Commemorative—commemorates events in life of Buddha or his disciples, may contain figurines
  - » Object—containing objects belonging to Buddha or disciples, e.g., begging bowl, robe, scriptures, etc.
  - » Relic—containing human relics of Buddha, his disciples, or lay saints
  - » Symbolic—symbolize aspects of Buddhism, may contain figurines or scripture
  - » Votive—small, constructed to commemorate visits to large stupa or gain spiritual benefits
- Railings encircling stupa

Synagogues

Architectural styles vary, but these elements are usually present in some combination:

- Aron Kodesh (Torah ark)
- Bimah (raised platform/lecturn)
- Entrances may be on Jerusalem-oriented wall or on opposite wall
- Façade, interior walls, and floors often highly decorated with Jewish symbolism and iconography including wall paintings of biblical scenes and folk tales based on biblical stories and mosaic flooring depicting biblical scenes and zodiac cycles. Inscriptions also commonly occur painted, incised, or in tesserae.
- Genizah (cemetery, coffin, or special storeroom for retired/worn out sacred texts)
- Library or study room
- May have adjoining or annexed building including schools, hostels, guest houses, ritual baths, and/or synagogue officials' residences
- Menorah
- Neir tamid (perpetual light above and before the aron Kodesh)
- Oblong hall divided by column rows into a central nave and surrounding aisles
- Periphery/backroom for holding Kiddush
- Stepped benches lining all walls facing inward
- Tebam (reader's platform)
- Torah shrine (aedicula—earliest form, niche, or apse—later form) built into wall of synagogue oriented to Jerusalem, which in turn dictated the orientation of the entire building. Sometimes there are two aedicule—one for Torah, one possibly for menorah.
- Triple portal entrance

Temples

Temples are religious structures common to a wide range of religious traditions across time and place. They vary greatly in size, complexity, detail, and function. They are found in monotheistic and polytheistic traditions. Because of their great variety, it is impossible to characterize a "typical" temple and its components. The following list includes attributes from several different temple types.

- Altars
- Ambulatory or cloister
- Amulets and written charms
- Banners and flags and banner poles
- Bells, gongs, chimes
- Burials
- Byobu screens
- Carved poles, columns, obelisks, stela, etc.
- Cella (sanctuary containing cult deity statue)
- Chambers accessible only to religious specialists or authorities
- Cinnabar
- Colors (usually white, red, gold, blue, green)
- Columns and colonnades
- Complex of structures (like a monastery) with dedicated functions
- Cosmic modelling
- Designated areas for purification rituals
- Fire features for burning offerings, sacred flames/light, candles
- Fire towers for maintenance of sacred flames
- Food offerings (fruit, wine, milk, honey, beer, meat and poultry)
- Gardens
- Gates, archways, or doors (often decorated) delineating entrance to sacred space
- Guardian statues at thresholds
- Imagery of sacred animals and creatures
- Incense and censors
- Metal vessels and decorative application (gold, bronze, brass, silver, copper)
- Mosaic or decorative tiling of symbolic colors and patterns
- Murals (mosaic, painted, friezes of sacred stories and/or events)
- Musical instruments (cymbals, drums, flutes, conch shells, harps, lyres, etc.)
- Numerical patterns (within measurements, arrangements, or repetition of motifs and elements)
- Offering tables or platforms
- Oracle speaking tubes or shafts
- Orientation corresponding to religious cosmological ideas
- Plant offerings (flowers, palm, tobacco, etc.)
- Prayer mats
- Prayer wheels
- Precious stones (jade, obsidian, turquois, etc.)
- Processional routes (often lined with statuary)
- Ropes and other twined or knotted objects
- Sacred animals (koi, carp, turtles, peacocks, monkeys, cattle, parrots, etc.)

- Sacred trees and groves
- Sacrificial tables, stones, scaffolds, or altars
- Situated on sites of cosmic power (e.g., lightning strikes) or places related to deities or religious events
- Situated on sites with natural sensorial elements (sounds, movement of wind, smells, over rushing water, view to other sacred landscape features)
- Situation variations: isolated and restricted; central and easily accessible
- Spatially or geographically linked in network of other temples or sacred features
- Specific types: worship of deity; mortuary; fire; oracle; healing
- Stages or performance platforms for religious plays
- Statues and figurines of deities
- Stupas
- Verticality and height of structures emphasized (reaching to realm of gods)
- Water features (fountains, lakes, oceans, ponds, pools, rivers, streams, water vessels)

Sacrificial

Sacrifice implies that something of value is given in exchange for a desired outcome or in payment of an obligation. There are various types of sacrificial rituals and objects as illustrated below.

Deposits

Hoard or cache depositions: Hoards may be a ritualistic offering or merely a cache of valuables intended for recovery at some safer, more convenient, or needful future time. They may be a one-time deposit or an accumulation of deposits over a longer time span. They may be of one material or object type (e.g., all silver or iron, all weapons or coins) or they may be a mixture of material, objects, or both.

Votive depositions: Votives are generally thought of as gifts dedicated to a supernatural or divine power/entity. They may be propitiations, entreaties (for either blessings or curses), gifts of gratitude, or obligatory commerce between humans and otherworldly beings. Votives deposits may be individual items or an accumulation of objects from one or more contributors over a short or prolonged time span. There may be significant time gaps between votive depositions events.

- In caves
  - » Bones (animal and human)
  - » Figurines (anthropomorphic, theriomorphic, or therianthropic)
  - » Painted and/or incised pebbles
  - » Weapons (full-sized or miniature made from soft, unusual, or non-functional material—e.g., stone axes of jadeite or chalk)

- In water (bogs, cenotes, ditches, lakes, rivers, springs, streams, wells). Depositions may be in the water or in the ground (banks/shoreline) of the waterbody. Often these are clustered around river mouths, fords, bridges, and confluences. In some cases, there is a fanned pattern of deposition in the water indicating a consistent throwing/casting of sacrifices into the water from a designated position on the shore, bank, or other water edge.
  - » Badges (lead pilgrim and secular badges)
  - » Booty (combination of materials and objects)
  - » Cauldrons and other vessels
  - » Coins
  - » Eggs (often ostrich, also made of stone, clay, porcelain, wood, and often decorated)
  - » Figurines and statues (anthropomorphic, theriomorphic, or therianthropic) often made of wood or metal
  - » Iron firedogs
  - » Keys
  - » Metal tablets with inscribed curses, prayers, or petitions
  - » Objects and victims often pinned or weighted in place
  - » Tools (agricultural, carpentry, smithing, weaving)
  - » Weapons (knives, shields, swords, spears: often intentionally bent or broken)
  - » Whetstones
- On altars or shrines
  - » Amphorae
  - » Baskets
  - » Blood
  - » Candles
  - » Figurines (animal, deities, human)
  - » Flowers
  - » Fruit
  - » Grain or rice
  - » Honey
  - » Images (carvings, drawings, paintings)
  - » Incense
  - » Milk
  - » Tobacco
  - » Vessels (bowls, goblets, plates, urns)
  - » Wine
- Other objects and ideas related to sacrifice and sacrificial rituals (human and animal)
  - » Dedicated area or structure for the detainment of sacrifices until time of ritual
  - » Dedicated area or structure for the purification and preparation of sacrifice
  - » Emphasis on skulls and leg bones
  - » Evidence of violence and overkill (peri- and postmortem)
    - – Constraints and trussing (feet, hands, neck)
    - – Crushing
    - – Disembowelment
    - – Dismemberment
    - – Multiple deaths: bludgeoning, strangling, throat cutting
    - – Torture
    - – Twisted, bent, broken weapons requiring excessive effort to so violently distort
  - » Excessively deep burials

» Gang chains (series of iron collars attached by chains)
» Hoods, blindfolds, or other vision obscuring devices
» Mixed human and animal remains (cremated or inhumed)
» Platforms, stones, or tables for conducting blood sacrifice
» Tools for dispatching blood sacrifices (made of various materials: bone, lithic, metal)

» Value of the sacrifice may lie in its materiality or attributes (e.g., age, color, deformity or uniqueness, material, sex, size, species, etc.)
» Vessels for the capture and/or containment of blood, organs, or other body parts

UNDERWATER

Magical and ritualistic items may be found in underwater sites. Some of these sites are specifically related to the water body itself (e.g., holy wells, rivers, lakes, ditches, bogs) and accumulate offerings at that specific location both above and below the water (See the section "Elementals" in Chapter 6 "Ritualistic, Sacred, and Magical Landscapes" or in this chapter, the section "Sacrificial" for more details). This section will be focused on submerged sites like shipwrecks, plane wrecks, and inundated human habitations and/or features.

Inundated Sites and Features

• Monoliths
• Mortuary features (gravestones, stone coffins, urns)

• Religious statuary (deities, demons, saints, spirits)
• Temple structures

Ship and Boat Wrecks

Seafaring and other water-based activities, either for travel or occupation, were risky propositions. As with other dangerous and unpredictable enterprises, sailors and fishermen often incorporated protective or "good luck" elements into their watercraft. Some of these elements would have been a structural part of the craft while others would have been objects or animals brought aboard.

• Carved deity figures
• Cats
• Coins, perforated or bent

• Colors (often red or blue painted designs)
• Figureheads

- Figurines
- Holed stones
- Horseshoe nailed to the mast
- Knotted rope
- Painted symbol on prow (often an "eye")
- Prayer beads
- Protective plants
- Silver coin nailed to the mast

Plane Wrecks

Similar to ship and boat travel, flying early aircraft was always a dangerous undertaking, especially in combat situations. During World War I and II, pilots often incorporated shielding or "good luck" elements into their aircraft drawing on both religious and magical protections. Many underwater plane wreck sites have not been surveyed or excavated, so any potential magico-religious artifacts associated with the pilot/crew and aircraft are likely still in place.

- Black cat images, buttons, and badges
- Catholic saints medals
- Chains and belts of strung coins
- Coin sewn into clothing over heart
- Crooked, bent, or perforated silver coins
- Crosses/crucifixes (commercially made or crudely fashioned out of virtually any material including bullets)
- Elephant with raised trunk images and charms
- Figa red coral charm
- Fumsup mascots
- Hand of Fatima images, charms, and badges
- Horseshoe images, charms, and badges
- Hunched back figurine charm
- Magical plants and their images or as charms (four-leaf clover, Edelweiss, fern)
- Miniature cast metal figures of Joan of Arc and the Virgin Mary in little lead capsules
- Modified personal gear marked with religious or magical symbols (e.g., padlocks, canteens, cigarette lighters)
- Number thirteen charms (while associated with bad luck by British and American soldiers, it was considered a lucky number by the French)
- Painted magical symbol or image on nose or tail of aircraft
- Pig images and charms
- Prayer beads, rosaries, paternosters
- Rings made from coffin nails
- Sacred Heart badges
- Scapular medals
- Swastika badges charms, keys, and pins
- Touchwood charms

CHAPTER 6

Ritualistic, Sacred, and Magical Landscapes

While some ritualistic, religious, or magical beliefs and practices may be confined to a particular feature, structure, or delineated site, many of these beliefs and practices play out on a much larger and entangled scale incorporating multiple elements across a landscape. Some of these elements are closely situated, others reach to the horizon, and still others involve more immaterial elements like sound, wind, and the flash of sunlight on water. Traditional Cultural Properties (TCPs), usually associated with Native American people, are a prime example of a culture's spiritual beliefs being embedded in an entire landscape. The following introduces various types of elements that constitute different ritual or sacred landscapes.

ASTRONOMICAL ASSOCIATIONS AND STRUCTURES

- Chamber tombs
- Long barrows
- Medicine wheels
- Menhirs
- Monoliths
- Stone circles/henges (also wood henges)
- Stone effigies (anthropomorphic or theriomorphic)

COSMOLOGICAL MODELING

- Intentional modeling of terrestrial world on the cosmos captures idea that this world is sentient and able to communicate or otherwise interact with the divine
- Numerological elements associated with cosmic ideas incorporated into dimensions, architectural structures, and distances of and between settlement and architectural components

- Settlements laid out in a symbolic design to embody the cultural idea of the cosmos (often repetitions of circles, crosses, squares, high and low points, left/right and forward/behind placements, and cardinal direction orientation)
- Structures designed as reflections of the cosmic elements (circles, squares, crosses, high and pointed, underground)
- Tombs or temples constructed of various stone from across landscape to mimic the larger sacred landscape
- Water courses or bodies that are perceived as cosmological interfaces or frameworks through which humans connect with the divine
- World trees considered the center of the world and connecting the whole of the universe through their roots, trunks, and branches

CULTURALLY MODIFIED ECOFACTS (CMEs)

- Trees (Culturally Modified Trees: CMTs) (living organisms also referred to as vivifacts)
  - » Bent
  - » Incised (known as arborglyphs or dendroglyphs)
  - » Scarred
- Incised stones
  - » Effigies
- » Eoliths
- » Manifestations of deities or spirits
- » Maps to sacred sites
- » Markers of the abode of deities or spirits
- » Protective boundary markers
- » Rune stones
- » Story stones

DIRECTIONAL ORIENTATION

- Directions and their association with deities or demons may be perceived as good or evil; interaction with a direction will be related to these perceptions and reflected in the ritual activities or structures associated with the area or as an avoidance of the area.
- Each direction may be associated with a particular deity and have land-forms or features that embody or are the manifestation of that deity.
- In some cultures, tombs/burials are oriented on a north-south axis, in others on an east-west axis. Some are not cardinal direction specific but are situated to face a designated holy center (e.g., Jerusalem or Mecca).

- Right/left positioning often indicates a complex network of concepts. As listed below, these ideas are similarly shared around the world with very few exceptions (e.g., Japanese attributions to right and left are generally the reverse of that stated here). On a landscape, what is right or left depends on one's orientation: if facing east, right is south and left is north, for example, so it is necessary to understand broader cultural ideas about orientation to recognize associated incorporations of right/left ideologies. At a site or site locus scale, this layout is more evident (e.g., facing the interior of a structure through its entrance already positions one to know what is right or left). Ritual circumambulations are usually done "sun-wise," that is moving in the path of the sun or to the right. This means that the space or object being circled is to the right-hand side of the participant, giving it the position of "righteousness" and keeping the "sinister" at bay.
  » Right: above, up, forward, male, righteous, good, active, intellectual, superior, dominant, divine
  » Left: below, down, behind, female, deceptive, sinister, passive, intuitive, inferior, subservient, chthonic
- Temples and other religious structures often face/open to the east.
- Tombs/burials are often located to the east, southeast, or south of settlements.
- Tomb structures usually open to the east.

ELEMENTALS (AIR, EARTH, FIRE, WATER)

Each of these elements has its own attributes, but they are often seen to work in consort in various ways as sacred or ritualistic sites. This is especially salient at points where two or more meet in intermedial zones:

- Field/forest boundaries
- Land/sky (mountain tops)
- Land/water (islands, shorelines)

Confluences of multiple strands of a single form, like the meeting of waterways or trails, are also perceived as powerfully charged and liminal.

Air

- Area or features that funnel air drafts over the ritual site or objects (this is experienced as the "breath of god," which is also enacted through the use of fans—often of bird feathers or sacred plants—or by blowing)

- Features (natural or human-made) may funnel air currents/wind to enhance the sound of the wind or amplify and carry the sound of the human voice
- Situation of sacred site in areas where the wind creates sound and visual dynamics through the rustling of tree branches and leaves or objects attached to tree branches
- Situation of sacred site in areas where the wind's force buffets participants creating a vestibular and tactile experience
- Situation of sacred site or manipulation of features to enhance and experience the wafting of scent as a component of ritual
- Situation of sacred site or manipulation of features to facilitate the up draught carrying of ritual smoke (incense or cremation) heavenward

Earth

- Cracks in rock faces (often associated with rock art) are conceived to be spirit portals and may be used for deposition of offerings, rock art, or as burial sites.
- Features constructed of both locally sourced and imported materials may have these familiar and unfamiliar materials alternated in bands or sections.
- Natural caves or caverns are often thought of as abodes of a deity or spirit or portals to the underworld; may be used for deposition of offerings, rock art, burials, ritual purification, inducing altered states of consciousness, and other ritual practices.
- Quarries or resource acquisition sites of minerals (e.g., ocher) or stones (e.g., jade) used in ritual or religious practices; this "earth" is itself sacred because it produces other earth-related sacred substances.
- Ritual or sacred sites/features may be situated at the interface of two distinctive soil/sediment/mineral zones.
- Soils, minerals, and stones may be intentionally transported over great distances to be used in ceremonial/sacred/ritualistic contexts. These materials are perceived as special, spiritual, or powerful in some sense due to their material attributes or associations with place, other special materials, or potent beings.
- Soils used in constructing burial mounds; may be brought from other places chosen for particular attributes or associations.
- Soils (whether imported or locally sourced) may be laid down in distinctive and deliberate layers of color, texture, luminosity, hardness/softness, or other qualities. These layers may be an inverse of the normal stratigraphic positions of the soils/sediments.
- Subterranean features (natural or human-made) that allow people to physically be enveloped in the earth: caves and rock shelters, kivas, mounds, tombs, tunnels and chambers

- Trees (as World Trees or Axis Mundis), or as sacred groves, are associated with the earth element as their roots are believed to stretch to the underworld and connect the human world to the supernatural world of the dead

Fire

- Ash from large or long-burning ceremonial/ritual fires may be collected and intentionally used as fill in other sacred sites or contexts (some far removed from original burning site).
- Fire is an important element in many rituals; large-scale ceremonial fires or funerary/sacrificial pyres may have dedicated fire pits or designated areas that leave discernable ash layers from repeated use. Fires were often lit in conjunction with particular rock art sites.
- Places and landscape features struck by lightning are often revered as sacred or spiritually powerful. Temples or shrines may be built on these sites.
- Volcanos, with their potential or perpetual flow of fire, are virtually always considered sacred abodes of fire deities.

Water

- A water course (rivers especially) may embody a belief system's primary creative life force or deity or manifest the cosmological structure of the world (e.g., the Ganges).
- A water course (river, stream, etc.) may symbolically demarcate mundane and sacred space.
- Deep pools (e.g., cenotes) or underground lakes are often thought of as portals to the underworld; may be used for deposition of offerings, sacrifices, or burials.
- Even if not visible, the sound of water (rushing, trickling, dripping, lapping of waves or crashing of surf, etc.) may be a contributing aspect of the sacred vitality of a landscape.
- Natural or human-made/modified features for pooling or collecting water are used for altars, offerings, scrying, purification rituals, or communication portals to the spirit world.
- Natural springs, wells, and bogs are often thought of as abodes of a deity or spirit or portals to the underworld; may be used for deposition of offerings or ritual purification.
- Particular water bodies are believed to possess healing powers and are, thus, pilgrimage destinations.
- Sacred sites may be situated above underground water courses that can be heard and/or felt on the surface.

- Spiritual seascapes may incorporate terrestrial elements like sea mammal (e.g., dugong) bone mounds, tidal zone stone arrangements, or sea-facing spirit/deity figures that express the cosmologies and linkages of marine-scapes.
- Terrestrial waters may be linked to "heavenly" waters (rain), so even in arid landscapes features may indicate through imagery, symbolism, or construction (catchment vessels) the sacred incorporation of water across the landscape.
- The shimmer qualities of water (and play of light) may play a role in the determination of ritual landscape meanings and beliefs.
- The situation of ritual features or structures on a landscape may be dictated by the association of water, directionality, and negative or positive forces.
- Water bodies and courses may create a symbolic pattern with ritualistic significance across a large landscape.
- Water bodies and courses may be the physical embodiments or abodes of deities or spirits.

FLORA AND FAUNA

Flora

- Crop fields of plants for specific use in ceremony/ritual
- Culturally Modified Trees (CMTs) either individually, as waymarkers, or as a copse
- Figures (often composed of flora materials) set in fields as fertility and protective beings (deity figures, harvest figures, scarecrows)
- Gathering areas for particular plants used in ceremony, ritual, or magic
- Groves or forests associated with spirits, deities, or cosmological ideas
- Individual tree designated as a world or axial tree, identified with a spirit or deity, or venerated as a marker of cultural territory or ancestral history
- Specific symbolic or magically protective trees planted in burial grounds/cemeteries

Fauna

- Caves associated with sacred animals like bears
- Forests associated with sacred animals like stags
- Giant terraglyphs of animals on plains and hillsides
- Landscape area designated as omphalos and represented by an animal as the cosmic foundation of the universe (e.g., a turtle or serpent), which may be manifested on the landscape by giant mound figures or stone arrangements

- Mountains or rock outcroppings shaped like giant or mythical animals
- Waterways (lakes, oceans, rivers, streams) as the embodiment or habitation of sacred fish (e.g., carp or salmon) or animal (e.g., crocodile, hippopotamus, whale)

GEOLOGICAL, GEOGRAPHICAL, AND OTHER NATURAL MARKERS (MOUNTAIN PEAKS, WATERWAYS, TREES, ROCKS, CLIFFS, CAVES)

- Cosmological cartography (mapping the landscape via natural markers perceived as deities, spirits, or cosmically marked spots to validate cosmological beliefs)
- Landscape features resembling anthropomorphic or theriomorphic beings (mountains or hills that look like giants, humans, or animals, etc.)

LIGHT/DARK

- Astronomically aligned dark subterranean structures pierced by shaft of light on solstices and equinoxes
- Bogs and other "dark" waters often were places where "light" colored or light reflecting objects were sacrificed or offered
- Caves and caverns (dark zones vs light-penetrated areas; manipulating rock art in dark zones via flickering torchlight)
- Deep, dense forests
- Reflective materials (e.g., quartz) inside dark zones catch the light of torches, flashing and blinking
- Situating of ritual/ceremonial areas in proximity or view of banded or other alteration of light and dark soils or stones
- Use of light and dark colored soils or stones in layers of mounds or other constructions
- White chalk figurines or stones placed in dark sacred places create a distinct light/dark visual experience

Ritual vs. Sacred Landscapes

Not all revered or specialized landscapes have a religious/sacred nature or purpose (or at least not as the primary usage). Some landscapes are secular, sociopolitical spaces meant to model hierarchies of status, authority, power, and social position. Secular landscapes used to ritually enact these hierarchies include:

- Academic campuses
- Fraternal halls
- Governmental building clusters
- Guildhalls
- Military installations
- Penal institutions
- Plantations
- Processional or parade grounds and routes
- Rehabilitation asylums/ institutions

Sociopolitical ritualized ceremonies performed in these landscapes include:

- Awards
- Dedications
- Graduations
- Inaugurations
- Inductions
- Initiations
- Inspections
- Parades
- Processionals
- Terminations/Abandonment

SEASONALITY

The seasonal round has occasioned ritualized practices to address concerns of fertility, productivity, success, and protection that play out on the landscape. These rituals are often associated with:

- Body fluids (blood, milk, semen)
- Feasting
- Figurines or statuary of deities, grain spirits, or saints
- Fire (bonfires, candles, torchlight processions)
- Noisemakers (bells and drums especially)
- Processions
- Sacred or apotropaic flora
- Sacred or magical symbols
- Salt
- Water (often bodies of water for immersion—lakes, ponds, rivers, wells) or for aspersion

Some seasonal rituals that may leave material traces include:

- Annual property boundary marking/blessing/purging
- Equinox, solstice, and cross-quarter day observances
- Fall/winter butchering
- First/last harvests
- Midwinter observances (Christmas, Hanukkah, New Year, Saturnalia, Yule, etc.)

- Moving herds to/from summer/winter pastures
- Periodic repainting of rock art images (the seasonality of plant dyes or growth around sites or high/low water levels of area water courses in the access paths to sites may be indicators of when these renewal events occurred)
- Sowing and threshing
- Spring birthing of livestock

SOUNDSCAPES

- Area chosen for its echoing characteristics
- Calcite forms (stalagmites, stalactites, and draperies) in caves tapped for their resonant sounds and often located in proximity to cave art or evidence of dancing or performative rituals
- Ringing rocks (lithophones), may be in water courses or outcroppings and quarries
- Ritual area situated in "soundless" areas (caves, canyons, dense forests, etc.) specifically for their unusual silence
- Ritual area situated to hear rushing water or blowing/moaning/singing wind
- Situation of a sacred structure or a ritual area to hear the rustling of sacred trees and groves as an oracular or divinatory event (phyllomancy)
- The sound of working (carving, chipping, incising) particular types of rock may be a significant element in the placement of some rock art

TRAVEL CORRIDORS (DANCE, CEREMONY, EMIGRATION, EXODUS, PILGRIMAGE, PROCESSIONAL, SUBSISTENCE, TRADE)

- Circular trodden paths may indicate the repetition of ritual dance or the circumambulation of a variety of ritual, religious, or magical ceremonies. These areas are often demarcated with some type of boundary marker (e.g., bones, posts, stalagmites stuck in the ground).
- Pilgrimage routes include a series of intermittent ritual points.
- Processional routes (may be visible as only a pounded down or vegetatively different course)
- Ritual points on the landscape can be and are used for both sacred and mundane purposes dictated by context and participants.

- Travel corridors associated with events like pilgrimages have a definite ritual destination point. Starting at the specific site and considering the importance of associated directions to magico-ritualistic belief can assist in locating the travel corridors leading to the site.
- Travel corridors often have ritualistic sites, structures, and/or materials integrated along the route. Identifying the corridor can assist in identifying the ritualistic elements; likewise identifying a series of ritualistic/magical elements can reveal travel corridors.
- Travel corridors that appear to take a circuitous or "out of the way" route between points may indicate the purposeful avoidance of sacred or taboo areas.

VERTICAL/HORIZONTAL ASSOCIATIONS

- May incorporate meanings associated with right/left; up/down; over/under; front/back; and forward/behind.
- Places of power are either centrally located within a settlement or ritual complex or alternatively situated at a peripheral end point to which the rest of the settlement or complex is orientated.
- Places of power (spiritual or political) are often situated on natural or human-built high points. These may be the spiritual or political structures and/or the residences of the spiritual or political leaders.
- Tombs/burials/excarnation sites often located in upper or lower areas associated with portals to the spirit world (caverns/caves, low lying land, mountain tops, near/in sinkholes, near/in bodies of water)
- Tombs/burials or other sacred sites may be situated along or aligned with major water courses.
- Tombs/burials or other sacred sites may run parallel to ridge contours or escarpments of paths of movement/pilgrimage.
- Tombs placed either higher or lower than settlements
- When facing east, the left-hand side (north) of a churchyard in Catholic tradition is the devil's domain; deviant burials are usually located in this left or "sinister" area.
- Women's birth and fertility/reproductive rituals are often situated in subterranean or other areas below the level of daily activities.
- Worship or other spiritual ceremonial activities conducted at high (mountain top) or low (subterranean) points

VIEWSHEDS

- Aversion to placing settlement in the viewshed of the dead (cemeteries/tombs)
- Battlefields strategically chosen to be overlooked by sacred mountain
- Creation of large burial mounds or other sacred structures or images to be prominently visible on the landscape, specifically from designated areas
- Mortuary and sacred structures situated to viewshed of particular and prominent landscape feature like a mountain or stone outcrop
- Ritual spaces/performances positioned to see particular and prominent sacred landscape feature(s)
- Situation of guardian/spiritual beings on a landscape in order to "face" or "see" the threatening forces they are to repel (for example, the giant stone figures of Easter Island (Rapanui) who all face toward the sea)

CHAPTER 7

Ritualistic, Religious, and Magical Material Culture by Material Type and Attribute

This chapter provides researchers with lists of objects and materials commonly used in ritualistic, ceremonial, religious, and/or magical practices. Sometimes these objects or materials may be easily recognizable as relating to such practices due to inscriptions, imagery, or obvious contexts. In other cases, it will be difficult to interpret the object/material as relating to such practices. In these situations, more nuanced attention must be given to the context and associated objects to understand the applicability of a ritualistic, religious, and/or magical interpretation.

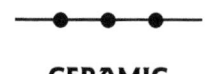

CERAMIC

Ceramic refers to anything constructed from a clay paste. While predominately associated with pottery vessels, the ceramics category also includes everything from beads and tiles to figurines. The malleability of ceramic paste prior to firing made it a versatile material to shape or incise, and its surface, either pre- or post-firing, provided a ready canvas for painting or other decorative application. Ceramics include terracotta and other low-fired clays, earthenware, stoneware, and porcelain. While susceptible to breakage, ceramics have an extremely high rate of survival in all archaeological contexts.

Adornments

- Beads
- Earrings
- Gorgets
- Pendants

Amulets

- Animal figures
- Crosses
- Deity images
- Eye images
- Holed discs
- Pendants
- Pilgrim badges
- Tokens

Figurines/Statues

- Animals
- Anthropomorphic/therianthropic figures
- Deities
- Demons/monsters
- Fertility figures (male or female with exaggerated genitalia, or animals associated with fecundity)
- Nkondi/Nkisi

Imagery

- Cylinder-seals
- Death masks
- Pendants
- Plaques
- Roofing tiles (*antefix*)
- Spirit masks
- Tablets
- Tiles

Vessels

- Anthropomorphic/theriomorphic/therianthropic vessels
- Bartmann/Bellarmine stoneware witch bottles
- Blood-letting sacrifice containers
- "Devil-trap" inscribed Babylonian and Hebrew bowls
- Canopic jars
- Censors
- Feasting vessels
- Goblets/chalices/cups
- Oil ewer
- Oil lamp
- Pitchers and jugs
- Plates or shallow dishes for offerings
- Pots
- Scrying bowls
- Spouted jars
- Tea ceremony sets
- Urns (burial or offering jars)

Other

- Flutes
- Pillows and head rests
- Pipes
- Whistles
- Wind chimes

COLOR

English has eleven basic color terms, but other cultures may have as few as three or four color categories or fewer, more, or different ways to distinguish colors. Regardless of the number of colors recognized within a culture, color affects people emotionally, psychologically, and behaviorally, and thus it figures prominently in the enactment of ritualistic, religious, or magical beliefs. Particular colors often symbolize or embody aspects of the paranormal world, and some are believed to possess inherent magical or divine power (red, white, black, blue, yellow, and green are the most common). Specific colors can represent deities, spirits, or demons and are often part of an integrated symbolic system that includes relationship to cardinal directions, divine attributes, celestial/terrestrial bodies or entities, and concepts of good and evil. Objects may be chosen for their natural coloration, have color applied to protect, influence, empower, or activate them, or be chosen because they derive from a particularly colored source.

- Beckoning cats (black, gold, white)
- Black animals (cats, bulls, dogs, horses, rams, etc.)
- Black fowl
- Blue and green bottles hung in trees
- Blue and white glass beads
- Blue or red doors, windowsills, and gates
- Blue, white, and yellow evil eye beads
- Candles (various colors in different ritualistic contexts)
- Eggs from a black or white hen
- Gemstones (various colors in different ritualistic contexts)
- Haint blue painted porch ceilings
- Mosaic or other tiles (various colors in different ritualistic contexts)
- Red cinnabar used in burials
- Red ocher placed in or used on burial materials and/or on corpse
- Red ocher used on weapons
- Red or yellow ocher rock art
- Red painted gateways to sacred paths or temples
- Red painted nail heads in and around thresholds
- Red painted symbols on doors, walls, ceilings, or objects
- Red string, thread, or scraps of cloth (embroidery, pom poms, ribbons, tassels, yarn)
- Religious authorities' or specialists' garb (e.g., red Cardinal robes, white Sufi gown)
- Stones used in sacred structure construction (various colors in different ritualistic contexts)
- White animals (bulls, cats, dogs, horses, rams, etc.)
- White fowl
- White, green, or red eggs
- White, black, or red stones marking sacred boundaries, entrances, or passageways

• • •

FAUNA

Animals and animal parts are a common aspect of ritualistic, religious, and magical practices. They may be revered as divine or be associated with deities or the spirit world; they may be used in divination, as sacrifices, as protective amulets, to ensure a successful hunt, or as instruments of maleficium. Livestock was deemed especially vulnerable to bewitchment, so some animal burials may indicate such affliction or an attempt to protect the rest of the livestock.

Additionally, presence or absence of particular faunal remains and their butchering patterns may be indicators of specific religious foodway associations, restrictions, or taboos.

Animal Carcass

- Bears
- Cats
- Cattle and oxen
- Dogs
- Fowl (chickens)
- Frogs and toads
- Goats and sheep
- Horses
- Mice and rats
- Pigs
- Rabbits and hares
- Squirrels

Bone

- Astragalas
- Beads
- Bones (animal or human)
- Bone mounds
- Buttons
- Component of medicine bundles
- Corno or cornicello (red coral horn-shaped amulet; alternatively made of silver or gold)
- Ear bones
- Figurines (animal, human, and spirits/deities)
- Harpoon heads
- Jewelry (earrings, nose piercing, pendants, chest plates)
- Oracle bones
- Remains of ritual sacrifice, feasting, or religiously/ritualistically prescribed foodways
- Tattoo tools

Claws/Talons/Hooves

- Component of medicine bundles
- Effigies
- Jewelry (earrings, necklaces)
- Sewn onto hats/clothing
- Wrist and ankle rattle bracelets

Feathers

- Attached to drums and rattles
- Attached to figurines
- Attached to tobacco pipes
- Attached to weapons
- Capes or simulated wings
- Component of Intentionally Concealed Object assemblages
- Component of medicine bundles
- Fan (e.g., used in smudging or prayer)
- Headdresses
- Quills for writing or illustrating

Fur/Hides

- Burial wraps
- Drum and rattle heads
- Fur hats (e.g., Shtreimel—Jewish Shabbat hat)
- Medicine-bundle wrap or pouch
- Miniature seal-skin kayaks
- Oracle bone or stone pouch or mat
- Shaman capes
- Tattooing kit wrap or pouch

Horn/Antler

- Attached to houses and outbuildings (barns, stables, byres)
- Drinking vessels
- Figurines (animal, human, and spirits/deities)
- Headdresses
- Rattles
- Spoons
- Trumpets

Other Body Parts

- Eyes
- Feet or paws
- Gut parkas
- Hair locks
- Hearts
- Scalps
- Trachea

Shell

- Buttons
- Censors and smudge vessels
- Cowrie shells (necklaces/bracelets, placed in masks or figurines as eyes, sewn onto hats/clothing)
- Eggs
- Jewelry (bracelets, earrings, hair adornments, nose rings, pendants)
- Mask gorgets (made from lightning whelks, *Busycon contrarium*)
- Masks made from whole turtle shells
- Musical instruments (flutes, horns, rattles)
- Wind chimes

Teeth/Tusks

- Animal and human
- Carved animal figures and heads
- Carved human/spirit figures and heads
- Handles for scripture pointers
- Harpoon heads
- Ice scratcher
- Jewelry (bracelets, earrings, necklaces)
- Medicine bundle component
- Tobacco pipes
- Sewn on hats and other clothing items

FLORA

Until the industrial revolution and development of synthetic materials, plants provided the raw material for virtually all human needs: shelter, food, clothing, medicine, tools, transport vessels, and other technologies, so they naturally also were used in numerous ways and manifestations in ideologically based practices. Although eggs may be the most universal of all ritually, religiously, or magically utilized objects, plants comprise the largest and most varied of all materials used in ritualistic, religious, or magical practices. In these practices, plants are used in their natural states, manufactured into objects, or illustrated through various mediums. Some plants have divine associations; some have magically protective, destructive, curative, or divinatory powers; and some are used to produce altered states of consciousness or other access to spirit worlds.

- Ancestral spirit poles (often marking a funerary site)
- Banner and flag poles or staffs (carved, incised, or modeled wood)—pole holes may be visible demarking cardinal directions, processional routes, sacred spaces, holy structures, funerary areas, or political/military ceremonial structures/areas
- Branches, leaves, and cones cast in bronze or gilded
- Burnt as offerings, protection, and purification
- Burnt then buried in crop and livestock fields and pastures
- Butter churns and paddles
- Coffins
- Consumed as mind-altering substance (ingested, smoked, sniffed, rubbed into cuts)
- Costumes
- Divining rods
- Door and window frames and sills
- Doors
- Fibers and stalks woven into figures and symbolic designs
- Floral imagery (carved, embroidered, woven, appliqued, tiled, painted in various mediums: ceramic, metal, stone, textile, wood)
- Flower offerings
- Food offerings (fruit, grain, and vegetables)

- Handles for scripture pointers
- Hazel branches, rods, and garrotes used in ritual (possibly sacrificial) burials
- Hung on and over doors and windows, over beds and cradles, over hearths, on and over stables
- Incense and censors
- Maiden's garlands
- Masks
- Oracle sticks
- Planted on rooftops, at house and yard corners and peripheries, at gateways, at field corners and boundaries
- Runic staves
- Runic talismans (usually yew)
- Staffs
- Strewn in rafters, along thresholds and boundaries
- Tattoo tools
- Totem poles
- Vessels for ceremonial eating and drinking
- Wands
- Wooden adornments (bracelets, earrings, hair ornaments, pendants)
- Wooden figurines and statues (anthropomorphic, theriomorphic, or therianthropic) of deities, demons, guardians, sacrificial victims, or spirits)
- Wooden hurdles used to secure corpses in bogs
- Wooden poles and pillars representing World Trees or other sacred trees
- Wooden vessels (mortar and pestles; feasting and offering bowls and plates)

Cultural Trees

CMTs (Culturally Modified Trees)

- Bent
- Incised
- Scarred

Memorial or Ceremonial Markers

- Birth
- Death
- Justice
- Marriage
- Pilgrimage
- Sacred groves

Sacred Tree Attributes (May Possess One or More of These Aspects)

- Associated with a deity or other spiritual being
- Associated with a religious or historical event
- Inhabited by a sacred animal
- Located in proximity to a sacred water source (river, spring, well)
- Marks a sacred site or landscape used for ritual and ceremony
- Possesses distinctive qualities that marks it as extra-ordinary

- Possesses healing or divinatory properties
- Provides a community with some indispensable product
- Site of an unusual event or phenomena
- Symbol of fertility, longevity, or immortality

Sacred Tree Species (May Be Considered World Trees Representing the Spiritual Center of a Culture and Often Believed to Connect or Communicate All Cosmic Levels)

- Acacia (*Acacia sensu lato*)
- Alder (*Alnus spp.*)
- Almond (*Amygdalus communis*)
- Apple (*Malus spp.*)
- Asam (*Kapaca guineensis*)
- Asas (*Bridelia grandis*)
- Aseng (*Musanga acropioides*)
- Ash (*Fraximus excelsior*)
- Asoka (*Saraca indica*)
- Azap (*Mimuspos djyve*)
- Azem (*Psilanthemus manii*)
- Balsam fir (*Abies balsamum*)
- Banyan (*Ficus bengalensis*)
- Baobab (*Adansonia digitala*)
- Beech (*Fagus gandiflia*)
- Bel (*Aegle marmelos*)
- Birch (*Betula spp.*)
- Bodhi (*Ficus religiosa*)
- Cedar (*Cedrus spp.*)
- Cotton (*Bombax malabericum*)
- Date palm (*Phoenix dactylifera*)
- Elder (*Sambucus spp.*)
- Elegalenga (*Ocimum americanum*)
- Elm (*Ulmus spp.*)
- Eteng (*Pycnanthus angolensis*)
- Eyen (*Distmananthus benthamianus*)
- Fig (*Ficus spp.*)
- Garjan (*Dipterocarpia*)
- Ginkgo (*Ginkgo biloba*)
- Hawthorn (*CrataegusI*)
- Hazel (*Corylus spp.*)
- Holly (*Carya spp.*)
- Juniper (*Juniperus spp.*)
- Karam (*Nauclea parvifolia*)
- Laurel (*Laurus*)
- Linden (*Tilia spp.*)
- Mango (*Manfifera indica*)
- Mbel (*Pterocarpus soyanxiî*)
- Mes (*Celtis australis*)
- Mfôl (*Enantia cholorantha*)
- Munrun (*Bassia latifolia*)
- Myrrh (*Commiphora myrrha*)
- Oak (*Quercus spp.*)
- Olive (*Olea spp.*)
- Ôtunga (*Polyalthia suaveolens*)
- Ôvung (*Guibourtia tessmanniî*)
- Peach (*Prunus persica*)
- Persea (*Persea*)
- Pine (*Pinus spp.*)
- Pipal (*Aegle marmelos*)
- Plane (*Platarius orientalis*)
- Pomegranate (*Punica granatum*)
- Rowan (Mountain Ash) (*Sorbus aucuparia*)
- Sal (*Shorea robusta*)
- Silk Cotton (*Ceiba pentandra*)
- Sycamore (*Ficus sycamorus*)
- Tamarind (*Tamarindus indica*)
- Tamarisk (*Tamarix spp.*)
- Terebinth (Turpentine) (*Pistacia terebinthus*)
- Walnut (*Juglans regia*)
- Willow (*Salix spp.*)
- Yew (*Taxus spp.*)

Ritual Materials Associated with Sacred or Spiritual Trees

- Altars
- Animal remains
- Baskets
- Candles
- Coins
- Cloth rags
- Eggs
- Figurines
- Flags
- Food remains
- Gems and jewelry
- Honey
- Incense
- Milk
- Musical instruments
- Nails hammered into tree
- Occupational tools
- Offering vessels
- Oil/oil lamps
- Pictures or images of religious figures
- Ribbons
- Ritual pits containing a live tree or a tree trunk and filled in with offerings
- Ritual shafts filled with pots, offerings, leaves, nuts, etc.
- Stones (may be manuports)
- Thread and yarn
- Votive tablets
- Weapons
- Wine

Psychotropic Plants

Hallucinogenic plants have a long history of use in ritual and magic. Evidence of these mind-altering substances can be found through archaeobotanical remains from either wild harvested sources or from cultivated areas, or from residue analysis of the tools and vessels used in their application or ingestion. Their representations are also visible in carvings, figurines, rock art, and textile imagery. (For nonpsychotropic ritual and magical plants, see "Glossary of Ritualistic, Religious, and Magical Plants.")

- Ayahuasca/Yajé (*Banisteriopsis caapi*)
- Bakana (*Scirpus atrovirens*)
- Blue Water Lily/Ninfa/ Quetzalaxochiacatl (*Nymphaea ampla*; *Nymphaea caerulea*)
- Chiricaspi/Chiric-Sanango (*Brunfelsia chiricaspi*)
- Copelandia (*Copelandia cyanescens*)
- Culebra Borrachero (*Methysticodendron amesianum*)
- Deadly Night Shade (Belladonna) (*Atropa belladonna*)
- Dhatura/Dutra (*Datura metel*)
- El Nene/El Ahijado/El Macho/ Maconha (*Coleus blumei*; *Coleus pumilus*)
- Epená/Nyakwana/Yakee/Paricá (*Virola calophylla*)
- Ephedra/ma-huang/Indian tea/ Mormon tea/popotillo (*Ephedra spp.*)
- Ergot (*Claviceps purpurea*)
- Esakuna (*Cymbopogon densiflorus*)
- Everlasting Coumarine (*Helichrysum foetidum*)

- Floripndio/Huacacachu/Maicoa/ Toá/Tonga (*Brugmansia arborea* and several others)
- Frijol de Playa (*Canavalia maritima*)
- Gaise Noru Noru (*Ferraria glutinosa*)
- Genista (*Cytisus canariensis*)
- Gi'-i-Wa/Gi'-i-Sa-Wa (*Lycoperdon marginatum*)
- Hemp/Marijuana (*Cannabis indica*)
- Henbane (*Hyoscyamus niger*)
- Hierba de la Pastora/Hierba de la Virgen/Pipiltzintli (*Salvia divinorum*)
- Hikuli Mulato/Bakana/Wichuri (*Epithelantha micromeris*)
- Hikuli Suramé/Chautle/Peyote Cimarrón/Tsuwiri (*Ariocarpus fissuratus*)
- Iboga (*Tabernanthe iboga*)
- Jimson Weed/Thorn Apple (*Datura stramonium*)
- Jurema/Ajuca (*Mimosa hostilis*; *Mimosa verrucosa*)
- Kieli/Hueipatl/Tecomaxochitl (*Solandra brevicalyx*; *Solandra guerrerensis*)
- Mandrake (*Mandragora officinarum*)
- Mescal Bean/Coral Bean/ Colorines/Frijoles/Red Bean (*Sophora secudiflora*)
- Mexican Buckeye/Texas Buckeye (*Ungnadia speciose*)
- Mushrooms (*Amanita muscaria*; *Conocybe siligineoides*; *Pslocybe mexicana*)
- Ololiuhqui/Badoh/MorningGlory/ Snake plant (*Turbina corymbosa*)
- Paguando/Totubjansush/Guatillo (*Iochroma fuchsioides*)
- Peyote (false) (*Coryphantha compacta*)
- Peyote (*Lophophora williamsii*; *Lophophora diffusa*)
- Piule/Badoh Negro/Tlililtzin (*Ipomoea violacea*)
- Rapé dos Indios (*Maquira sclerophylla*)
- San Pedro/Aguacolla/Gigantón (*Trichocereus pachanoi*)
- Screw Pine (*Pandanus* sp.)
- Shang-La (*Phytolacca acinosa*)
- Soma/Fly Agaric (*Amanita muscaria*)
- Taglli/Hierba Loca (*Pernettya furens*)
- Taique/Borrachero (*Desfonainia spinosa*)
- Takini (*Helicostylis pedunculata*)
- Teonanacatl/Hongo de San Isidro/ She-to/To-shka (*Conocybe siligineoides*; *Panaeolus sphictrinus*; various other mushrooms)
- Toloache (*Datura inoxia*)
- Torna Loco (*Datura ceratocaula*)
- Vilca/Cebil (*Anadenanthera colubrine*)
- Wichuriki/Hikuli Rosapara (*Mammillaria grahamii*)
- Yahutli (*Tagetes lucida*)
- Yopo/Cohoba (*Anadenanthera peregrine*)
- Yün-Shih (*Caesalpinia sepiaria*)
- Zacatechichi/Thle-Pelekano/Bitter grass (*Calea zacatechichi*)

GLASS

The reflective and shimmering characteristics of glass make it a prime material for supernaturally endowed objects. Its malleability enabled its use in a wide range of objects found in ritualistic, magical, and religious settings. Although fragile and susceptible to degradation in buried contexts, glass does survive well in many terrestrial and underwater archaeological sites.

- Amulet case pendants
- Beads
- Blue or green bottles for "bottle trees"
- Buttons
- Decanters
- Eggs
- Evil eye beads
- Flasks and beakers for alchemical work
- Inlaid on important holy or political book covers/bindings
- Inlay material for metal objects
- Inlay material on masks
- Goblets/chalices
- Jewelry (armbands, bracelets, earrings, pendants, rings)
- Marbles
- Mirrors
- Orbs
- Phials
- Scrying bowls
- Scrying glass
- Shards (often blue) found in magical assemblages
- Stained glass windows
- Symbols incised, scratched, or embedded into windowpanes
- Tesserae
- Witch balls
- Witch bottles

METAL

Iron has been revered by many as a supernaturally powerful and protective substance; hence, any object constructed of or enhanced with iron embodies this power. Precious metals also have supernatural or divine associations. Part of their power is connected with their reflective or shimmering characteristics. The sound producing qualities of metal also made it an ideal material for empowered objects. As a result, metal religious and magical objects appear in a vast array of forms and expressions. Many types of metal (even ferrous iron) survive well in the archaeological record, and virtually every type has been used for ritual, religious, or magical objects (gold, silver, copper, bronze, brass, tin, nickel, iron, cast and wrought iron, steel, lead, pewter).

Adornments (Many of These Function as Amulets)

- Beads
- Brass tacks
- Buttons
- Coins
- Crowns and circlets
- Gorgets
- Hair ornaments and combs
- Jewelry (arm bands, bracelets, brooches, earrings, nose rings, pendants, pins, rings, torcs)
- Perforated discs
- Pilgrim badges
- Tinkle/jingle cones

Amulets

- Architectural hardware (door knockers, strap hinges, and cock's head hinges)
- Corno or cornicello (gold or silver horn-shaped amulet; alternatively made of red coral)
- Crosses/crucifixes
- Cylinder-seals
- Firearm side plates
- Hand pendants (Hamsa, Hand of Fatima, Figa)
- Spoons

Imagery

- Armor breastplates, helmets, etc.
- Coins
- Cylinder-seals
- Door knockers
- Figurines and statues (animals, deities, spirits)
- Firebacks
- Firedogs
- Floral images and objects
- Hinges
- Locks
- Masks
- Plaques
- Seal stamps
- Signet rings and stamps
- Staff heads
- Sword pommels
- Vessels (cauldrons, goblets, plates, etc.)

Sharp Objects

- Agricultural implements (axes, hoes, plows, scythes, etc.)
- Hearth pot hooks
- Knives and daggers
- Nails (bent and included in witch bottles, driven into figurines, driven around door and window frames, studded into doors, red-painted heads)
- Needles and pins
- Sacrificial tools
- Scissors
- Spears
- Styluses
- Swords
- Tattoo needles

Sound Producing

- Bells, cymbals, gongs
- Buttons
- Door knockers
- Flutes
- Gridirons and other cooking pots/ pans
- Horns
- Perforated discs or coins
- Pipe organ pipes
- Prayer wheels
- Rattles
- Singing bowls
- Tinkle/jingle cones
- Trumpets
- Wind chimes

Vessels

- Cauldrons
- Censors (brass, bronze, copper, silver)
- Feasting vessels
- Goblets/chalices
- Mortar and pestle
- Offering/collection plates
- Oil ewers
- Oil lamps
- Reliquary boxes
- Wine ewers

Other

- Indicator head (attached to a wooden or ivory rod used to point to word or line in scripture)
- Buckles
- Candlesticks
- Holy book/scripture covering/ binding
- Horse brasses
- Horseshoes
- Keys
- Lead curse tablets
- Locks
- Mirrors (brass, gold, silver)
- Mosaic tiles
- Orbs
- Scepters
- Scrying plates
- Thimbles

MINERAL/LITHIC/SOIL

Earth elements—minerals, stones, and soils—feature in many enactments and expressions of ritual and belief. They may be used as mediums for painting or staining in rock art or in funerary contexts, or the particular substance may be believed to have inherent magical or divine power. Some minerals (ash, chalk, and mud for example) are used as body paint in ritual or warfare contexts. Stone lends itself to various modes of modification to express or activate these powers. Other sensorial aspects of stone may also play a role in its use in religious, ritualistic, or magical practices.

- Ash
- Chalk
- Charcoal
- Fossils
- Gypsum (white)
- Lime
- Mud
- Phosphorus
- Ocher
- Salt
- Sand
- Soot
- Stone (Carved images on stones enhances the stones' power) (see "Glossary of Ritualistic, Religious, and Magical Gems and Other Stones").
  » Altars
  » Apotropaic (protective)
  » Astronomical alignment markers
  » Coronation stones (reveals rightful rulership)
  » Crop/digestive/head stones (from the inside of animals and fish)
  » Fetishes
  » Figurines and statues
  » Grave markers
  » Handfasting and other Stones of Accord (large, holed stones through which parties shook hands in agreement and commitment)
  » Lithophones (naturally sound-producing stones)
  » Lithotherapy (healing stones)
  » Medicine wheels
  » Picture stones
  » Portals to spiritual realms
  » Punishment/law (identifiers of thieves and other criminals and also implement of punishment)
  » Ritual tools
  » Sacred space markers
  » Sacrificial tables
  » Sensorial aspects indicative of religious, ritual, or magical association (color, hardness, reflective qualities, sound, temperature, texture, weight)
  » Sigil stones
  » Standing stones
  » Stone circles
  » Victory stones (predict or ensure victory over enemies)
  » Visionary/divinatory stones
  » Virtue testing stones
  » Weapons (full-sized or miniature) made from soft, unusual, or nonfunctional stone as sacrifices or offerings (e.g., stone axes of jadeite or chalk)

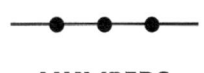

NUMBERS

All major religious belief systems, and undoubtedly most rituals and magical practices, incorporate numerological elements. These may be numbers with divine significance or some other perceived powerful resonance. The use of these numbers can be straightforward and obvious (e.g., two guardian statues at a temple gate), but they can also be embedded with the measurements of objects or structures, the distances between sacred features, or the repetition of particular motifs or attributes comprising sites, objects, and landscapes. Look for the following as indicators of such beliefs:

- Dimensions of ritual/religious structures following scriptural numerology
- Dimensions of town or temple complexes following numerological pattern
- Measurements of objects incorporating designated numerals
- Numbers are used in their base forms as well as with or in their multiple forms (e.g., four: four, eight, twelve, etc.)
- Objects or motifs recurring in particular numerical groupings
- Particular attributes of a motif occurring in spiritually powerful number sequences
- Placement of apotropaic objects at similarly measured distances
- The number three (and its multiples six, nine, twelve, etc.) is used almost universally and is the most frequently noted in religious/ magical practices

Other number-related objects used in ritual, religion, or magic:

- Astrological charts
- Astronomical markers
- Byobu (usually six-paneled screen)
- Calendars (carved, painted, written)
- Divining sticks (e.g., *I Ching*)
- Geometric numeric figures (hexagons, octagons, pentagons/ pentagrams, triangles)
- Numerical symbols
- Royal measuring devices
- Time devices
- Triptychs

SYMBOLS, DESIGNS, AND IMAGES

While virtually anything could be used by an individual as a symbol or design to designate an abstract correlation or meaning within a ritualistic, religious, or magical context, there are several symbols and designs that have been frequently repeated and widely adopted, substantiating their usage as powerful elements in the practice of various rituals, religious observances, or magical traditions. Symbols can be either abstract images or clearly articulated representations. Symbols and designs can be multivalent, often expressing a range of meanings simultaneously; therefore, similar or identical symbols or designs may not necessarily be intended as ritualistic, religious, or magical in every context or application.

The medium upon which symbols, designs, or images are wrought, or in the case of three-dimensional figural images, the material of which they are made are especially important aspects of their ritualistic, religious, or magical meaning and power. Many times these materials have special value due to their rareness or uniqueness, their association with particular deities/spirits, or their part in a complex network of other powerfully charged associations.

Animals

The use of animals to symbolize particular attributes (e.g., strength, wisdom), concepts (e.g., cultural identity, authority), persons, or spiritual beings dates to humankind's earliest expressive endeavors. Animal symbolic images manifest in every medium, form, and context. They are usually animals found within a cultural territory and with which the culture is directly familiar; however, they may also be mythological, legendary, or extinct creatures. While all animals (extant, extinct, or mythical) could be used symbolically, the most oft occurring include:

- Alligators and crocodiles
- Antelope
- Bats
- Bears
- Big cats (jaguars, leopards, lions, etc.)
- Bird of paradise
- Boars
- Bulls (domesticated and wild)
- Cats
- Dogs
- Doves
- Dragons
- Eagles
- Elephants
- Fish
- Frogs and toads
- Goats
- Horses
- Lambs
- Lizards
- Monkeys
- Owls
- Rabbits and hares
- Rams
- Rats and mice
- Ravens
- Roosters
- Seals and sea lions
- Snakes
- Stags
- Turtles and tortoises
- Wolves

Composite Figures (Also Called Trans-species)

Combining attributes of humans, animals, and plants in various configurations allowed complex relationships and concepts to be expressed in a single image. Animals or plants can appear with human characteristics, in human postures, or engaging in human behaviors. Human figures may appear with animal or plant characteristics or behaving like plants or animals. Some figures may be combinations of multiple animals and/or plants. Composite figures represent a variety of entities and ideas:

- Alchemical concepts
- Allegorical vices and virtues
- Ancestral spirits
- Astrological beings
- Cosmological realms
- Deities and divine beings
- Demons
- Divine rulers
- Fertility

- Interconnectedness of spiritual, human, animal, and plant domains
- Landscape spirits (e.g., foliate heads for forest spirits)
- Liminality
- Mythological creatures
- Sexuality and Gender
- Spirit world
- Transformation

Gender/Sex Variation Images

Depiction of sexual morphology or notions of gender are common attributes of imagery utilized in ritualistic, religious, or magical contexts. These images function in a multiplicity of ways from the most direct (e.g., emphatic genitalia = fertility) to obscure and complex (e.g., female depicted with normally attributed male accoutrements engaged in male-related activity). They may even be wholly symbolic (e.g., female = idea of Mother Land). Even in ambiguous imagery, it is sometimes possible to see gendered reference in other details such as left and right positioning.

- Androgynous figures
- Animal hermaphroditic figures
- Emphatic portrayal of genitalia
- Gender identity reiterated through repetition of gender-associated objects, animals, behaviors, and symbols within the overall image
- Gendered images may represent concepts like dominance vs. subjugation, nationality, or territory
- Hermaphroditic figures
- Inversion of gendered appearance and behavior or mixed gender motifs (sometimes this indicated a shaman or two-spirit person)
- Left or right imagery (e.g., female warriors wielding weapon in left hand whereas men usually depicted wielding weapon in the right hand)
- Particular nonreproductive age groups (children, postmenopausal women, the elderly) may be considered genderless and may be depicted as androgynous or marked by specific clothing, hair styles, or other details to indicate that status
- Therianthropic figures (often incorporating antlers or horns or melding humans and animals to emphasize sexuality and/or gender)

Geometric Images

Several geometric figures recur throughout the world and across time as powerful symbols of the divine or as magical elements generating their own forces or channeling power from some other benevolent or malevolent source. These images can appear as drawn, painted, burned, incised, embroidered, carved, formed, molded, or represented on every conceivable material or surface.

- Circles
- Crosses (see Figure 9.2 "Template of cross style examples" in Chapter 9)
- Crosshatches
- Dots
- Grids
- Hexagons
- Lines (straight, wavy, zigzag)
- Octagons
- Pentangles/pentagrams
- Spirals
- Squares
- Stars (usually created by overlapping triangles)
- Swastikas
- Triangles

Hyperbole and Distortion

Imagery with intended ritualistic or belief-centered meanings and uses often depicted subjects with exaggerated, emphasized, or otherwise distorted features. This focus on deformity or skewed perspective mirrors the common preference for sacrificial victims with physical abnormalities or perceived otherness as particularly suited to be mediators in the spirit world. These hyperbolic and distorted images manifest in a wide range of motifs, including:

- Asymmetry of features
- Bodily deformities
- Dimorphism
  » Body disproportionate in itself or in relation to other objects and subjects in the image
  » Overly large body parts in relation to normal or undersized parts
    – Most common hyperbolic parts: eyes, genitalia, hands, heads, legs, lips, and mouths
- Disarticulated limbs and body parts (arms, eyes, feet, hands, legs)
- Extra limbs
- Polydactyly
- Presence of some but not all features/details (e.g., blank face; eyes and nose but no mouth; body but no arms or legs)
- Reversed faces (two different faces seen by inverting the image)
- Schematic (minimalistic and somewhat abstract) portraying only the essential features in an exaggerated way
- *Tête coupée* (severed head)
- Tricephalic heads

Mystical

Many religious or spiritual traditions (like alchemy) used secret or esoteric symbol systems whose meanings and use were restricted to a particular group or class of initiated practitioners. These symbols were often complex combinations that may include:

- Abbreviations or acronyms
- Animals, composite animals, or therianthropes
- Celestial images
- Geometric figures
- Human body parts (eyes, hands, legs)

- Made up alphabet/script
- Made up words
- Numbers
- Plants
- Word squares

Other Ritual Marks

Found in both formal religious settings and in domestic or mundane contexts, various ritual marks have been documented that appear to act apotropaically. In some circumstances, marks may also indicate curse spells or hexes. In addition to geometric and mystical markings, look for the following:

- Burn marks (some teardrop-shaped caused by the flame of a candle)
- Dots
- Gridirons
- Hearts

- Images (for imitative magic, e.g., a ship to ensure a safe sea voyage)
- Initials
- Labyrinths
- Ladders
- Scrolls

Rock Art

Rock Art can generally be divided into two broad application types: surface and incised. Surface applications (pictographs) are painted or drawn images on rock wall surfaces inside caves or rock shelters or on cliff wall faces. These may range from the complex and realistic images found at Paleolithic sites like Lascaux and Chauvet to the abstract and schematic imagery from across African, Asian, Australian, and North American sites to the nineteenth-century and early twentieth-century historic inscriptions in the North American West. Incised applications (petroglyphs) are pecked, carved, chipped, or scratched into either the rock surface itself or the rock's surface coating called "desert varnish."

The images often express motifs of transformation, transition, and liminality. They may also be linked to the immediate and wider landscape. For example, imagery of water birds may proliferate at sights close to or in sight/

sound of water sources or images of water spirits or "offerings" to those spirits may be situated along shorelines where they will be "washed" by the lapping waves or submerged during high tides.

Many regions and countries require permits to access rock art sites. Please consult the proper authorities in your area for the required permits and protocols. Rock art is extremely fragile and any engagement with it and its recordation requires particular care. Keep impact to the rock surfaces to the absolute minimum, which means:

- Do not remove turf from buried rock surfaces or mosses, lichens, or other plant growth from panels. The removal of these growths weakens the rock surface or exposes the surfaces to erosive processes. Also, do not remove surrounding plants as they may also form part of the system of meaning in conjunction with the rock art.
- Do not attempt to remove graffiti, chalk, or other media from the rock.
- Do not remove wasp nests as they can sometimes be used to date rock art.
- Do not use substances (including water) to clean rock surfaces.
- Only use soft brushes or your hands to gently whisk away leaves or bird droppings; Never use stiff or hard bristled tools or metal tools (trowels or knives) to attempt to clean surfaces.
- Do not try to enhance images with chalk or any other substance.
- Do not use any recording method that would have direct or repeated contact with the rock surface or use adhesives/tapes on the rock to affix tracing material or photographic scales.
- Do not deface or endanger the rock by writing your name or messages on the panels, walking or driving over panels, or lighting fires or candles on or close to the rock.

Rock attributes may be important elements in the overall meaning, function, and power of the imagery. Such attributes include:

- Color
- Cracks
- Curvature
- Inclusion of other materials like quartz or gold
- Patterning
- Resonance
- Shadowed and illuminated areas
- Shine
- Texture

Pictograph media (excepting charcoal, media was usually mixed with water, animal fat, blood, urine, or egg yolk as a binding agent). The choice of medium and its additive(s) was often dictated by the image, meaning, placement, and function of the pictographs.

- Bat guano (white, brown)
- Chalk (white)
- Charcoal (black, grey)
- Copper ore (green)

- Diatomaceous earth (white)
- Gypsum (white)
- Hematite (red)
- Kaolinite clay (white, grey)
- Lime (white)
- Lizard or bird dung (white or yellow)
- Manganese (black)
- Ocher (yellow, orange, red, brown)
- Shells (white)

Common Pictograph and Petroglyph Images

Animals

- Antelope
- Aurochs
- Badgers
- Bears
- Birds
- Bison/buffalo
- Bulls
- Deer/elk/moose
- Dogs/coyotes
- Dragonflies
- Fish
- Frogs
- Horses
- Insects
- Lions
- Lizards
- Mammoth/mastodons
- Rabbits
- Reptiles
- Rhinos
- Sheep and goats (domestic and wild)
- Snakes
- Spiders
- Squirrels
- Tracks
- Turtles

Humans

- Apparel and adornment
- Birthing
- Corn maidens
- Eyes
- Dancing
- Feet and footprints
- Genitalia
- Hands and handprints
- Headdresses and masks
- Human forms
- Hunters
- Shield warriors
- Squatting man

Objects and Other Images

- Activities (dancing, flying, games, hunting, music)
- Anthropomorphic creatures
- Boats
- Bows and arrows
- Circles
- Celestial (sun, moon, stars)
- Clubs (claviforms)
- Crenellations
- Crescents

- Crosses
- Cup marks
- Dots
- Drums and drumsticks
- Flutes and other musical instruments like horns
- Flywhisks
- Geometric symbols/designs
- Grids
- Horned and other monsters/demons
- Ladders
- Lightning bolts
- Lines
- Number systems
- Maps
- Maze/labyrinth
- Medicine bags
- Plants
- Shields
- Sleds
- Spears
- Spirals
- Staff or crook/crosier
- Swastika
- Tectiforms (house-shapes)
- Theriomorphic creatures
- Tree of Life
- Water/waves
- Weapons
- Weather (clouds, lightning, rain, rainbows)
- Wheels
- Zigzags

Rock art stylistic traditions are the specifically regional variations and/or suites of image subjects, artistic style types, colors, pigments, surfaces, and positioning. Within these traditions the common artistic style types include:

- Abstract
- Naturalistic
- Outline
- Realistic
- Schematic
- Solid (positive)
- Stencil (negative)
- X-Ray

Text

Like abstract symbols, text itself is a symbolic system. Words, actual or nonsense, play an especially significant role in ritualistic, religious, and magical practice as virtually all cultures believe in their innate power. This may stem from the connection between speaking (breathing) and the idea that the breath is the soul or life-force. Many religious traditions include creation stories of deities "speaking" or breathing the world into existence. In past historic periods when writing and reading were skills possessed by only an elite chosen few, words (especially written ones) carried additional weight as mysterious and influential purveyors of divine (or demonic) power.

While virtually all rituals would have included some spoken incantations, prayers, or enchantments as part of their enactment, there are various material manifestations of the written word that indicate their ritualistic, religious, and/or magical character.

- **Charms:** written charms on clay, cloth, paper, papyri, parchment, wax, or wood. (Often concealed around thresholds for protection, or attached to other objects)
- **Curses:** may be written on a variety of material, but often on lead. They are often folded or bent and concealed (e.g., thrown in water, placed in hole in tree trunk, buried, inserted into grave monuments or cavities in burial ground, etc.)
- **Magical words:** usually nonsense words, sometimes unpronounceable, sometimes misspelled or altered foreign words, they are used alone or in conjunction with actual divine names and/or prayers.
- **Names:** the power inherent in a deity's name is virtually universal and is called upon in both religious and magical practice as the ultimate empowering element in the rite. Also, equating one's true name with one's essence or soul is a widespread and ancient belief; thus, great effort has always been expended to circumvent the use of the true name of deities, rulers, religious personages, and individuals. This name aversion may be visible as:
  - » Euphemistic names or descriptions on statues, structures, or in books
  - » Initials or surname only on grave markers
  - » Obliterating names on statues or structures upon a person's death
- **Scripture:** all formal religions have some type of written texts espousing their tenets, creation stories, and holy biographies. Some of these are gathered into books or manuscripts; however, excerpts, citations, or quotations are often inscribed, written, painted, or mosaicked into/onto walls, floors, tablets, fonts, stelae, statues, grave markers, thrones, gemstones, amulets, jewelry, or other structures or objects.

TEXTILES AND CLOTHING

Although textiles are fragile and do not generally survive well in the archaeological record, they do surface from arid or anaerobic contexts in appreciable numbers. The religious, ritualistic, or magical aspect of textiles/clothing may reside in their forms, material composition, colors, applied symbolic designs, or usages.

- Altar cloths
- Animal figures
- Aprons
- Banners and flags
- Bed curtains
- Belts
- Bibs
- Blankets and bed linens
- Canopies
- Cerecloths
- Clothing (shirts, dresses, pants, cloaks, shawls, robes, tunics)

- Cord (usually knotted)
- Curtains
- Cushions
- Dolls
- Felt or cloth hearts (usually red)
- Footwear
- Fringes
- Hats, head bands, and headdresses
- Horse accoutrements (martingales, saddle blankets, tail and mane amulets)
- Pendants
- Pom poms
- Pouches and bags
- Prayer cloths
- Prayer rugs
- Rags (often red, white, blue, yellow, or green)
- Religious vestments
- Sarongs
- Sashes
- Scarves
- Scrolls
- Shrouds
- Stuffed triangle amulets
- Thread, string, yarn (usually red)
- Towels
- Veils and masks
- Worn or damaged clothing
- Worn or damaged footwear

CHAPTER 8

Sensory Elements in Ritual, Religion, and Magic

The senses, both physical and affective, play a major role in the enactment and experience of ritual, religious, and magical practices. Sometimes these components are easily recognized; however, often these elements are taken for granted and overlooked leaving critical aspects of human ritualized behavior misunderstood or entirely unconsidered.

Although specific sensory elements may be emphasized and recognized as the following lists illustrate, sensory stimuli usually act in tandem. Wind, for example, is itself tactile (one feels the sensation of temperature and motion across the skin) and vestibular (the strength can push or sway); but it is also the catalyst for other sensory experiences: auditory (as it rustles the trees or howls/moans through objects); visual (its travel seen in the objects it moves); olfactory (it carries and intermingles the scents of whatever it passes over); and affective (its role in carrying prayers to the ancestors and gods through rising or disseminating smoke evokes emotional responses).

Often in religious and ritual practices, it was believed one could commune with the spirits or divine only when in a state of altered consciousness, which necessarily implies that one's sensory experiences needed to be manipulated in some way. Altered states of consciousness (ASC) can be achieved in various ways:

- Chanting
- Controlled breathing
- Dance
- Hyperventilation
- Ingestion (intoxicating beverages or psychotropic plants)
- Isolation

- Meditation
- Music
- Repetitive vestibular motion (jumping, rocking, swaying, swirling)
- Sensory deprivation
- Sleeplessness

Some of these behaviors are seen depicted in figural objects and imagery or can be deduced through the material remains of vessels, plant residues, or activity in isolated or dark contexts.

AFFECTIVE

- Structures designed to manipulate light levels and quality (brightness of sunlight, darkness/shadows) to produce emotional states of joy, fear, anxiety, etc.
- Structures or natural sites that block or limit participants' visual or auditory scopes, which can generate feelings of anxiety
- Use of color to induce desired emotional states appropriate to the ritual or the sacred setting
- Use of psychotropic substances to achieve altered states of consciousness or altered emotional states
- Use of tactile features (hardness or softness of seating, kneeling surfaces; temperature of ritual space and surfaces, etc.) to create feelings of comfort/discomfort, calm/anxiety

AUDITORY

- Bells and chimes
- Ceremonial structures (e.g., chamber tombs) that produce infrasound (low frequency vibration). Infrasound can cause feelings of awe, fear, and/or perception of supernatural events.
- Chambers constructed to channel sound in temples or other ritualistic structures
- Conch shells
- Cymbals
- Garment attachments: bones, buttons, claws, coins, discs, shells, teeth
- Gongs
- Horns and trumpets
- Musical instruments (drums, flutes, harps, rattles, tambourines, whistles)
- Oracle speaking tubes
- Osteophones
- Prayer wheels
- Rain sticks
- Religious buildings constructed to acoustically amplify choral singing and chanting
- Ringing rocks (lithophones)
- Ritual area situated to hear rushing water or blowing/moaning/singing wind or wind in trees
- Singing bowls
- Tinkle/jingle cones
- Wind chimes and rattles (glass, shell, wood)

GUSTATORY (TASTE)

- Anthropophagy (cannibalistic ritual consumption—butcher marks or pot-boiling evidence on human bones)
- Communion wafers

- Ritual feast offerings (bread, fruit, honey, meat, milk, cacao, tea, or foods not usually consumed in everyday contexts)
- Wine, beer, mead, and other intoxicating drinks

OLFACTORY

- Anointing oils
- Fragrant flowers
- Censors
- Incense used by
  » Africans
  » Arabians
  » Asians
  » Buddhists
  » Christians (Anglican, Catholic, Orthodox)
  » Egyptians
  » Greeks
  » Hindus
  » Jews
  » Mesoamericans
  » Muslims
  » Native Americans
  » Romans
  » Scandinavians
- Incense ingredients
  » Aloe
  » Ambergris
  » Balm of Gilead
  » Bear root
  » Bdellium
  » Benzoin and other gum resins
  » Camphor

» Cassia
» Cedar
» Cinnamon
» Copal
» Coriander seed
» Costus
» Cypress
» Dried flowers, seeds, roots
» Fir
» Fragrant woods (cedar, citrus, myrtle, sandalwood)
» Frankincense (Olibanum)
» Galbanum
» Juniper
» Kyphi or khyphi (Egyptian incense comprised of: honey, wine, raisins, sweet rush, resin, myrrh, frankincense, seselis, calamus, asphalt, thryon, dock, arcouthelds, caramum, orris root, tchet oil)
» Ladanum
» Lavender
» Mastic
» Musk
» Myrrh
» Myrtle

- » Olive leaves
- » Onycha
- » Rose
- » Sage
- » Sandalwood
- » Stacte
- » Storax
- » Sweetgrass
- Perfumes
- Sites with natural pungent or acrid smells (bogs, hot springs, sulfur pools, swamps, volcanos, etc.)

TACTILITY/HAPTIC

- Abraded surfaces
- Carved or incised surfaces
- Exposed sites where participants experience intensity of rain, snow, sun, and wind on their skin
- Fire ordeal sites (e.g., walking on burning coals)
- Naturally rough or smooth surfaces explained through mythic or divine events
- Pecked surfaces
- Protruding sharp objects (teeth, rocks, metal) attached to masks, figurines, or other objects or features
- Rigid and hard furniture for worshippers (e.g., wooden benches and pews)
- Sites or objects with discernable temperatures (cold caves, cool metal, hot springs, burning needles, windy sites of hot, cool, cold breezes/blasts, etc.)
- Smoothed surfaces
- Stinging insect ordeal sites and paraphernalia (e.g., bullet ant ordeal)
- Subterranean narrow passageways requiring full-body contact—crawling, slithering, squeezing—to navigate to sacred interior
- Viscous substances (e.g., henna paste, honey)
- Water bodies or vessels for participant immersion, anointment, or cleansing

VESTIBULAR

- Ceremonial spaces for spinning, jumping, bouncing, rocking, swinging ritual performances
- Ceremonial structures (e.g., chamber tombs) that produce infrasound (low frequency vibration)
- Ritual space accessed via a swinging suspension bridge
- Ritual space over a rushing underground water course
- Ritual space situated to experience buffeting winds
- Twisting/turning ritual procession or access path

VISUAL

- Use of color to symbolize or activate sacred or magical elements and powers
- Use of colossal features, structures, or images to visually engage and dominate viewers
- Use of gateways, guardian statuaries, distinctive trees and rocks, walls, and other features to visually demarcate the entrance to or boundary of sacred space
- Use of light/dark to focus, emphasize, or obscure participants' view of ritual or ritual components

- Viewshed created to focus the gaze on or direct the view toward a sacred feature, site, or direction
- Viewshed created to intentionally obstruct view of sacred or ritual site or feature
- Viewshed manipulated to view numerically significant landscape (e.g., duality—light/dark elements or two sacred mountain peaks; trinity—vista of sky, earth, and water)

CHAPTER 9

Forms and Templates

This chapter is comprised of various recordation forms and templates that may be reproduced or altered to fit the context specific needs of the researcher. Even if a site does not obviously contain ritualistic, religious, or magical components, using these forms, or variations of them, will ensure that data necessary for determining the enactment of such belief-based practices will be captured and available for future analysis and interpretation.

The templates provide basic visual examples of some common types of ritualistic, religious, and/or magical objects and symbols. As there are literally thousands of variations of such objects/symbols, these examples represent a very small percentage and are intended to give researchers a general idea of what objects/symbols in particular categories may look like.

Forms

- Burial Site Survey Form
- Burial Recordation Form
- Conflict and Battlefield Site Recordation Form
- Individual Figurine/Statuary/Figural Vessel Recordation Form
- Intentionally Concealed Object (ICO) Recordation Form
- Plant Recordation and Collection Form
- Quotidian and Occupational Site Recordation Form
- Religious, Ceremonial, and Formal Ritual Building Recordation Form
- Ritual Landscape Recordation Form
- Ritual/Magical Assemblage Recordation Form
- Rock Art Recordation Form

BURIAL SITE SURVEY FORM

Site # _____ Recorded by _____ Date _____

Site Name _____ Site Type_____

Location Information _____

Coordinates: Township _____ Range _____ Section _____ Block _____ Lot # _____

Site Orientation and Situation on Landscape_____

Alignment (with ritual/sacred landscape features, structures, astronomical elements, habitation, ecofeatures)

_____

_____

_____

Accessibility (e.g., restricted access to particular individuals, seasonal or other temporal restrictions)

_____

_____

_____

Surrounding/Associated Plants _____

_____

Surrounding/Associated Structures and Their Functions _____

_____

_____

Religious, Ceremonial, Ritual Affiliation(s) of Burials _____

_____

_____

Existing Plat Maps _____

Original or Early Images/Drawings of Site_____

Designated Areas (e.g., cultural groups, religious groups, gender, organizational groups, children, criminals, suicides, social deviants) _____ - _____

_____

_____

_____

Ordered or random distribution of burials_____

_____

_____

_____

BURIAL SITE SURVEY FORM

INDIVIDUAL MARKERS/GRAVES—Use a separate sheet for each marker/grave

Marker: Photograph each marker/grave and assign an ID number to each.

Marker ID Number: _____

Names on Marker: _____

Birth Dates: _____ Death Dates: _____

Number of Inscribed Surfaces: _____ Inscriptions: _____

_____

Condition of Inscribed Surfaces: Mint   Clear but worn   Trace   Illegible   Mostly legible

Male   Female   Child   Infant   Ethnicity _____

Orientation (facing direction):   N   S   E   W   NE   SE   NW   SW   Undeterminable   (Circle most appropriate)

Footstone: yes   no   Footstone Inscription _____

Measurements/Dimensions (inches):

Main = Width _____ Height _____ Thickness _____

Base = Width _____ Height _____ Thickness _____

Grave= Width _____ Length _____ Distance between burials _____

Material Identification

Stone: Sandstone   Limestone   Marble   Granite   Other: _____

Masonry: Brick   Stucco   Cast stone   Concrete   Other: _____

Metal: Iron   White Bronze   Other: _____

Other material (describe): _____

Marker Style

Tablet   Tablet w/base(s)   Footstone   Box tomb   Table tomb   Obelisk   Cradle   Tree Stump   Rock Cairn

Government issue   Civil War   WWI   WWII   Spanish-American   Korean   Statuary   Monument   Plaque   Modern

Bedstead   Ledger   Grave depression   Barrow   Mound

Other: _____

Offerings Associated with Marker/Grave:

Fresh flowers   Artificial flowers   Stones   Food   Clothing/Cloth   Paper/Text   Balloons   Stuffed animals   Figurines

Ocher   Tobacco   Religious icons/objects   Water   Salt

Other: _____

BURIAL SITE SURVEY FORM

Enclosure Identification

Style: None   Fence   Wall   Coping   Cradle   Plantings   Curb

Material: Iron   Brick   Stucco   Stone   Concrete   Wood   Soil

Vegetation: Shrubbery   Trees   Groundcovers   Bulbs   Grass   None   Other: _____ __

Marker Condition: Sound   Cracked

Eroded 1 2 3   Sunken/tilted 1 2 3   Exfoliated 1 2 3 Delaminated 1 2 3

Broken _____ # of pieces   Voids/losses 1 2 3 Stained 1 2 3 Moss/lichen 1 2 3

Structure or footing unsound   Structure failure

Other: _____

Causes: Settling   Weathering   Vegetation   Paint/graffiti   Vandalism   Structure failure

Other: _____

Other Patterns:

Right: Male _____   Female _____   Left: Male _____   Female _____

Other Right/Left patterns _____

_____

Symbol

Skull   Faces   Bones   Plant/Flower   Cross   Dove   Lamb   Other animal   Religious iconography

Wreath   Masonic symbol   3D statuary   Geometric symbol   Urn   Willow   Book/Scroll   Organizational symbol

Finger pointing   Inverted torch   Family crest   Astronomical symbols   Occupational symbols/images

Other: _____

Numerical Patterns (within measurements, arrangements, or repetition of motifs and elements: often 2, 3, 4, 5, 7 and multiples)

_____
_____
_____
_____

Comments and Notes:

BURIAL SITE SURVEY FORM

Sketches of Grave/Marker; Map of Burial(s); Sketch of Burial in Greater Landscape

BURIAL RECORDATION FORM

Site # _____   Recorded by _____   Date _____

Site Name _____   Site Type_____

Location information _____

Coordinates: Township _____ Range _____ Section _____ Block _____ Lot # _____

Site Orientation and Situation on Landscape_____

Alignment (with ritual/sacred landscape features, structures, astronomical elements, habitation, ecofeatures)

_____

_____

_____

Accessibility (e.g., restricted access to particular individuals, seasonal or other temporal restrictions)

_____

_____

_____

Surrounding/Associated Plants _____

_____

Surrounding/Associated Structures and Their Functions _____

_____

_____

Religious, Ceremonial, Ritual Affiliation(s) of Burials _____

_____

_____

Existing Plat Maps _____

Original or Early Images/Drawings of Site_____

Designated Areas (e.g., cultural groups, religious groups, gender, organizational groups, children, criminals, suicides, social deviants) _____

_____

_____

_____

Ordered or random distribution of burials_____

_____

_____

_____

BURIAL RECORDATION FORM

Use a separate sheet for each burial

Assign an ID number to each burial. Take multiple photographs of each burial with scale and north arrow.

Burial ID Number: _____ Number of bodies _____ ☐ Primary burial ☐ Secondary burial

Type of Burial: In-ground Above-ground Cave/rock shelter Cliff Tree Other _____

Burial Container: Coffin Casket Vault Urn Basket Log Boat None Other _____

Grave Cut: _____ Fill: _____

Articulated: Y N Details: _____

Disturbed: Y N Details: _____

Sex and Age: Male Male ? Female Female ? Adult Adolescent Child Infant

Orientation (facing direction): N S E W NE SE NW SW Undeterminable (Circle most appropriate)

Head location: N S E W NE SE NW SW

Body Attitude: Supine (face up) Prone (face down) Fully extended Kneeling Sitting Standing Semi-flexed (loose fetal) Tightly-flexed (tight fetal) Lying on left side Lying on right side Arm(s) crossed over chest Arm(s) crossed over pelvis Arm(s) extended to side Arm(s) extended overhead Ankles crossed Legs crossed

Describe details including right/left elements: _____

_____

Burial Dimensions

Maximum length _____ Maximum width _____ Maximum Depth _____

Burial Container Measurements

_____
_____
_____
_____

Associated Grave Goods (List and describe in detail noting positioning and associations)

Object	Description

BURIAL RECORDATION FORM

Skeletal Record of Bones Present in Burial

NOTES:

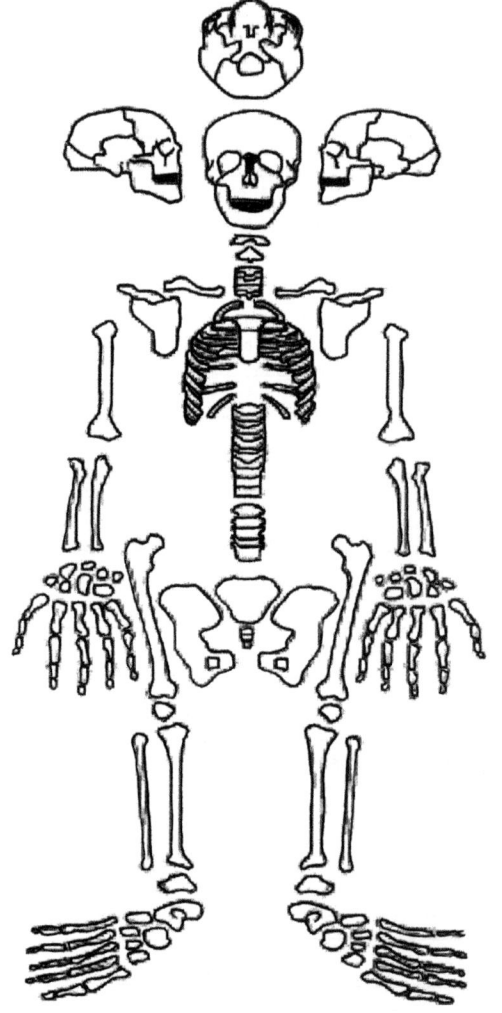

BURIAL RECORDATION FORM

Sketch/Map of Burial(s) including associated Grave Goods and references to greater ritual landscape

CONFLICT and BATTLEFIELD SITE RECORDATION FORM

Site # _____ Recorded by _____ Date _____

Site Name _____ Type of Conflict _____

Location information _____

Coordinates: Township _____ Range _____ Section _____

Orientation _____

Alignment (with ritual/sacred landscape features, structures, astronomical elements, habitation, ecofeatures)

_____
_____
_____

Accessibility (e.g., degree of difficulty to access; restricted access to particular individuals; seasonal or other temporal restrictions) _____

_____

Surrounding/Associated Plants _____ _____

_____

Surrounding/Associated Structures _____

_____
_____

Other Uses _____

_____

Topographical Features _____

_____
_____

Maps _____

_____

Original or Early Images/Drawings of Site _____

_____
_____

Known conflicts or battle events at site (include dates and participants if known) _____

_____
_____
_____
_____
_____

CONFLICT and BATTLEFIELD SITE RECORDATION FORM

Site Description _____

_____

_____

Colors (what colors, where used, associated with what forms and materials) _____

_____

_____

Features (e.g., shrines, cairns, stone or wooden markers, etc. indicating protection, prayer, or other ritual practice)

_____

_____

Site and Feature Measurements _____

_____

_____

_____

Numerical Patterns (within measurements or repetition of motifs and elements)

_____

_____

Symbols or Motifs (carved, painted, inscribed, etc. either formally or informally and their measurements, alignments, orientations, and/or associations with the building, the landscape, or other features)

_____

_____

_____

Wear patterns (from ritual/ceremonial participation: movement, dancing, sitting routes and places) _____

_____

Burials (locations and their measurements, alignments, orientations, and/or associations with the landscape or other features)

_____

_____

Concealed Objects (location and their measurements, alignments, orientations, and/or associations with the site, the landscape, or other features)_____

_____

Sensory Elements (attributes of site that create, manipulate, or otherwise affect sensory experience, e.g., visual, auditory, olfactory, tactile, gustatory (taste), temperature, pain) _____

_____

_____

Artifacts (appropriated enemies' clothing; talismans/amulets, altered ammo and weaponry, religious icons, enemies' body parts, trench art, totems, etc.) _____

_____

CONFLICT and BATTLEFIELD SITE RECORDATION FORM

Mapping/Illustrating (site elevations and plans from all sides, alignment with landscape features; details of symbolic, color, sensory, and numeric elements)

INDIVIDUAL FIGURINE/STATUARY/FIGURAL VESSEL RECORDATION FORM

Site # _____   Recorded by _____   Date _____

Site Name _____   Site Type_____

Location information _____

Coordinates: Township _____ Range _____ Section _____ Unit _____ Level _____

Deposition situation _____ _____

_____

Figurine Type

Figurine ID Number: _____

Human: Male   Female   Androgynous   Child   Infant   **Animal:** _____   Composite _____

Therianthrope (human/animal composite): _____

Mythical Being (deity, spirit, demon, etc.): _____

Figurine Attributes

Form: Full body   Partial body   Head   Hand   Foot   Leg   Arm   Phallus   Vulva   Other _____

Posture: Standing   Sitting   Squatting   Reclining   Crawling   Swimming   Flying   Other _____

Arms: Folded/crossed   Straight to sides   Bent to sides   Extended overhead   Outstretched to side   Outstretched to front

Legs: Crossed   Straight   Bent   Extended   **Feet:** _____

Eyes: Open   Closed   Partially open   No eyes   Extra large   Extra small

Mouth: Open   Closed   No mouth   Extra large   Extra small   Teeth   Tongue

Ears: Human   Animal _____   No ears   Extra large   Extra small

Horns or antlers (from what animal?) _____

Material

Ceramic/clay   Stone   Jade   Bone   Horn/Antler   Shell   Wood   Wax   Cloth   Grain   Rubber   Dough   Copal   Metal

Other material (describe): _____ _____

Decoration

Colors: _____

Inscriptions: _____

Clothing: _____

Symbols: _____

Other: _____

INDIVIDUAL FIGURINE/STATUARY/FIGURAL VESSEL RECORDATION FORM

Figurine Form

Statuette	Whistle	Vessel	Pendant	3-D	Flat	Natural Object

Other: _____

Molded	Modeled	Carved	Woven	Cast	Forged

Vessel:	Pitcher	Urn	Box	Bowl	Basket	Other:_____

Measurements/Dimensions

Width _____ Height _____ Thickness _____

In grouped depositions, distances between figurines _____

Distances between figurine(s) and other features

_____

_____

Symbolic Associations

Orientation (facing direction): N   S   E   W   NE   SE   NW   SW   Indeterminate   (Circle most appropriate)

Numerical symbols (e.g., 3, 4, 5, 7 or multiples of these) or recurring numerical patterns, occurrences, or motifs

_____

_____

_____

Association with thresholds or boundaries _____

Association with particular features _____

Artifacts associated with figurine

_____

_____

Photographs: _____

_____

Comments and Notes:

INDIVIDUAL FIGURINE/STATUARY/FIGURAL VESSEL RECORDATION FORM

Sketches of figurines; sketches of figurines in situ

INTENTIONALLY CONCEALED OBJECT (ICO) RECORDATION FORM

Site # _____   Recorded by _____   Date _____

Site Name _____   Site Type _____

Location information _____

Coordinates: Township _____   Range _____   Section _____   Unit _____   Level _____

Individual Object ☐   Multiple Similar Object Assemblage ☐   Multiple Mixed Object Assemblage ☐

Single Deposition Event ☐   Multiple Deposition Event ☐   Time Span of Multiple Deposition Event _____

Objects Contained in Multiple Object Assemblage _____

_____

Location of Deposit _____

_____

Provenience Data _____

Accessibility After Deposition:

☐ Inaccessible   ☐ Accessible with extreme difficulty (would require structural disturbance/destruction to access)

☐ Accessible with moderate difficulty (minor removal of structural element or in area not easily or normally reached)

☐ Accessible with ease (open hole/niche or area easily reached and available)

Object Description (Describe each object separately; use additional form if needed to document each artifact)

ID # _____   Object Form: _____

Material(s): _____

Color(s): _____

Symbols/Inscriptions/Markings: _____

_____

Decoration: _____

_____

Condition: ☐ Complete   ☐ Fragment   ☐ Worn/Deteriorated   ☐ Cut   ☐ Pierced   ☐ Bent   ☐ Mummified

☐ Burnt   ☐ Melted   ☐ Corroded   ☐ Articulated   ☐ Disarticulated   ☐ Flattened   ☐ Broken/Shattered

☐ Other _____

Gender/Sex/Age Attribution: ☐ Undetermined Adult   ☐ Female Adult   ☐ Male Adult

☐ Undetermined Child   ☐ Female Child   ☐ Male Child   ☐ Infant

Right or Left Associations: _____

Width _____   Height _____   Length _____   Thickness _____   Circumference _____   Diameter _____

Weight _____   Other _____

INTENTIONALLY CONCEALED OBJECT (ICO) RECORDATION FORM

Arrangement and Measurement (Always include measurement units appropriate to historic period and culture)

Orientation (alignment for each object: **N   S   E   W   NE   SE   NW   SW** Indeterminate)

Object 1 _____   Object 2 _____   Object 3 _____   Object 4 _____

Placement Details: _____

_____

In grouped depositions, distances between objects: _____

Distances between object(s) and other features: _____

_____

Associations with Right or Left: _____

_____

Symbolic Associations

Numerical symbols (e.g., 3, 4, 5, 7 or multiples of these) or recurring numerical patterns, occurrences, or motifs)

_____

_____

_____

Association with thresholds or boundaries _____

_____

Association with particular features _____

_____

Any obvious or known religious associations _____

Any obvious or known ethnic associations _____

History of Structure

Date(s) of Construction: _____   Date(s) of Renovation: _____

Original Builders: _____

Subsequent Owners/Residents and Dates: _____

_____

_____

Structure Type: ☐ Residential ☐ Religious ☐ Civic ☐ Commercial ☐ Medical ☐ Industrial ☐ Entertainment

☐ Agricultural ☐ Governmental ☐ Educational ☐ Mortuary ☐ Memorial ☐ Transportation

Specific Building/Structure Form: _____

INTENTIONALLY CONCEALED OBJECT (ICO) RECORDATION FORM

History of Structure, continued

Building/Structure Description: _____

_____

_____

Building/Structure Materials: _____

_____

_____

Historic or Current Association with or Proximity to:

☐ Water Feature _____

☐ Subterranean Space _____

☐ Trees _____

☐ Other Distinctive Natural Features _____

☐ Other Distinctive Structures or Features _____

Historical Events Related to Time, Place, or Individuals Associated with Structure: _____

_____

_____

_____

_____

_____

_____

_____

Photography Log Information: _____

_____

_____

_____

_____

Notes: _____

_____

_____

_____

_____

INTENTIONALLY CONCEALED OBJECT (ICO) RECORDATION FORM

Object Description (Describe each object separately; use additional forms if needed to document each artifact)

ID # _____ Object Form: _____

Material(s): _____

Color(s): _____ _____

Symbols/Inscriptions/Markings: _____

_____

Decoration: _____ _____

_____

Condition: ☐ Complete ☐ Fragment ☐ Worn/Deteriorated ☐ Cut ☐ Pierced ☐ Bent ☐ Mummified

☐ Burnt ☐ Melted ☐ Corroded ☐ Articulated ☐ Disarticulated ☐ Flattened ☐ Broken/Shattered

☐ Other _____

Gender/Sex/Age Attribution:　　☐ Undetermined Adult　　☐ Female Adult　　☐ Male Adult

　　　　　　　　　　　　　　　☐ Undetermined Child　　☐ Female Child　　☐ Male Child　☐ Infant

Right or Left Associations: _____ _____

Width _____ Height _____ Length _____ Thickness _____ Circumference _____ Diameter _____

Weight _____　　　　Other _____

Object Description (Describe each object separately; use additional forms if needed to document each artifact)

ID # _____ Object Form: _____

Material(s): _____

Color(s): _____ _____

Symbols/Inscriptions/Markings: _____

_____

Decoration: _____ _____

_____

Condition: ☐ Complete ☐ Fragment ☐ Worn/Deteriorated ☐ Cut ☐ Pierced ☐ Bent ☐ Mummified

☐ Burnt ☐ Melted ☐ Corroded ☐ Articulated ☐ Disarticulated ☐ Flattened ☐ Broken/Shattered

☐ Other _____

Gender/Sex/Age Attribution:　　☐ Undetermined Adult　　☐ Female Adult　　☐ Male Adult

　　　　　　　　　　　　　　　☐ Undetermined Child　　☐ Female Child　　☐ Male Child　☐ Infant

Right or Left Associations: _____ _____

Width _____ Height _____ Length _____ Thickness _____ Circumference _____ Diameter _____

Weight _____　　　　Other _____

INTENTIONALLY CONCEALED OBJECT (ICO) RECORDATION FORM

Sketches of ICOs and sketches of ICOs in situ

PLANT RECORDATION and COLLECTION FORM

Plant ID and Report—Project Name:	
Collector's Name:	Date:

Please insert information into each field provided; if no information is present for your particular species, enter N/A. Press your specimen and attach to this form in the space provided.

Common Name(s):	
Scientific Name:	
Physical Description:	

Plant Characteristics:	
Height:	
Width:	

Plant Type:	Flower Description:
Tree	
Shrub	Color:
Herbaceous	Size:
Vine	Month of Bloom:

Plant Uses: Food, Medicinal, Ritual, Magic, Construction, etc.

Attach Plant Specimen Here	On back of page draw map and indicate location of find

PLANT RECORDATION and COLLECTION FORM

Plant ID and Report—Project Name:	
Collector's Name:	Date:

GPS Coordinates:	Location Description (include other plant communities, associations, features, etc.):
T R S	
Access: Road Trail Water Cross-country	

Map Notes or Legend:	Draw Map Here

QUOTIDIAN and OCCUPATIONAL SITE RECORDATION FORM

Site # _____   Recorded by _____   Date _____

Building or Site Name _____   Domestic _____   Occupational _____

Address _____   _____

County _____   Township _____   City _____

Other Location information _____

Coordinates: Township _____   Range _____   Section _____   Block _____   Lot # _____

Orientation _____

Alignment (with ritual/sacred landscape features, structures, astronomical elements, habitation, ecofeatures)

_____
_____

Accessibility (e.g., restricted access to particular individuals, seasonal or other temporal restrictions)

_____
_____

Surrounding/Associated Plants _____

_____

Surrounding/Associated Structures _____

_____

Relationship of Building to Surroundings _____

_____

Date of Original Construction _____   Builder _____

Religious, Ceremonial, Ritual Affiliation of builders/residents: Original _____

Subsequent _____

Other Uses _____

Alterations _____

Additions/Removals _____

Maps _____

Original or Early Images/Drawings of Structure _____

References _____

_____
_____
_____

Gender Associated Areas or Tasks _____

_____

QUOTIDIAN and OCCUPATIONAL SITE RECORDATION FORM

Building Description _____

_____

Building materials _____

_____

Colors (what colors, where used, associated with what forms and materials) _____

_____

_____

Threshold/Openings/fences/boundaries (note materials, designs, colors, plants, artifacts associated with windows, doors, corners, chimneys, rafters, roofs)_____

_____

_____

Building Measurements _____

_____

_____

_____

Numerical Patterns (within measurements or repetition of motifs and elements)

_____

_____

Symbols or Motifs (carved, painted, inscribed, etc. either formally or informally and their measurements, alignments, orientations, and/or associations with the building, the landscape, or other features)

_____

_____

_____

Wear patterns (from ritual/ceremonial participation: movement, dancing, sitting routes and places) _____

_____

Burials (location within or near building and their measurements, alignments, orientations, and/or associations with the building, the landscape, or other features)

_____

_____

Concealed Objects (location within or near building and their measurements, alignments, orientations, and/or associations with the building, the landscape, or other features)

_____

_____

Sensory Elements (attributes of site that create, manipulate, or otherwise affect sensory experience, e.g., visual, auditory, olfactory, tactile, gustatory (taste), temperature, pain)

_____

_____

QUOTIDIAN and OCCUPATIONAL SITE RECORDATION FORM

Mapping/Illustrating (Building/site elevations from all sides, alignment with landscape features; exterior plan and interior plan; details of symbolic, color, sensory, and numeric elements)

RELIGIOUS, CEREMONIAL, and FORMAL RITUAL BUILDING RECORDATION FORM

Site # _____   Recorded by _____   Date _____

Building or Site Name _____

Address _____ _____

County _____ Township _____ City _____

Other Location information _____

Coordinates: Township _____ Range _____ Section _____ Block _____ Lot # _____

Orientation _____

Alignment (with other ritual/sacred landscape features, structures, astronomical elements, habitation, ecofeatures)

_____

_____

Accessibility (e.g., isolated location, restricted access to particular individuals, physically challenging to reach, seasonal or other temporal restrictions)

_____

_____

Surrounding/Associated Plants

_____

_____

Surrounding/Associated Structures

_____

_____

Relationship of Building to Surroundings _____

_____

Date of Original Construction _____ Builder _____

Religious, Ceremonial, Ritual Affiliation: Original_____

Subsequent _____

Other Uses _____

Alterations _____

Additions/Removals _____

Maps _____

Original or Early Images/Drawings of Structure _____

References _____

_____

_____

_____

RELIGIOUS, CEREMONIAL, and FORMAL RITUAL BUILDING RECORDATION FORM

Building Description _____
_____

Building materials _____
_____

Colors (what colors, where used, associated with what forms and materials) _____
_____
_____

Threshold/Openings (note materials, designs, colors, plants, artifacts associated with windows, doors, corners, chimneys, rafters, roofs) _____
_____
_____

Building Measurements _____
_____
_____
_____

Numerical Patterns (within measurements or repetition of motifs and elements)
_____
_____

Symbols or Motifs (carved, painted, inscribed, etc. either formally or informally and their measurements, alignments, orientations, and/or associations with the building, the landscape, or other features)
_____
_____
_____

Wear patterns (from ritual/ceremonial participation: movement, dancing, sitting, routes) _____
_____

Burials (location within or near building and their measurements, alignments, orientations, and/or associations with the building, the landscape, or other features)
_____
_____

Concealed Objects (location within or near building and their measurements, alignments, orientations, and/or associations with the building, the landscape, or other features)
_____
_____

Sensory Elements (attributes of site that create, manipulate, or otherwise affect sensory experience, e.g., visual, auditory, olfactory, tactile, gustatory (taste), temperature, pain, iewscape, soundscape, smellscape, etc.
_____
_____

RELIGIOUS, CEREMONIAL, and FORMAL RITUAL BUILDING RECORDATION FORM

Mapping/Illustrating (Building elevations from all sides, alignment with landscape features; exterior plan and interior plan; details of symbolic, color, sensory, and numeric elements)

RITUAL LANDSCAPE RECORDATION FORM

Instructions and Information

Recording ritual landscapes is a complex and time-consuming endeavor. Because such landscapes can cover extremely large areas and incorporate numerous tangible and intangible ritualistic, cosmological, and/or sacred components, it is never possible to capture everything in a brief survey. To thoroughly record such sites may require several visitations at different times of year, under various conditions, and from different vantage points. Likely, such recordation will also require ethnographic or historical documentation research to reveal the ritual/sacred importance of particular features and elements of a landscape. Additional survey and research may be necessary to situate one landscape into a network of associated ritual sites across a much more extensive landscape.

This form is meant to be a template applicable or amendable for any ritual landscape regardless of cultural, geographical, or temporal associations. While not every component will be relevant for every site, the critical importance of the form is to draw recorders' attention to the subtle, embedded, and sensorial elements that often define ritual/sacred landscapes. There may certainly be human-made features readily observed, recognized, and recorded that proclaim a ritualistic or sacred purpose of the landscape, but the features are there only because of underlying or associated attributes of the landscape that mark it as a numinous or otherwise special or powerful place.

The form includes five pages of recordation components meant to be used to address the landscape as a whole (or as much as can be perceived); the sixth page is to record in more detail individual features within the landscape; and finally, the last page provides a graph to sketch maps or draw features, landscape elevations, or artifacts. Recorders should use as many of these individual or sketch forms as necessary. Each page has a place for the site number, the recorder's name, and the date of recordation. It is important that this information be filled in on each page as a precaution against individual pages becoming separated from the rest of the packet. This cross-referencing on each page allows the documentation to be retrieved or reconciled if need arises.

GLOSSARY OF TERMS

Anthropomorphic—having human form
Axis mundi—a marker of the center of the universe that often connects and is the conduit for the earth to the spiritual realm(s)
Barrow—large mound of earth or stones over the dead (also called a tumulus)
Cenote—a deep sinkhole in limestone having a pool at the bottom
Culturally Modified Trees (CMT)—humanly manipulated for cultural reasons: bent, scarred, incised
Dolmen—megalithic tomb or structure with large flat stone laid across upright stones
Ecofact—biological or other natural objects or remains, usually refers to non-living natural elements
Henge—a Neolithic monument usually containing a circle of standing stones or wooden posts
Manuport—an object (usually a natural object) transported out of its natural environment and taking on special power in its new setting
Menhir—tall, upright monumental block of stone
Monolith—single block of stone usually shaped like a pillar or monument
Numinous—filled with a sense of the divine, supernatural, sacred, mysterious
Orientation—the direction something faces
Palimpsests—a layering of site use/occupation over time; rewriting over the top of previous writing
Sink or sinkhole—a cavity in the earth into which a stream or other water course disappears
Therianthropic—having a combined human and animal form
Theriomorphic—having animal form
Toponym—place name
Vestibular—bodily motion and vibration (rocking, swaying, swinging, bouncing, twirling, etc.)
Viewshed Aspect—looking at a ritual feature from an outside point
Viewshed Prospect—looking out from a ritual feature
Vivifact—living elements (e.g., trees and other plants) that are either humanly modified or culturally indicative

RITUAL LANDSCAPE RECORDATION FORM

Site # _____   Recorded by _____   Date _____

Site Name _____

County _____ Township _____ City _____ State _____

Other Location Information _____

Coordinates: Township _____ Range _____ Section _____ Block _____ Lot # _____

Primary Orientation E ☐ W ☐ N ☐ S ☐ NE ☐ NW ☐ SE ☐ SW ☐

Alignments (with other ritual/sacred landscape features, sites, structures, astronomical elements, habitation, ecofeatures)

_____
_____
_____
_____
_____

Vertical or Lateral positioning (including right/left, up/down, above/below, front/back, forward/behind)

_____
_____
_____
_____

Palimpsests (layering of ritual/sacred usage or features across time and/or cultural groups)

_____
_____
_____
_____

Associations (with other ritual/sacred landscape features, structures, habitations, ecofeatures, artifacts)

_____
_____
_____
_____

Accessibility (e.g., isolated location, restricted access to particular individuals, physically challenging to reach, seasonal or other temporal restrictions, open and easy access to larger groups)

_____
_____
_____
_____

Surrounding/Associated Plants

_____
_____
_____
_____

RITUAL LANDSCAPE RECORDATION FORM

Associations with spiritual thresholds (e.g., caves/caverns, mountain peaks, water sources, sink holes, cenotes, high/low places, dark or illuminated places)

_____
_____
_____
_____
_____

Associations with spiritual forces or abodes (e.g., windy areas, mountain peaks, water sources or rushing water, high/low places, dark or illuminated places, forests, caves/caverns, designated trees or stones, phosphorescent stones or outcrops)

_____
_____
_____
_____

Cosmological cartographic features or associations (e.g., natural features with or without human modification believed to be markers of cosmic creation; axis mundi, world trees, etc.)

_____
_____
_____
_____

Numerical Patterns (within measurements, distances, or repetition of elements) Describe the measurement system used (metric, standard, indigenous, ethnic, historical, etc.)

_____
_____
_____
_____

Do multiple features, when plotted and the dots connected, create a figure?

Symbol ☐ Description _____

Anthropomorphic (human form) ☐ Description _____

Theriomorphic (animal form) ☐ Description _____

Therianthropic (human-animal form) ☐ Description _____

From what vantage point is the figure discernable?

_____
_____
_____

Known toponyms (place names) for places or features

_____
_____
_____
_____

Site # _____   Recorded by _____   Date _____

RITUAL LANDSCAPE RECORDATION FORM

Indications of possible taboo sites or areas? (e.g., no evidence of use although seemingly similar to utilized areas; concentration of artifact offerings or features at perimeter of area but absent from within the area)

_____

_____

_____

Sensory Elements (attributes of site that create, manipulate, or otherwise affect sensory experience, e.g., visual, auditory, olfactory, tactile, vestibular)

Visual:

Viewshed Aspect (looking at a ritual feature from an outside point, include what is obstructed)

_____

_____

_____

Viewshed Prospect (looking out from a ritual feature, include what is obstructed)

_____

_____

_____

Aerial or overhead view

_____

_____

_____

Levels of visibility (light, darkness, shadow, illuminated elements at certain daily or seasonal times)

_____

_____

_____

_____

Colors and Shimmer (naturally occurring or added through offerings or human modifications)

_____

_____

_____

_____

_____

_____

_____

Site # _____   Recorded by _____   Date _____

RITUAL LANDSCAPE RECORDATION FORM

Auditory:

Natural Soundscape (e.g., wind, water, creaking trees, ringing rocks, bird song, thunder, cracking ice, etc.; include absence or muffling of surrounding sounds)

_____
_____
_____
_____
_____

Human Soundscape (e.g., bells, gongs, drums, chanting/singing, whistling, etc.; include absence or muffling of surrounding sounds)

_____
_____
_____
_____
_____

Olfactory:

Smellscape (include both pleasant and unpleasant aromas: flowers, trees, Sulphur, fire, decaying bodies (animal or human), salty sea, stagnant water, etc.)

_____
_____
_____
_____

Tactility:

Texture and Feel (e.g., smoothness or roughness of natural or human-made features; also the temperature sensation of a thing or place; wet, dry, humid; painful sensations—bare feet on sharp or hot rocks, etc.)

_____
_____
_____
_____
_____

Vestibular:

Bodily motion or vibration (e.g., from buffeting winds, underground rushing water, earth tremors, swinging suspension from trees, walking across rope bridges, etc.)

_____
_____
_____
_____
_____

Site # _____   Recorded by _____   Date _____

RITUAL LANDSCAPE RECORDATION FORM

Human-made Features (For each feature checked, provide a detailed description on attached pages)

☐ cairns   ☐ fasting/vision quest beds   ☐ eagle traps   ☐ stone or chalk effigies   ☐ medicine wheels

☐ rock art (use dedicated rock art recordation form)   ☐ culturally modified trees (CMT)   ☐ shrines

☐ temples   ☐ houses of religious worship   ☐ hermit cells   ☐ pilgrimage trails/roads   ☐ processional routes

☐ monoliths   ☐ henges   ☐ menhirs   ☐ colossal statues   ☐ dolmen   ☐ barrows   ☐ tombs

☐ burial features   ☐ offerings (e.g., rags or other items attached to trees or left at a site)   ☐ artifact caches

☐ other _____

Natural Features (For each feature checked, provide a detailed description on attached pages)

☐ designated trees   ☐ sacred plant gathering area   ☐ manuports   ☐ non-local material

☐ mountains/boulders/trees perceived as anthro- or theriomorphic   ☐ phosphorescent marker stones

☐ other _____

Water deemed sacred: ☐ spring   ☐ waterfall   ☐ hot spring   ☐ sinkhole   ☐ cenote   ☐ ditch   ☐ bog

☐ river   ☐ lake   ☐ stream   ☐ sea   ☐ watering hole   ☐ water meadow   ☐ slough   ☐ well

Nighttime and Dark Zone Observances

Sensory elements (include description of physical sensations: temperature, echo, visibility restrictions, heightened hearing)

_____

_____

_____

_____

Affective elements (include description of emotional/psychological sensations: anxiety/fear, calm, vulnerability, empowerment, invigoration, lassitude, transcendence, etc.)

_____

_____

_____

_____

_____

Astronomical (these are general observations; detailed archaeoastronomical data must be gathered by trained archaeoastronomers)

_____

_____

_____

_____

_____

RITUAL LANDSCAPE RECORDATION FORM

Individual Feature Descriptions (Use one sheet per feature)

Site # _____   Recorded by _____   Date _____

Feature name _____

Provenience: GPS _____

Other locational data _____   _____

Primary Orientation   E ☐   W ☐   N ☐   S ☐   NE ☐   NW ☐   SE ☐   SW ☐

Vertical/Lateral Placement   High ☐   Low ☐   Under ☐   Above ☐   Forward ☐   Behind ☐   Left ☐   Right ☐

Feature description (include sensory elements)

_____
_____
_____
_____
_____
_____
_____
_____
_____

Feature measurements (use whatever measurements are relevant and acquirable for the particular feature: height, length, width, circumference/girth, depth, surface area, volume, etc.)

_____
_____
_____
_____
_____
_____

Distances between this feature and other features or associations

_____
_____
_____
_____

Modifications, markings, symbolic forms

_____
_____
_____

Associated artifacts, ecofacts, vivifacts

_____
_____
_____
_____
_____

RITUAL LANDSCAPE RECORDATION FORM

Mapping/Illustrating (Create several maps and illustrations at different scales to encompass the broadest landscape and also individual features or groups of features to capture their details as well as their associations and relationships to each other.)

Site # _____   Recorded by _____   Date _____

RITUAL/MAGICAL ASSEMBLAGE RECORDATION FORM

Site # _____   Recorded by _____   Date _____

Site Name _____   Site Type _____

Location Information _____

Coordinates: Township _____   Range _____   Section _____

Orientation _____

Alignment (with ritual/sacred landscape features, structures, astronomical elements, habitation, ecofeatures)

_____

_____

_____

Accessibility (e.g., degree of difficulty to access; restricted access to particular individuals; seasonal or other temporal restrictions) _____

_____

Surrounding/Associated Structures _____

_____

_____

Other Uses _____

_____

Topographical Features _____

_____

Citations of Original or Early Images/Drawings of Site _____

_____

Known stressful events at site (include dates and participants if known) _____

_____

_____

_____

_____

Sensory Elements (attributes of site that create, manipulate, or otherwise affect sensory experience, e.g., visual, auditory, olfactory, tactile, gustatory (taste), temperature, pain) _____

_____

_____

RITUAL/MAGICAL ASSEMBLAGE RECORDATION FORM

Number of Objects in Assemblage_____ Location of Assemblage _____

Arrangement of objects _____

_____

_____

Single deposition event Yes _____ No _____ Interminable _____   Concealed deposition Yes _____ No _____

Other Intentionally Concealed Objects (ICOs), symbols, or ritualistic, magical, or religious related objects on site _____

_____

_____

_____

_____

List of photographs and drawings _____

_____

_____

_____

_____

Condition types for object chart:

Complete, undamaged

Complete, disarticulated, pierced, bent, folded, etc.

Fragmented or partial (part _____)

Burnt

Mummified

Worn out through use or wear

Corroded

Cut, slashed

Broken

RITUAL/MAGICAL ASSEMBLAGE RECORDATION FORM

Object Number	Form	Material(s)	Color(s)	Decoration	Additional Markings/ Symbols	Measurements	Condition	Numerical Elements	Additional Details

RITUAL/MAGICAL ASSEMBLAGE RECORDATION FORM

Mapping/Illustrating (site elevations and plans from all sides, illustration of assemblage in contextual relationship)

ROCK ART RECORDATION FORM

Instructions and Information

Rock art sites exist around the world, dating from the Paleolithic to modern historic times. They occur in various settings, including dark zone caves, rock shelters, exposed cliff walls, and freestanding stones. Recording rock art can be a complex and time-consuming endeavor that will be dictated by numerous factors: accessibility, lighting, rock surface, rock art condition, and seasonal variation to name a few. To thoroughly record such sites may require several visitations at different times of year, under various conditions, and from different vantage points. Likely, such recordation will also require ethnographic or historical documentation research to reveal the ritual/sacred importance of particular features and elements of the greater landscape within which the rock art sites are integrated. Additional survey and research may be necessary to situate one site into a network of associated rock art and other ritual sites across a much more extensive landscape.

This form is meant to be a template applicable or amendable for any rock art site regardless of cultural, geographical, or temporal associations. While not every component will be relevant for every site, the critical importance of the form is to draw recorders' attention to both the observable and the more subtle, embedded, and sensorial elements that often define ritual/sacred sites. There are certainly human-made features (the rock art itself) readily observed, recognized, and recorded that proclaim a culturally significant, ritualistic, or sacred purpose of the site, but the features are there only because of underlying or associated attributes of the environment and landscape that mark it as a numinous or otherwise special or powerful place.

Glossary of Rock Art Terms

There are several terms used in rock art study that are region or culture specific. The following is a brief list of commonly used terms in rock art study and documentation.

Dry pigment: a dry pigment like a crayon or charcoal piece used to draw; it creates a streaky color application on the rock surface, especially if the rock surface is rough.

Friction: the engraving technique created by abrading, grooving, rubbing, or scratching.

Motif: the design or pattern of figures. Most rock art assemblages have limited ranges of motifs.

Parietal art: a general term for rock art that includes finger markings, bas-relief sculptures, engraved images, and paintings.

Petroforms (also called geoglyphs): figures outlined with large rocks/boulders (portable glacial erratics); very large and usually in wide open locations. They may have been designed and situated with an aerial (spiritual) view in mind. These figures are often found in fields or pastures with scattered glacial debris; thus, petroform locations can be difficult to interpret.

Petroglyphs: carved, pecked, or incised figures; the most numerous type of rock art recorded. Usually found in caves and rock shelters or on bluff faces. Most are found on vertical faces, although may be on cave floors. They are primarily outline figures, but may contain interior designs such as heart lines. A large majority are geometric designs.

Pictographs (also called pigment art): painted figures (using a variety of pigments) on vertical rock faces and ceilings in caves and rock shelters and on bluff faces. They often entail more detail and interior design than petroglyphs. Petroglyphs and pictographs can sometimes be found at the same sites, and some figures combine both carved and painted designs.

Percussion: the engraving technique created by pecking, pounding, or pitting.

Rotation: The engraving technique created by drilling.

Stenciling: while the object or hand is held against the rock surface, wet pigment is blown or applied around it creating a negative image of the object.

Superimposition: overlapping of newer images on top of older images.

Wet pigment: a wet pigment mixture used as paint; it creates a relatively even color application on the rock surface.

ROCK ART RECORDATION FORM

Site # _____ Recorded by _____ Date _____

Site Name _____

County _____ Township _____ City _____ State _____

Other Location Information _____

Coordinates: Township _____ Range _____ Section _____ Block _____ Lot # _____

Primary Orientation E ☐ W ☐ N ☐ S ☐ NE ☐ NW ☐ SE ☐ SW ☐

Rock Surface Type

☐ sandstone   ☐ limestone   ☐ granite   ☐ other _____

Texture of the surface

☐ smooth   ☐ slightly rough   ☐ very rough   ☐ irregular   ☐ fractured

Rock deterioration (natural) (check all that apply)

☐ none   ☐ poorly cemented   ☐ surface spalling   ☐ water erosion   ☐ sun exposure   ☐ mineral accretions

☐ wind erosion   ☐ cracking   ☐ rock fall   ☐ animal nesting/burrowing   ☐ plant root intrusion   ☐ blackened by fire

Presence of lichen, worts, or moss (check all that apply)

☐ lichen   ☐ worts   ☐ moss

Types and extent of coverage

_____

_____

Rock deterioration (cultural) (check all that apply)

☐ modern graffiti   ☐ removed images or panels   ☐ burned surface   ☐ disturbances to cave/rock shelter floors

☐ evidence of modern campfires   ☐ litter   ☐ erosion from recreational vehicles tracks   ☐ chalked   ☐ logging

☐ livestock   ☐ visitor use   ☐ bullet holes   ☐ other _____

Caves and Rock Shelters:

Direction of the opening E ☐ W ☐ N ☐ S ☐ NE ☐ NW ☐ SE ☐ SW ☐

Direction of bluff face in which the cave or shelter is found E ☐ W ☐ N ☐ S ☐ NE ☐ NW ☐ SE ☐ SW ☐

Length (range) and Width (range) of the cave or shelter interior _____

Height (range) from floor to ceiling _____

Bluff faces:

Direction of the bluff face E ☐ W ☐ N ☐ S ☐ NE ☐ NW ☐ SE ☐ SW ☐

Length (range) and Width (range) of the ledge below the rock art _____

Any protective overhang and the height between the bottom ledge and the overhang _____ _ _

Petroform sites or Petroglyphs/ Pictographs on a horizontal rock outcrop:

Orientation of the image/form on the landscape E ☐ W ☐ N ☐ S ☐ NE ☐ NW ☐ SE ☐ SW ☐

ROCK ART RECORDATION FORM

Type and size of the boulders along with any lichen, wort, or moss growth

_____
_____
_____

Acreage/size of the site _____

If the site is located on a discrete landform, a description of that landform

_____
_____
_____

<u>Imagery</u>

Number of figures

Pictographs _____   Petroglyphs _____   Complete figures _____   Partial figures _____

Animal figures _____   Anthropomorphic figures _____   Geometric figures _____   Plant figures _____

Composite figures _____   Spiritual figures _____   Other _____

Styles (check all that apply)

☐ abstract   ☐ naturalistic   ☐ outline   ☐ realistic   ☐ schematic   ☐ solid (positive)   ☐ solid (negative)   ☐ X-ray

Pigments Used (check all that apply)

☐ chalk   ☐ charcoal   ☐ bat guano   ☐ copper ore   ☐ gypsum   ☐ hematite   ☐ kaolinite clay   ☐ lime

☐ ocher   ☐ shell   ☐ manganese   ☐ diatomaceous earth   ☐ lizard or bird dung   other _____

Imagery present

(An **Individual Feature Description** form should be filled out for each image, which is found at the end of this document.)

_____   _____   _____   _____
_____   _____   _____   _____
_____   _____   _____   _____
_____   _____   _____   _____
_____   _____   _____   _____
_____   _____   _____   _____
_____   _____   _____   _____
_____   _____   _____   _____
_____   _____   _____   _____
_____   _____   _____   _____
_____   _____   _____   _____
_____   _____   _____   _____
_____   _____   _____   _____
_____   _____   _____   _____

If hand or feet are depicted, also indicate whether they are right or left.

ROCK ART RECORDATION FORM

In addition to the actual rock imagery, it is important to record details of the broader site and landscape.

Alignments (with other ritual/sacred landscape features, sites, structures, astronomical elements, habitation, ecofeatures)

_____
_____
_____
_____
_____

Vertical or Lateral positioning (including right/left, up/down, above/below, front/back, forward/behind)

_____
_____
_____
_____
_____

Palimpsests (layering of ritual/sacred usage or features across time and/or cultural groups)

_____
_____
_____
_____
_____

Associations (with other ritual/sacred landscape features, structures, habitations, ecofeatures, artifacts)

_____
_____
_____
_____
_____

Accessibility (e.g., isolated location, restricted access to particular individuals, physically challenging to reach, seasonal or other temporal restrictions, open and easy access to larger groups)

_____
_____
_____
_____
_____

Surrounding/Associated Plants

_____
_____
_____
_____
_____
_____
_____

ROCK ART RECORDATION FORM

Associations with spiritual thresholds (e.g., caves/caverns, mountain peaks, water sources, sink holes, cenotes, high/low places, dark or illuminated places)

_____
_____
_____
_____
_____

Associations with spiritual forces or abodes (e.g., windy areas, mountain peaks, water sources or rushing water, high/low places, dark or illuminated places, forests, caves/caverns, designated trees or stones, phosphorescent stones or outcrops)

_____
_____
_____
_____

Cosmological cartographic features or associations (e.g., natural features with or without human modification believed to be markers of cosmic creation; axis mundi, world trees, etc.)

_____
_____
_____
_____

Numerical Patterns (within measurements, distances, or repetition of elements). Describe the measurement system used (metric, standard, indigenous, ethnic, historical, etc.)

_____
_____
_____
_____

Do multiple features, when plotted and the dots connected, create a figure?

Symbol ☐ Description _____

Anthropomorphic (human form) ☐ Description _____

Theriomorphic (animal form) ☐ Description _____

Therianthropic (human-animal form) ☐ Description _____

From what vantage point is the figure discernable?

_____
_____
_____

Known toponyms (place names) for places or features

_____
_____
_____
_____

Site # _____   Recorded by _____   Date _____

ROCK ART RECORDATION FORM

Indications of possible taboo sites or areas? (e.g., no evidence of use although seemingly similar to utilized areas; concentration of artifact offerings or features at perimeter of area but absent from within the area)

_____
_____
_____
_____

Sensory Elements (attributes of site that create, manipulate, or otherwise affect sensory experience, e.g., visual, auditory, olfactory, tactile, vestibular)

Visual:

Viewshed Aspect (looking at a rock art feature from an outside point, include what is obstructed)

_____
_____
_____
_____
_____

Viewshed Prospect (looking out from a rock art feature, include what is obstructed)

_____
_____
_____
_____

Aerial or overhead view

_____
_____
_____

Levels of visibility (light, darkness, shadow, illuminated elements at certain daily or seasonal times)

_____
_____
_____
_____
_____

Colors and Shimmer (naturally occurring in the rock or pigments or added through offerings or human modifications)

_____
_____
_____
_____
_____
_____
_____

Site # _____   Recorded by _____   Date _____

ROCK ART RECORDATION FORM

Auditory:

Natural Soundscape (e.g., wind, water, creaking trees, ringing rocks, bird song, thunder, cracking ice, etc.; include absence or muffling of surrounding sounds)

_____
_____
_____
_____
_____

Human Soundscape (e.g., bells, gongs, drums, chanting/singing, whistling, etc.; include absence or muffling of surrounding sounds)

_____
_____
_____
_____
_____

Olfactory:

Smellscape (include both pleasant and unpleasant aromas: flowers, trees, Sulphur, fire, decaying bodies (animal or human), salty sea, stagnant water, etc.)

_____
_____
_____
_____

Tactility:

Texture and Feel (e.g., smoothness or roughness of the rock or human-made features; also the temperature sensation of a thing or place; wet, dry, humid; painful sensations—bare feet on sharp or hot rocks, etc.)

_____
_____
_____
_____
_____

Vestibular:

Bodily motion or vibration (e.g., from buffeting winds, underground rushing water, earth tremors, swinging suspension from trees, walking across rope bridges, etc.)

_____
_____
_____
_____
_____

Site # _____   Recorded by _____   Date _____

ROCK ART RECORDATION FORM

In addition to the rock art, are there additional human-made features? (For each feature checked, provide a detailed description on attached pages) (check all that apply)

☐ cairns ☐ fasting/vision quest beds ☐ eagle traps ☐ stone or chalk effigies ☐ medicine wheels

☐ culturally modified trees (CMT) ☐ shrines ☐ rune or picture stones

☐ temples ☐ houses of religious worship ☐ hermit cells ☐ pilgrimage trails/roads ☐ processional routes

☐ monoliths ☐ henges ☐ menhirs ☐ colossal statues ☐ dolmen ☐ barrows ☐ tombs

☐ burial features ☐ offerings (e.g., rags or other items attached to trees or left at a site) ☐ artifact caches

☐ other _____

Natural Features (For each feature checked, provide a detailed description on attached pages) (check all that apply)

☐ designated trees ☐ sacred plant gathering area ☐ manuports ☐ non-local material

☐ mountains/boulders/trees perceived as anthro- or theriomorphic ☐ phosphorescent marker stones

☐ pigment resourcing area ☐ other _____ _____

Water deemed sacred (check all that apply)

☐ spring ☐ waterfall ☐ hot spring ☐ sinkhole ☐ cenote ☐ ditch ☐ bog

☐ river ☐ lake ☐ stream ☐ sea ☐ watering hole ☐ water meadow ☐ slough ☐ well

Nighttime and Dark Zone Observances

Sensory elements (include description of physical sensations: temperature, echo, visibility restrictions, heightened hearing)

_____
_____
_____
_____

Affective elements (include description of emotional/psychological sensations: anxiety/fear, calm, vulnerability, empowerment, invigoration, lassitude, transcendence, etc.)

_____
_____
_____
_____
_____

Astronomical (these are general observations; detailed archaeoastronomical data must be gathered by trained archaeoastronomers)

_____
_____

ROCK ART RECORDATION FORM

Individual Feature Descriptions (Use one sheet per feature)

Site # _____   Recorded by _____   Date _____

Feature name _____

Provenience: GPS _____

Other locational data _____   _____

Primary Orientation E ☐   W ☐   N ☐   S ☐   NE ☐   NW ☐   SE ☐   SW ☐

Vertical/Lateral Placement   High ☐   Low ☐   Under ☐   Above ☐   Forward ☐   Behind ☐   Left ☐   Right ☐

Image/feature description (include sensory elements)

_____
_____
_____
_____
_____
_____
_____
_____
_____

Image/Feature measurements (use whatever measurements are relevant and acquirable for the particular feature: height, length, width, circumference/girth, depth, surface area, volume, etc.)

_____
_____
_____
_____
_____
_____

Distances between this image/feature and other images/features or associations

_____
_____
_____
_____
_____
_____
_____

Associated artifacts, ecofacts, vivifacts

_____
_____
_____
_____
_____

ROCK ART RECORDATION FORM

Mapping/Illustrating (Create several maps and illustrations at different scales to encompass the broadest landscape and also individual details of rock art images, image groups, and complete panels and their associations and relationships to each other.)

Site # _____ Recorded by _____ Date _____

Templates

CENSORS

Incense has been used almost universally in ritual and belief practices through time and across the world. The burning of aromatic substances (plants and resins) necessitated the use of some type of vessel or holder that would be fire-resistant, hold the incense material securely, and facilitate the dispersal of the resulting smoke in the desired direction and manner. These holders (censors) were made of ceramic, metal, bone, shell, or stone. They can range in style from wholly natural and unadorned to elaborately carved, molded, or cast vessels. They vary in size from small containers for personal ritual use to extremely

Figure 9.1. Template of censor style examples. *Left to right, top row:* Aztec turkey claw vessel, Egyptian boat; *middle row:* Japanese ceramic bowl, Native American natural half shell, Minoan pottery jug, Iron Age ceramic pot; *bottom row:* brass Catholic thurible, Etruscan standing vessel, Chinese bronze-footed pot, handheld brass Indo Persian burner. Drawing by Isabeau Newbury. Published with permission.

large to accommodate great quantities of burning material in communal ritual settings. Censors are often bowl-shaped vessels, but they can also be figural shapes of animals, buildings, or other objects. Some censors are obvious, but other less-obvious forms may be revealed through chemical residue analysis that indicates evidence of the burning of aromatic substances. The images presented here illustrate just a few of the many variations of censors found around the world.

CROSSES

The cross—or symbol comprised of crossed lines—has been utilized in various forms by numerous cultures to express a range of religious and magical beliefs. It is often a symbol of the divine or associated with specific religious figures. In some cases, a particular cross symbol has come to stand for an entire religious tradition (e.g., Christianity). The cross also symbolizes cosmological concepts of earthly quatrains like cardinal directions and the four seasons of the yearly cycle, and, in its swastika variations, represents the sun and the continuous turning of the wheel of life. There are virtually infinite possibilities for the cross representation from the most basic two crossed lines to highly complex, ornate, or stylized variations. This graphic illustrates just a smattering of the various cross symbols found in different traditions.

FIGURINES

One of the most common of all objects representing religious or magical belief and/or used in ritual practices is the three-dimensional figurine. Figurines include animal (theriomorphic), human (anthropomorphic), animal-human combinations (therianthropic), or monsters, demons, deities, spirits (mythic) forms. They may be extremely realistic representations or more stylized portrayals. Sometimes figurines are merely a bone, stick, or stone that "suggest" a being through its natural shape or features. Some are fully rounded 3-D images, while others may be flat and impressionistic. In many cases, the figurines are highly crafted objects with intricate details that express specific meanings and associations. Still others are just a particular body part: arm, leg, hand, foot, head, or penis, for example. They can be made of clay/ceramic, bone, stone, wood, plant parts (roots, tubers, or fruits), plaster, papier-mâché, straw, cloth, shell, hooves, resin, ivory, metal, glass, or plastic. The variations in figurine at-

Figure 9.2. Template of cross style examples. Drawing by Isabeau Newbury. Published with permission.

tributes, positioning, posturing, and gesturing are too numerous to list here but include sitting, standing, squatting, crawling, swimming, flying, jumping, and dancing with every conceivable configuration of arm and leg gesturing. Figure 9.3 gives a few examples of figurine styles and postures.

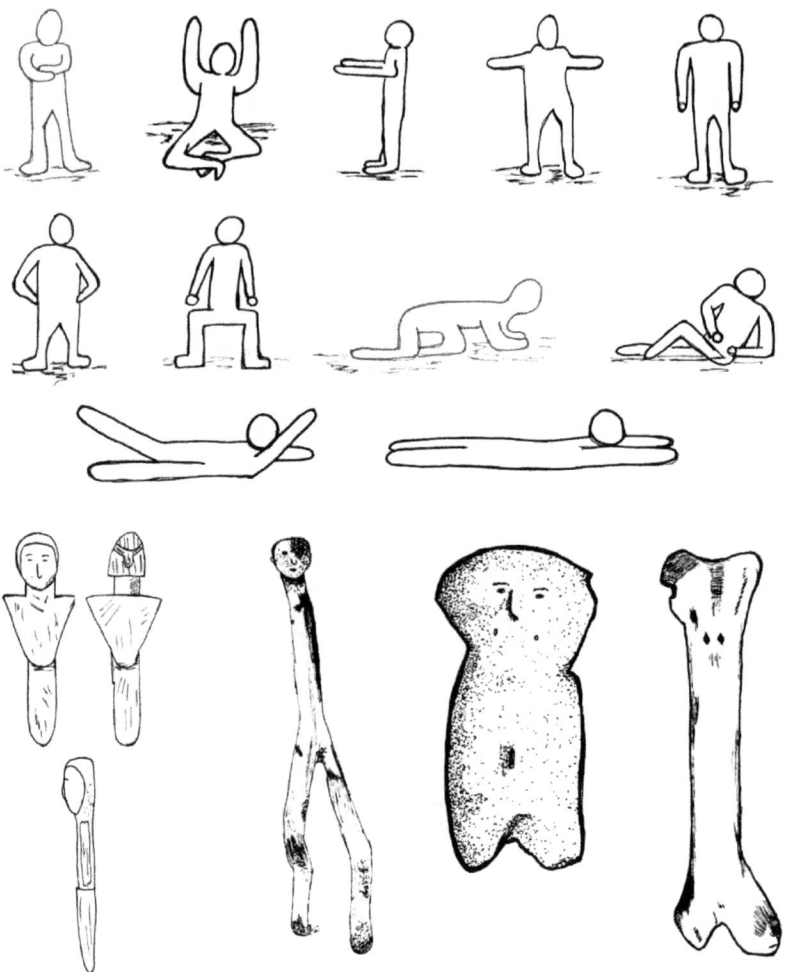

Figure 9.3. Template of figurine posture and style examples. Drawing by Isabeau Newbury. Published with permission.

CHAPTER 10

Technologies, Methodologies, and Analyses

Material evidence for ritualistic, religious, or magical practice may not be immediately observable in the archaeological record. In order to reveal such practices, more sophisticated analysis may be necessary. All the standard archaeological methodologies, technologies, and analytical tools used for discovering evidence of human behaviors in the past can be used to ascertain indications of ritual, religion, or magic belief and related behaviors. The following sections provide some examples of how the particular "tool" may be applied to archaeological sites, landscapes, artifacts, and/or ecofacts to record, reveal, or analyze potential evidence of past beliefs.

3-D SCANNING

- CT Scanning (Computed Tomography)—3-D digital x-ray
  - » Scan/x-ray cremation urns, witch bottles, or other vessels with ritualistic contents
- Texture analysis—3-D scanning can reveal or enhance surface textures. Texture can be a significant or determinate factor in particular objects or materials chosen for ritualistic, religious, or magical use.

ACCESSIBILITY ANALYSIS

Access to the places, materials, and practices associated with ritual, religion, and magic are all restricted in some way: who has access, how difficult is the access; and what factors influence the access. Understanding these restrictions is the goal of accessibility analysis. The following list illustrates some of the concerns of accessibility analysis:

- Access influenced or determined by religious/ceremonial calendar
- Access influenced or determined by season, climate, or cosmological event
- Access to appropriate areas/spaces to create, deposit, perform, or monitor ritualistic, religious, or magical practices
- Access to material resources for creation of ritualistic, religious, or magical objects
- Access to tools, technologies, and/or knowledge to create objects/materials or perform ritualistic, religious, or magical practices
- Restrictions on access to sacred sites, artifacts/ecofacts, or performances by class, caste, rank, age, gender, or profession

BOTANICAL ANALYSIS

Identifying the plant materials from a site may reveal ritual feasting, offering/sacrificing rituals, or other ritual use of plants.

- Macro botanical analysis (seeds, pits, husks, reeds, twigs, leaves, living plants specimens placed in/on structures or grown in/around structures for magical protection or religious associations)
- Palynology (pollen analysis)
- Phytoliths (microscopic silica bodies)

CHEMICAL RESIDUE ANALYSIS AND DNA ANALYSIS

Testing visible or microscopic residues on artifacts can reveal a range of organic substances used in ritualistic, religious, magical, or ceremonial contexts.

- Ash or charcoal residue from cremation (in urns/jars, on altars, pyre platforms, or in burials)
- Blood as element in magical charms or other ritual practices
- Blood from sacrificial victims (human or animal)
- DNA from bodily fluid residue on ritual artifacts to determine sex or lineage of individual user
- DNA from human burial remains may help explain aspects of atypical burials (e.g., age, lineage, pathology, sex)
- Foods used for ritual offerings or feasting or in magical charms
- Ocher used in mortuary, rock art, or other ritualistic contexts

- Plant or resin materials used for incense, smudging, or purification
- Plants placed in/on structures or grown in/around structures for magical protection
- Psychotropic plant/animal use
- Urine as element in magical charms or other ritual practices

GEOPHYSICAL SURVEY

Each type of geophysical or subsurface testing technology has its advantages and limitations. The terrain, soil, vegetation, and climatic or other environmental conditions can all affect the usefulness of the technology.

- Ground Penetrating Radar (GPR): detects speed of radar signals bouncing off buried features or voids
  - » Can indicate the depth of buried objects or features, which may help in determining if the readings suggest a funerary or other belief associated feature
  - » Locate subsurface anomalies that may indicate burials, funerary structures, feasting pits, caches, or hordes
- Magnetometry: detects the magnetic fields of buried objects that differ from the natural background
  - » Locate subsurface anomalies that may indicate burials, funerary structures, feasting pits, statuary, caches, or hordes
- Metal Detector: detects the presence of metal either on the surface or below surface levels
  - » Locate metal objects with possible magical associations (especially along threshold/boundary areas, under floors/foundations, buried at crossroads, at offering sites, along waterways, in conflict sites)
  - » Locate metal objects with possible political/military ceremonial associations (especially along threshold/boundary areas, in battlefields, prison camps, parade grounds, treaty sites, military forts or encampments)
  - » Locate metal objects with possible religious associations (especially within and around religious structures and cemeteries, along threshold/boundary areas, under floors/foundations, at offering sites, along waterways, in conflict sites)
- Resistivity: records the level of electrical resistance when a current hits buried features
  - » Best used to locate the solid remains of structures (e.g., religious building foundations, crypts, tomb structures, etc.)

- Sonar: detects underwater objects and water depth through the emitting of sound pulses and measuring their reflected return
  - » Locate structures and objects in underwater contexts (temples, statuary, intentionally submerged features, sacrificial materials or skeletal remains, etc.)

SOIL AND MINERAL ANALYSIS

- Geochemical analysis: used to determine the origin and source of minerals and soils to identify local versus imported materials
  - » Soils, stones, and minerals used in and for ritual/sacred structures and objects are often imported from places/areas with particular divine or cosmically powerful associations; likewise, locally sourced materials may indicate the placement of structures/objects in that place as being directly related to that place's significance.
  - » Source determination can reveal larger conceptualizations of worldviews and other-than-human ontologies and relationships to the landscape.
- Soil micromorphology: generally used to microscopically analyze the soil composition of floor deposits/layers in archaeological contexts
  - » Can reveal layers of particular soils used in construction and plastering because of or associated with concepts of the divine, purity/impurity, ritual spaces and events, or apotropaically empowered attributes (colors, reflective properties, etc.)

MAPPING

Maps come in a wide variety of types and can reveal ritualistic, religious, or traditional beliefs, ideas, and sites.

GIS Analysis

The various applications of GIS can reveal complex spatial associations either embedded within or existing as the structural frameworks for belief systems and their enactments.

- Analyze environmental and geographical characteristics of religious, ceremonial, or ritualistic landscapes or sites

- Determine the degree of isolation or difficulty of accessibility of spiritual places
- Map crisis events, their intensity, and duration
- Map flow and distribution of folk belief, traditions, religious groups, and ethnic groups
- Map sensorial and affective data over landscapes or sites with associated historical events
- Reveal spatial patterns alignment, distribution, association, layout, and orientation of religious, ceremonial, ritualistic or magical places, structures, landscapes, and artifact/ecofacts
- Track viewsheds, soundscapes, and scentscapes

Map Types

- Bird's eye view maps
  - » Illustrate the importance and relationship of church/worship buildings to political and social infrastructure
  - » Show the location, orientation, and relationship of cemeteries/burial grounds to the neighborhoods and landscape of a town
- Pilgrimage maps
  - » Indicate the official paths trodden by innumerable people to a built or natural site believed to be imbued with sacred and/or healing powers
- Town maps
  - » May reveal underlying numerical or symbolic organization of the town's design layout (e.g., Masonic symbolism)
  - » Show the location, orientation, and relationship of cemeteries/burial grounds to the neighborhoods and landscape of a town
- Tithe maps
  - » Delineate church-owned lands and possibly the designated functions of particular land sections

Patterns

- Areas avoided, undeveloped (which may indicate a spiritual association or taboo)
- Numerical (distance) relationships between ritual/sacred sites or between ritual/sacred and mundane sites
- Situation of mortuary sites in relationship to settlements
- Situation of sacred buildings/features on landscape
- Ritual site placement

Placenames (Toponyms)

- May designate ceremonial or other ritual performance sites
- May designate pilgrimage routes
- May identify gathering areas for sacred plants
- May identify spiritual transformation sites of important individuals (places of revelation or transcendence)
- May indicate cosmological modeling or creation myths
- May indicate sites or features associated with sacred or mythological spiritual beings
- May mark sites or features of sacred healing
- May reveal sites or features deemed spiritually dangerous or taboo

MEASUREMENTS

Divine or magical numbers may be incorporated into a ritualized context through the measurements of the objects or the measured distances from each other or from a significant datum point. To reveal these embedded measures requires knowing and using the measurement system and devices utilized by the originating culture of the site under study. Even if the original system is unknown, relative measuring can still reveal patterns.

Manual Measuring

- Measuring tapes can certainly be used for small distances but be aware that temperature actually contracts or expands steel tapes.
- Distance measuring wheels work well for relatively smooth areas clear of obstructions (e.g., plants, rocks, rough and pitted terrain). These wheels come in different sizes and are either totally manual (limited units and basic counter) or electronic models that measure in multiple units of measure. The advantages of these wheels are their affordability, ease of single person operation, and no dependence on satellite signals.

Range Finding

- While marking coordinates with GPS can assist in calculating estimated distances between features, it is not always an accurate measuring strategy. When distances between features may reveal embedded religious numerology, it is necessary to have a more accurate measuring device. For greater distances or for more ease in difficult terrains, using a range finder rather than measuring tapes can produce instant measurements in feet, yards, meters, kilometers, and miles (depending on the quality of the device). Range finders are handheld and compact, and they don't require satellite availability, making them versatile and useful in any location.

- There are also GPS range finder apps for phones or tablets that can instantly plot the distances between multiple features, which may reveal ritualistic patterns with embedded numerical measurements or intentional relative spacing.
- Another handheld digital device is called a laser distance measurer. These are battery-powered and do not require satellite availability. They come in basic to deluxe models that can measure in English or metric units. Unlike range finders, these can accurately measure distances from a fraction of an inch up to hundreds of feet (or centimeters and meters).
- Total stations, of course, can also be used for measuring greater distances, but these are dependent on reliable satellite availability and can be persnickety devices as well as expensive.

PHOTOGRAPHY

- D-Stretch software
  » Enhances carved, incised, or painted images that are otherwise difficult or impossible to discern with the naked eye
- LIDAR (Light Detecting and Ranging; a form of aerial photography)
  » Locate connecting or associated features on a large landscape like waterways, travel corridors, and structures
  » Locate structures like temples and ceremonial complexes under dense vegetation
  » Locate use patterns like circumambulation tracks or pilgrimage routes
- Multispectral imaging
  » Enhances inscribed images or writing that may be worn or faded to point of illegibility or invisibility
- Photogrammetry
  » Facilitates abstracting measurements of features and spatial distribution from photographs
- RTI (Reflectance Transformation Imaging)
  » Enhances inscribed images or writing that may be worn or faded to point of illegibility or invisibility

CHAPTER 11

Resources

DOCUMENTARY RESOURCES

Numerous historical sources may be used to glean knowledge about, evidence for, and insight into the form and use of ritualistic, religious, and magical material culture. Some sources are textual while others may be more symbolic or material. Below are several sources that can provide researchers invaluable information.

- Almanacs
- Astrological works
- Botanical works
- Broadsides
- Church records
- Court documents
- Diaries
- Embroidery
- Ethnographies
- Family histories
- Folklore (stories, superstitions, planting and weather lore; proverbs)
- Furniture
- Grave markers
- Greeting cards
- Grimoires
- Herbals
- Law statutes
- Leechbooks (medicinal recipes)
- Letters
- Literature
- Maps
- Medical books
- Mercantile/commercial inventories
- Mother's advice books
- Newspapers
- Oral histories
- Paintings and other artwork (all media and genres)
- Photographs
- Placename studies
- Poetry
- Probate records
- Receipt (recipe) books
- Religious texts
- Sermons
- Songs
- Treatises

SCHOLARLY ASSOCIATIONS

American Anthropological Association (AAA): www.aaanet.org
American Cultural Resources Association (ACRA): www.acra-crm.org
American Folklore Society (AFS): http://www.afsnet.org
Archaeological Institute of America (AIA): www.archaeological.org
European Association of Archaeologists (EAA): www.e-a-a.org
The Folklore Society: http://www.folklore-society.com
Societas Magica: http://www.societasmagica.org
Society for American Archaeology (SAA): www.saa.org
Society for Church Archaeology (SCA): www.churcharchaeology.org
Society for Ethnobiology (SoE): www.ethnobiology.org
Society for Historical Archaeology (SHA): www.sha.org
World Archaeological Congress (WAC): www.wac.uct.ac.za

SCHOLARLY JOURNALS

American Antiquity: www.saa.org/publications
Archeoastronomy: The Journal of Astronomy in Culture: http://escholarhship
.org/uc/jac
Church Archaeology: www.churcharchaeology.org/journal
Church Monuments: https://churchmonumentssociety.org/the-journal
Comitatus: A Journal of Medieval and Renaissance Studies: http://
escholarhship.org/uc/cmrs_comitatus
Ethnology: http://www.pitt.edu/˜ethnolog
Fabula: https://www.degruyter.com/journal/key/FABL/html
Folklore: http://www.folklore-society.com
Historical Archaeology: www.sha.org
Hoodoo and Conjure Quarterly: http://planetvoodoo.com
International Journal of Historical Archaeology: www.kluweronline.com/
issn/1092-7697/current
Journal of American Folklore: https://www.afsnet.org/page/JAF
Journal of Contemporary African Studies: https://www.ru.ac.za/iser/jcas/
Journal of Ecclesiastical History: http://www.cambridge.org/core/journals/
journal-of-ecclesiastical-history
Journal of Ethnographic Theory: http://www.haujournal.org/index.php/
hau/issue/current

Journal of Ethnology and Folkloristics: http://www.jef.ee/index.php/journal

Journal of Feminist Studies in Religion: http://www.fsrinc.org/jfsr

Journal of Folklore Research: https://iupress.org/journals/jfr

Journal of Material Culture: http://journals.sagepubcom/home/mcu

Journal of Medieval and Early Modern Studies: http://www.dukeupress.edu/
journal-of-medieval-and-early-modern-studies

Journal of Modern African Studies: http://www.cambridge.org/core/
journals/journal-of-modern-african-studies

Journal of Religion: http://www.press.uchicago.edu/ucp/journals/journal/
jr.html

Journal of Religion in Africa: http://brill.com/view/journals/jra/jra-
overview.xml

Journal of Ritual Studies: http://www.pitt.edu/~strather/journal.htm

Journal of the Royal Anthropological Institute (formerly *Man*): http://www
.therai.org.uk/publications/journal-of-the-royal-anthropological-institute

Material Religion: The Journal of Objects, Art and Belief: http://www
.tanfonline.com/toc/rfmr20/current

Medieval Archaeology: http://www.tanfonline.com/toc/ymed20/current

Medieval Ceramics: http://medievalceramics.wordpress.com

Method and Theory in the Study of Religion: http://brill.com/view/journals/
mtsr/mtsr-overview.xml

Myth, Ritual, and Witchcraft: http://magic.pennpress.org

Numen: International Review for the History of Religions: www.brill.com/
numen

Paranthropology: Journal of Anthropological Approaches to the Paranormal:
www.paranthropology.co.uk

Past and Present: https://academic.oup.com/past

Post-Medieval Archaeology: http://www.tanfonline.com/toc/ypma20/
current

Preternature: www.psupress.org/Journals/jnls_Preternature.html

The Archaeological Journal: http://www.tanfonline.com/toc/raij20/current

*The Journal for the Academic Study of Magic as Preternature: Critical and
Historical Studies on the Preternatural*: http://preternature.org

World Archaeology: http://www.tanfonline.com/toc/rwar20/current

ORGANIZATIONS AND BLOGS

There are numerous local and regional groups—some academic/professional,
some amateur enthusiast—in many countries. Please explore your local area
for additional contacts for organizations, blogs, and databases.

African Diaspora Archaeology Network: http://www.diaspora.illinois.edu/
Norfolk Medieval Graffiti Survey Blog: medival-graffiti.blogspot.com
Witch Bottles—Museum of London Archaeology: https://www.mola.org
   .uk/witch-bottles-concealed-and-revealed

RITUAL AND MAGIC DATABASES

Apotropaios: www.apotropaios.co.uk
Campbell Bonner Magical Gems Database: www.2.szepmuveszeti/hu/
   talismans/tour/1806
Material Culture of Magic (MC) Database: www.couragetoenlighten.com
The Northampton Museum Concealed Shoe Index: museumservices@
   northampton.gov.uk
Suffolk Medieval Graffiti Survey: www.medieval-graffiti-suffolk.co.uk
UK Detector Finds Database: http://www.ukdfd.co.uk/

TECHNOLOGY

DStretch software: www.dstretch.com
RTI: http://culturalheritageimaging.org/Technologies/RTI

REPORTING AND DOCUMENTING ICOs, SYMBOLS, OR OTHER ENIGMATIC DISCOVERIES

Access to the many occurrences of intentionally concealed objects (ICOs), symbols, objects, or other enigmatic indicators of belief has always been a major problem as there has never been a centralized place or mechanism for the systematic documentation and dissemination of information regarding these discoveries. To address this need, a database has been created to provide a place for the documentation of any of these finds.

Material Culture of Magic (MCM) Database

This is a clearinghouse database for the recordation of magical material culture finds. Anyone who has discovered: concealed objects in buildings, structures, or other places; symbols or marks; buried or oddly displayed animal remains; or other objects displayed or situated in a potentially meaningful place is asked to record those discoveries here. You may be an archaeologist, a house renovator or builder, a site demolition person, a historic preservationist, a hobbyist, or someone who has just found something interesting. Whoever you are, your discoveries are important to those specialists attempting to accumulate documented evidence of the historic belief in and practice of magic. By submitting the information about your find(s) to this database, researchers will have access to data they would otherwise be unaware of.

The database is divided by region; within each region it is further organized by object type. The database will be updated as new submissions are received. Please help us document, preserve, and disseminate the valuable and irreplaceable evidence you have discovered that speaks to the fears and hopes of historic people and their attempts to protect and provide for themselves and their families.

Please submit the information to: www.couragetoenlighten.com/material-culture-of-magic-database. Information needed from contributors:

- Date of Find
- Date of site/structure
- Location (city, county, state)
- Site type
- Object(s), symbol(s) found and description
- Where object(s), symbol(s) were found, be very specific (e.g., behind chimney, under back door threshold)
- Where is/are the object(s) now?
- Contact information
- Further comments
- Two to three pictures or drawings

Glossary of Ritualistic, Religious, and Magical Gems and Other Stones

The following annotations are drawn from several historical and folkloristic sources of documentation concerning the belief in and use of stones as objects of power and agency in magical, religious, and/or ritualistic practices. For a list of these sources, see the Further Reading section "Artifact Material Types and Attributes: Minerals/Lithics/Soils." This is not a comprehensive list in scope or detail, as people around the world certainly have imbued many stones (and other objects) with powers without recording those ideas. Knowing how, in what contexts, with what associations, and for what purposes people used these stones may assist archaeologists in their artifactual interpretations.

Aetites (eagle stone or pregnant stone): laid upon or attached to pregnant women—sometimes left wrist—to prevent abortions, protect the woman and fetus, and ease childbirth; also wrapped in skins of sacrificial animals for protection. Worn around neck to prevent drunkenness, increase wealth, ensure victory, and influence others to one's favor. Carrying the stone wrapped in a wolf pelt makes the carrier fearless in the face of evil. If carved with an eagle or fish, the stone protects against sea creatures and illness.

Agate: protects and overcomes poisonous wounds; those with an inclusion of a tree ensure good crops if attached to the ploughman's arm or the oxen's horns; used to avert storms and command the flow of rivers; protects from witchcraft and thunder.

Alabaster (also nicomar and marble): especially in its pure white form, used to make funerary monuments, vases, and urns because it preserves perfume and diminishes the stink of corpses.

Alectorias (cock stone or capon stone): created in the belly of a rooster. Wearers are imbued with strength, boldness, invincibility, and invisibility (especially if worn on a helmet). Also bestows eloquence and congeniality. Supposed to be set in gold and displayed on the right side, but it has power only if the wearer is chaste.

Almandine: expels all poisons, makes one invisible, and bestows insight into mysterious matters including conferring the ability of prophecy.

Amber: worn as an amulet or powdered and added to drink, treats madness; if touched it prevents drunkenness. Yellow amber gives the power of invisibility and unflagging physical strength. When rubbed, amber produces a static charge and gives off a distinctive smell.

Amethyst: prevents intoxication, stops magical charms, destroys poison, prevents demonic harm, and increases wealth; magical properties are amplified if it is set in gold or silver and etched with the image of a man on horseback with a scepter or sword in his right hand. If set in iron or lead with this same image, the stone makes the wearer master of all spirits and they will be impelled to answer all questions and divulge hidden treasures.

Ammonite: a fossil from the Jurassic and Cretaceous periods that was added to a milking bucket to increase a cow's milk output.

Androdamas (also argyrodamas): casts a fog over the sight of those close to the stone's bearer.

Anthracite: a hard fossil stone that when carried throughout one's life, prevents drowning from shipwreck.

Anthropocrinus: suspended from a multicolored string, this stone releases one from enchantments and possession.

Antipathites: countermagic against fascinations and enchantments.

Aphroselenite (moon foam): often engraved with the image of Isis, Hathor-Hecate, or other head topped with bull horns or crescent moon; when engraved with a man seated on an eagle and wielding a baton, the stone allows its bearer to overpower his enemies.

Argyrophylax: placed on threshold of treasure-store, it emits a trumpet sound at a thief's approach.

Arnostetite: held in the left hand, this stone is used to calm and control the wrath of kings or judges.

Arsenic (realgar): used by alchemists in their chemical experiments; used in magical concoctions against the plague (believed to be caused by demons); fed to livestock to protect them from demonic harm; burned to ward off evil forces, especially vampires.

Asbestos (also Amiantos, white variety): ward against witches' poisons and enchantments.

Astroites: valued in Zoroastrian magic.

Azurite: bestows the power of visions and prophetic dreams and helps in communicating with spirits.

Beryl: carved with an image of Neptune in a chariot with two horses it will protect one on sea voyages; gives the wearer a 1,000-foot radius field of vision in both light and darkness; carved with a Venus image it is an amulet to protect travelers. To summon water spirits or raise the dead and induce them to answer questions, the stone must be etched with an image of the hoopoe and herb *dracontea*.

Betyl: the standing stone in Jacob's dream (Genesis 28:10–15) on which he rested his head and received divine visions (*beit El*=dwelling of God).

Bezoar: means "antidote" or "counter-poison" in Persian. Used to nullify poisons. Alchemists called it the white oxide of antimony *bezoar.*

Calorite: set in iron, this stone was used by magicians as a general catalyst for magical spells.

Carbuncle: protects one from fire, water, captivity, and poisons; associated with dragons and serpents as glowing eyes; it gives the bearer power over rivals and enemies.

Carnelian: often engraved with images that direct its powers toward a particular end, usually some form of obedience to the wearer; also protects against storms, lightning, and enchantment.

Caste coq: from the head of a chaste rooster, this stone carried in the hand makes one invisible and victorious.

C(h)elidonia: the black variety protects one from animals; carried in the mouth it provides invisibility or, with honey, prophetic abilities.

Ceraunia, Ceranitis (lightning or thunder stone): at sea or on a river protects from storms, drowning; allows one to capture an enemy's city or fleet; protects houses and property from lightning; protects flocks if placed in sheepfolds; Icelandic bearers of the thunder stone (*skruggustein*) have the power to see the entire world.

Chalazias: reveals the future; protects the bearer from poverty and from evil harm all around.

Chalcedony: perforated and worn as a ring or pendant, it ensures victory in all things. Set in gold, it protects against venoms, drowning, storms, and fire; it will increase wealth if etched with a stag or billy goat image and stored in a moneybox.

Chalcophonos: a lithophone that chimes like brass when struck; used to construct ritual bells.

Chelonia: after rinsing the mouth with honey, the placing of this stone in the mouth at the new or full moon gives one divinatory powers for a day.

Chelonitis: can calm storms (or raise them if the gold-speckled variety is boiled with a scarab beetle); placed under the tongue, it gives divinatory powers.

Chlochitis: protects children from the devil and adults from demons and misfortune.

Chrysolite (topaz or jacinth?): perforated, threaded on donkey or ewe hair or blue silk thread, and worn on left wrist, it protects against night demons; set in gold it repels ghosts, gives wisdom, and shelters one from fear; it prevents one from unjust accusations and insures victory in legal proceedings. Etching it with various images activates different powers: an ass—prophecy; seated man with candle—brings wealth; vulture—imprisons demons and winds. Demons obey its bearer.

Citrine: known as the merchant's stone, it attracts wealth and success.

Coral: multipurpose amulet: drives away storms; banishes ghosts, witches, demons, and monsters; and protects against enchantments and spells. In conjunction with a seal skin and attached to a mast, it protects against wind and waves, lightning, demons and evil spells, and all manner of dangers like pirates. Most effective in protecting infants from the evil eye.

Corvia (crow stone): could open locks, turn iron to silver, ensure victory in legal cases, and make one invincible and invisible if carried in the mouth or pocket.

Crystal: brings the possessor good fortune, divine favor, and influence over others. Like other gems, crystal stones were often engraved with various images that related to specific uses and powers. Often found in graves.

Cytherins: worn around the neck or on the finger, this stone protects against evil spells, ensures safe journeying, and generates honor and fortune for the wearer.

Demath (Del Mach): protects against evil spirits and sudden death, and also ensures holy grace.

Dendrachates: gives its bearer prosperity, especially in gardening and cultivation where it is worn on one's arm or attached to the plow.

Dendritis: as an amulet it is carved with a sea dragon surmounted by a mountain and it will give one power over wild animals, success in ventures, and influence over men.

Diadochos: used in hydromancy to make demons appear in water; used in necromancy but loses potency if it actually touches a corpse; often used in conjunction with lead, mugwort, and fennel root.

Diamond (also adamas, anancite, and synecite): used in hydromancy and impels demons to appear before the stone's possessor while being unable to inflict harm.

Emerald: worn as a necklace or ring amulet it bestows the power of prophecy; attracts riches; repels demons; and stimulates one's memory. It is associated with angels and Mars.

Eumeces: placed under a bed at the head, it engenders prophetic dreams.

Faihâr: destroys magical charms and if drunk as an elixir, releases one from spirit possession.

Fossils: fossils of many types were believed to possess inherent magical properties; some were misidentified as actual stones: toadstone (tooth of the *Lepidotes*); jet (fossilized coniferous wood); amber (fossilized tree sap). Others that captured the skeletal imprint of an ancient creature (fish, snails, and insects) were likely thought to be animate and possess special powers.

Galatites (milk stone): worn as an amulet it defends one against the evil eye and bewitchment; it eases childbirth when attached to the leg of a woman in labor.

Galena (lead glance): shiny, silvery crystal mineral; deposited in burial mounds.

Garnet (type of carbuncle or jacinth): protects its bearer from dangers associated with traveling.

Heliotrope (green chalcedony or blood jasper): gives the power of invisibility and prophecy, summons rain, expels poison, and grants long life; if engraved with the image of a bat, the owner has power over evil spirits.

Hematite: worn as amuletic ring, it ensures business success; if etched with the image of a man wielding a sword and astride a dragon, it will allow the wearer to command all evil spirits to reveal where treasures are hidden.

Hephestites (also vulcan stone, festinus): set in gold or silver, often as a ring, and engraved with a flamingo and scorpion it is an amulet against venom, witchcraft, enchantment, and evil nighttime visions.

Jacinth (hyacinthos): held under the tongue, the jacinth bestows the power to foretell the future; worn as a necklace or ring, it protects one from strangers, the dangers of the sea, travel, and pestilence; it also grants wishes; these stones were often engraved with images of horses, crocodiles, and half woman–half fish figures.

Jade (nephrite): used as an amulet against kidney stones; used in mosaic burial masks, figurines, beads, and amulet jewelry as magically and divinely protective devices and as offerings to the gods; celts made of nephrite were carved with magical inscriptions.

Jasper: green jasper set in silver banishes ghosts; it is often etched with various images to create amulets and talismans for specific purposes.

Jet: used in axinomancy (divination by axe); as an amulet, it wards against demons and breaks enchantments and protects women in childbirth; used to make dice for gaming and chess pieces and protect gamers from deceit. When rubbed, jet produces a static charge and gives off a distinctive smell.

Lapis lazuli: used in love philters and as a contraceptive; used in treatment of epilepsy.

Lychnis: buried in fields, it protects them from hail and pestilence; worn around the neck, it grants prophetic power; it is worn as a healing agent for menstrual problems.

Magnet (load stone): placed under the pillow of a sleeping wife, it will reveal her fidelity (causing her to fall out of bed if she is untrue); used in rituals to conjure ghosts; kept in a house, it will bar the entrance of thieves and wild beasts; whoever carries the stone will have the power of persuasion; it attracts good luck and the granting of wishes.

Malachite: placed in cradles, it protects infants from evil spells; carrying or wearing the stone protects its bearer from accidents.

Margul: a stone from the Nile that is possessed as an aphrodisiac.

Melas (black stone): an amulet against enemies, evil spells, potions, and ill-fortune; it promotes success and victory.

Mica: sheets of mica covered floors and structures; found in burial mounds; valued for and perceived to be cosmically divine due to its reflective shininess.

Nemesitis (stone of destiny): engraved with the image of Nemisis, this stone protected one from nightmares and nightly demons, especially potent for guarding children.

Obsidian: in conjunction with burning pine resin, incense, and lepidota (wild licorice), it grants prophetic vision; it has regenerative powers that can restore youth; protects against nightmares; gives owner the power to fatally curse others; used for ritual/ceremonial sacrificial knives and lances, in graves, and as offerings to the gods.

Onyx: usually carved with magical images each of which gives the stone different powers; used in dream necromancy and to summon and imprison demons.

Opal (ophthalmius): "thief's stone" enshrouds its wearer in a thick fog making him invisible while sharpening his eyesight; the bearer cannot be arrested or bound.

Orite: the green variety is considered the strongest in protecting its bearer from danger; rubbed with rose essence, it protects one from venomous reptiles; carried in conjunction with an iron rod it prevents pregnancy or induces abortion.

Panchrus: a multicolored hyaline quartz, it was often engraved with the image of Lato and Harpocrates and three greyhounds; this amulet stone protected against all magical arts.

Pearl: habitual consumption of pearls protects one from sudden or poisonous death; pearls worn or carried sooth anger.

Pyrite: if crushed and added to water, it counteracts evil spells; if put in holy water, it can summon demons who will be compelled to answer their summoner's questions.

Quartz: used by numerous cultures across the world, quartz is often found in burials, used in divination, and believed to strengthen and balance life forces.

Ruby (carbuncle, garnet): in Christian practice, this stone should be set in gold and worn on the left side; it protects against seduction and danger, banishes sorrow, shields houses from lightning, and safeguards fruits and crops. It also has prophetic power: if its brightness fades, it presages something terrible to come.

Sapphire: in the Christian church, this stone is a symbol of purity. Cardinals and bishops were required to wear a sapphire ring on their right hands (the hand used for blessing) and is called "the sacred stone." As a divine stone, it ensures God's favor in prayers. It has the power to unlock doors and undo bonds, protect one from poisoning; and when pulverized and drunk in milk, it heals all illness. Asterite (star sapphire) was especially powerful with its internal, shifting light.

Sarda or Sardius: often carried by ferrymen for protection; if of twenty-barley grain weight and worn on finger or at throat, the wearer will have no frightful dreams or be vulnerable to curses or evil spells. Stone often etched and mounted in gold.

Sardachates: keeps wickedness at bay; attracts love and congeniality; powers activated by etching it with magical letters.

Sardonyx: used to break curses and enchantments and ensure success in all endeavors; most effective if set in silver.

Selenite: worn by pregnant women, it ensures a full-term and healthy infant; placed under the tongue, it gives the gift of prophecy; it protects thieves; and it safeguards sea travelers from storms.

Topaz: effective against insanity, neutralizes curses upon a house, improves one's memory, and attracts financial success. It is used in hydromancy.

Turquoise: varying shades of blue-green, the bluer the more powerful; changes color when poison is present and protects its bearer from poisoning, drowning, or being murdered (but only if the bearer leads a life of honesty and integrity); also protects horses from ill.

Table G.1. Biblical association of stones in Christian and Hebrew traditions. © C. Riley Augé.

Stone	Christian	Hebrew
Sardonyx	Matthew	Judah
Topaz	Peter	Simon
Emerald	Bartholomew	Ephraim
Ruby	Andrew	Ruben
Sapphire	Philip	Issachar
Jasper	James the Greater	Zebulon
Amber	Judas	Nephtali
Agate	Matthias	Dan
Amethyst	John	Gad
Chrysolith	Thaddeus-Simon	Asher
Onyx	James the Lesser	Benjamin
Beryl	Thomas; Virgin Mary	Manassus
Chalcedony	Virgin Mary	

Glossary of Ritualistic, Religious, and Magical Plants

This glossary lists some commonly cited plants used in magic, religion, or ritual from cultures around the world. Possible locations, uses, and properties are noted for each plant as they relate to magical or ritualistic use. The glossary is intended as an aid and introduction for archaeologists surveying sites to bring to their attention potentially magical or ritualistic plant use. For specifically hallucinogenic plant usage, see the section "Psychotropic Plants" in Chapter 7.

Acacia (*Acacia seyal*): sacred to the Hebrews, it could not be used for secular purposes like furniture, private dwellings, or mundane objects.

Aconite/Monkshood (*Aconitum spp.*): carried in pouches for invisibility; used in Ainu shamanic bear ceremonies on arrow points; drunk in potions and philters.

Acorus (*Acorus calamus*): anointment oil made from its roots; leaves strewn on floors of temples and churches.

Aloe (*Aloe barbadensis*): burned as incense; salve stored in shells; used in amulets and talismans; made into magical tea.

Amaranth (*Amaranthus spp.*): placed on tombs; hung in temples and churches.

Amate (*Ficus spp.*): bark made into paper used to make magical figures: these plant figures may be buried in fields oranthropomorphic figures worn as amulets or used for image magic when pierced with maguey, torn, and buried.

Angelica (*Angelica archangelica*): grown in house garden; burnt in hearth, on bricks, and in chafing pans; roots worn as amulets.

Apple (*Malus domestica*): grown in orchards and around houses; branches used for divining rods; sites of seasonal fertility rites and offerings; pips and peelings used in divination.

Arbor vitae (*Thuja occidentalis*): twig burned in sweat baths and carried to protect against magic; planted in cemeteries and near graves.

Areca (*Areca catechu*): nuts used to adorn Hindu gods.

Artemisia (*Artemisia spp.*): sacred to deities like Vishnu, Siva, and Artemis/Diana; used by Native American shamans in rituals to banish evil.

Asafoetida (*Ferula asafetida*): burned as incense; used by Himalayan shamans to exorcise demons; made into amulets; pouches of leaves hung around children's necks.

Asoka (*Savaca Indica* or *Jonesia asoka*): used to decorate Hindu and Buddhist temples.

Bamboo (*Bamusa spp.*): made into divination sticks; crosses erected in crop fields.

Bay laurel (*Laurus nobilis*): bushes planted around house perimeter; attached to doors; burned as incense.

Beans (*Leguminosae*): used in divination; carried in amulet pouches; represented as anthropomorphic apotropaic bean figures; grown in gardens; included in and on graves; used in ritual ceremonies.

Benzoin (*Styrax tonkinense*): burned as incense; used in alchemy.

Betel (*Areca catechu*): used in amulets; offering to gods; burned as protective incense.

Birch (*Betula pendula*): crosses cut from birch placed above front door; planted in front of houses; branches hung on barn/stable doors and placed on manure piles.

Blackthorn (*Prunus spinosa*): planted along fence lines as magical protection.

Broom (*Cytisus scoparius*): used for household brooms that magically protected the house.

Buckthorn (*Rhamnus frangula*): planted near doors and windows to ward off evil.

Calamus (*Acorus calamus*): burned as incense; spread along house thresholds.

Camphor (*Cinnamomum camphora*): used as protective incense.

Canella (*Cannella alba*; *C. winteriana*): used for divination; planted at a child's naming ceremony; branches burned during shamanic rituals; ingredient in Santeria initiation rite drink.

Carlina thistle (*Carlina vulgaris*): used in philters and love potions.

Cedar (*Cedar libani*; *Pinus cedrus*; *Juniperus spp.*; *Cedrella Mexicana*): *see Juniper*; *North American Cedar*; *Red Cedar*

Chicory (*Cichorium intybus*): grown in house garden; placed under bed of pregnant women.

Coca (*Erythroxylon coca*): included in graves; burned as incense; leaves read as oracles.

Coffee (*Coffea arabica*): drunk by religious devotees to stay awake during prolonged worship; grounds read as oracles.

Cola (*Cola nitida*; *Cola acuminate*; *Cola spp.*): nuts used in amulets.

Copal (*Bureseru microphylla*): tree pitch; burned as incense; sits on altars of shrines; used by Mayans and Aztec to fill the teeth of royal family members; burned during divination; offering to gods at household shrines and at initiation ceremonies; burned as food offering for the dead during Dia de Los Muertos.

Crocus (*Crocus sativus*): adorned marriage beds; used in love potions.

Cypress (*Cupressus sempervirens*): used for mummy cases and Greek coffins; planted around cemeteries and at the head of graves; branches carried by mourners at funerals.

Date palm (*Phoenix dactylifera*): seeds used in magical preparations; panicles used as amulets and magical weapons; palm wine used as ritual beverage; branches carried to churches and blessed; fronds made into apotropaic figures and hung near entrances; hung in houses.

Deadly nightshade (*Atropa belladonna*): garlands hung over doors and windows.

Desert sage (*Artemesia tridentate*): used as part of ceremonial dancer's regalia and as wreaths, anklets, and bracelets; carried in medicine pouches and bundles; tobacco pipes wrapped in sage before bundled; burned as incense and purifier; covered floors of sweat lodges.

Dill (*Anethum graveolens*): grown in house garden, near doors; mixed with trefoil, St. John's wort, and vervain and placed at house entrance; hung over doors, all as witch wards.

Dita (*Alstonia scholaris*; *A. venenata*): bark used to make parchment for amulets; seeds used for Tantric sexual rituals; wood used to construct altars.

Dragon tree (*Dracaena draco*): its resin—dragon's blood—used in numerous magical applications in the South Sea Islands; Europeans used it for incense in love magic.

Elder (*Sambucus nigra*): planted around house and yard perimeters; planted on and placed in graves; coffins made of elder wood; believed to be the abode of spirits, which deterred its cutting or burning.

False mandrake (*Allium victorialis*): substitute for mandrake; used as amulet to protect against injury, black magic, evil spirits, ghosts, avalanches, and battle wounds.

Fennel (*Foeniculum vulgare*): wreaths hung over doors and windows; seeds stuffed in keyholes; grown in house garden.

Flax (*Linum usitatissimum*): used as amulet; spun into cloth used for religious garments and shrouds.

Foxglove (*Digitalis purpurea*): grown in house garden to protect the household; used in love potions; associated with fertility; the dew from foxglove would allow one to communicate with the fairies.

Garlic (*Allium sativum*): worn as an amulet; hung on and over doors and windows; buried at or placed on rock piles at crossroads; grown in house gardens.

Ginger (*Zingiber officinarum*): in South Pacific, used in numerous magical rituals; used in amulets and fetishes.

Ginseng (*Panax ginseng*; *Panax quinquefolium*): dried, carved, clothed root used as an amulet.

Hawthorn (*Crataegus oxyacartha*): hung over windows, on doors, and in rafters; hung outside cowsheds; grown in house garden; bedecked marriage altars; put in cradles; burned at weddings.

Hazelnut (*Corylas aveilana*): branches used as torches at wedding ceremonies; nuts placed on windowsills; cross twigs placed on grain bundles and in barns; nuts carried as amulets; nuts thrown in hearths for divination; branches used as divining rod to locate treasure, water, and ores.

Hellebore (*Helleborus officinalis; Veratrum album*): worn as an amulet; strewn around houses; burned as incense.

Henbane (*Hyoscyamus niger; H. spp.*): used in divinatory incense; ingredient in love philters; used in rain rituals; burned as apotropaic incense; smoked; included in graves.

Henna (*Lasonia inermis*): used to dye skin, hair, and fingernails; used for wedding, birth, and circumcision rituals.

Holly (*Ilex aquifolium*): planted along house edges, under windows, and as hedges along property lines and roads; used to construct thresholds.

Houseleek/hens-and-chicks/stonecrop (*Sempervivum tectorum*): planted on roofs to protect the house from lightning sent by witches and demons.

Hyssop (*Hyssopus officinalis*): used in cleaning and purifying sacramental vessels; burned as incense to purify lepers; stalks used as sprinklers for sacrificial blood onto doorposts.

Incense cedar (*Libocedrus descurrens*): burned as incense in religious and ritual ceremonies.

Iris (*Iris florentina*): planted on graves, especially women's.

Ivy (*Hedera helix*): grown on exterior walls of house and barns; guarded cattle from evil and ensured their fertility and plentiful milk yield; associated with Dionysus and wine.

Job's tears (*Coix lacryma-jobi*): used for rosary beads and amulet necklaces.

Juniper (*Juniperus ssp.*): burned as incense; carried by persons as apotropaia; burned in ceremonial fires; berries were dried and made into bracelets worn by infants; wood used to construct ritual items; leaves used in sweat lodges; burned as incense during childbirth to prevent fairy substitution of a changeling; leaves carried in pouches.

Laurel (*Daphne laureola*): leaves chewed to induce oracular powers; worn as ceremonial garlands, wreaths, and chaplets.

Lavender (*Lavandula officianalis*): burned as incense; carried by persons to avert the evil eye; grown in house garden.

Leek (*Allium porrum*): worn by warriors in battle to protect against wounds.

Lily (*Lillium ssp.*): decorate sacred wells; grown in house gardens to protect against witches and ghosts; planted on graves.

Live-forever (*Sedum purpureum*): planted on roofs; hung in houses.

Lotus (*Nelumbo spp.*): associated with religious deities from several traditions (Hindu, Egyptian, Buddhist, Mayan, Greek); often depicted in architectural and religious artworks.

Maguey (*Agave americana*): leaves used in blood-letting ceremonies; leaves and tips used as amulets attached to houses.

Maize (*Zea mays*): used as grave goods; kernals used in amulets; food offering; ears hung on house walls.

Mandrake (*Mandragora officinarum*): roots fashioned into poppets and oracle figures; ingredient in love potions and philters; worn as charm; used in fetishes.

Marijuana (*cannabis sativa*): smoked, drunk as tea, ingested as medicine, and used in ritual foods.

Maté (*Ilex paraguariensis*): leaves included in graves; associated with silver-lined gourd vessels in graves provided for the making of maté tea on the afterlife journey; used in ritual and shamanic ceremonies.

Misteltoe (*Viscum album*): used in ritual ceremonies; suspended from house ceilings; burned in bonfires at midsummer rituals.

Moloucca beans (*Guilanderia bonduc* and *Guilanderia major*): known by many names: nickernuts, nikar nuts, sea pearls, eaglestones, and Virgin Mary bean; are beans or seeds from the warri tree indigenous to the Caribbean that are carried on the ocean currents and wash up on the beaches of faraway places like Ireland, Scotland, and Scandinavia where they are used as amulets for good luck, to banish ill-fortune, ease childbirth, or protect one from drowning, counter witchcraft and the evil eye, and unbewitch cattle and purify their milk.

Moonwort/honesty (*Lunaria annua*): used in potions to ward off evil; spread on locks and chains and inserted in keyholes to undo them; strewn on paths to unshoe passing horses.

Mugwort (*Artemisia vulgaris*): hung over doors; grown in house gardens; burned as incense; burned in ceremonial fires on the summer solstice; sewn into pillows to induce prophetic dreams.

Mullein (*Verbascum thapsus*): stem dipped in tallow used as a torch in religious processions; used in potions and carried as apotropaia; placed in shoes as contraceptive.

Myrtle (*Myrtus commuis*): Hebrews covered Tabernacle tents with boughs; sprigs worn by brides and grooms; garlands carried in processions; decorated tombs.

North American cedar (*Cedrus juniperus*): burned as incense in religious and ritual ceremonies; bark shredded and used as tinder to light ritual fires; wood burned in winter ceremonies; branches used to sweep/purify houses; spread on floor of sweat lodge.

Oak (*Quercus spp.*): sacred groves used for ritual ceremonies; used for doors, jambs, and windowsills; acorns carried as amulets.

Onion (*Allium cepa*): hung on walls and from ceilings to attract and capture ill forces; grown in house gardens.

Osha (*Ligusticum poteri*): root carried as talisman or charm.

Parsley (*Petroselinum crispum*): wreaths adorned tombs; grown in house gardens; apotropaic wreaths at weddings.

Peony (*Paeonia officinalis*): grown in house gardens; placed around beds to ward off incubi and succubae and other nightmares.

Pinecones (**any variety of pine**): affixed to garden gate posts as ward against ill-fortune.

Piñon (*Pinus ssp.*): pitch used to anoint corpses; burned as incense; wood used to construct ceremonial corrals and enclosures, hogans, cradles, weaving looms, and wands; branches and needles carried by ceremonial participants; Piñon wood charcoal used as black sand for sand paintings.

Poppy (*Papaver somniferum*): used as grave goods; burned as incense; smoked.

Primrose (*Primula vulgaris*): grown in house gardens; placed in temples and private ritual spaces.

Red cedar (*Juniperus scopulorum*): burned as incense; made into coffins; wood oil used in mummification process; used to make temple doors; branches used to sweep/purify houses; spread on floors of sweat lodges; downed cedar trees bestowed with offerings; included in graves.

Red clover (*Trifolium pratensa*): four leaves lucky (five unlucky); four-leaf clover placed in shoes; sprigs carried by travelers to protect from harm.

Red willow bark (*Salicaceae ssp.*): used to make wands and prayer sticks and other ceremonial objects and amulets; found as grave goods and votive offerings.

Reed (*Arundo donax*): used to make wind instruments played in magical or spiritual contexts.

Rice (*Oryza sativa*): used in ritual ceremonies; food offering; shrines in rice paddies.

Rose (*Rosaceae*): decorate sacred wells; bedeck tombs; planted on graves; grown around houses.

Rosemary (*Rosmarinus officinalis*): strewn on doorsteps; grown in house garden and near house door; placed under beds; carried in funeral processions; buried with the dead.

Rowan/mountain ash (*Sorbus aucuparia*): planted at house corners; butter churns made from rowan wood; rowan twigs attached to butter churns and milk buckets all as wards against witchcraft.

Rue (*Ruta graveolens*): grown in house garden and planted in window boxes or under windows; rubbed on house floors; brushes made from rue used in Catholic churches to sprinkle holy water before Mass; apotropaic wreaths at weddings.

Sage (*Salvia officinalis*): grown in house garden; hung in windows; burned as a purifier (smudge) to cleanse objects, people, and spaces; planted on graves.

St. John's wort (*Hypericum perforatum*): wreaths thrown on roofs; flowers hung over doors; grown in house garden; used by Christian priests in exorcisms; sprig carried to repel witches.

Sandlewood (*Santalum album*): used in embalming; burned on funeral pyres; used in construction of temples; burned as incense.

Snapdragon (*Antirrhinum majus*): grown in house gardens; worn as amulet.

Sunflower (*Helianthus annuus*): bowls of seeds placed on graves; venerated in rituals; ritual offerings.

Sweetgrass (*Hierochloe odarata*): burned as incense or purifier; usually plaited into long braids; pieces thrown on hot rocks during sweat ceremonies.

Sycamore (*Ficus sycamorus*): sacred to Hathor and Nut, offerings including water jugs, food, and flowers were placed at their roots.

Tagetes (*Tagetes lucida*): burned in healing rituals; woven into a cross and nailed to houses; used in purification ceremonies; flowers used as offerings.

Thornapple (*Dature spp.*): used as grave goods; used in amulets; flower offering to Siva.

Tobacco (*Nicotiana ssp.*): ceremonially smoked to communicate with the spirits; left on altars or at sacred places like shrines, rock art sites; springs and wells; cultivated in gardens; given as offering at Native American sacred sites and events; depicted in Native American rock art; included in graves.

Tulasi/holy basil (*Ocimum sanctum*): worshipped as a Goddess in India; drunk as a protective tea; planted around temples; included in graves.

Valerian/garden heliotrope (*Valerianan officinalis*): hung on door; grown in house garden to protection against evil.

Vervain (*Verbena officinalis*): planted in house gardens and around doors; carved on amulets; made into brooms; used in divination; bridal wreaths; burned to purify temples.

Wormwood (*Artemisia pontica*): spread around the inside perimeter of the house to protect against evil.

Yarrow (*Achillea millefolium*): as a protection against negative forces it was grown in house gardens, strewn on doorsteps, suspended over cradles, hung in houses, and nailed to doorways; found on graves; smoked in Native American ceremonies; used in Chinese divination; bestows second sight when held against the eyes; used in ayurvedic medicine.

Yaupon (*Ilex vomitoria*): used as a bitter black tea as a ceremonial drink.

Yerba santa (*Eriodictyon californicus*): known as the holy herb or sacred herb, it was scattered along boundaries; burned as incense; used as an altar offering.

Yew (*Taxus spp.*): planted in graveyards; buried with dead as protection from witches; wood used for funeral pyres.

Glossary of Ritualistic, Religious, and Magical Terms

Abbey: a complex of buildings to house and support a religious community of monks or nuns; synonymous with monastery, convent, or nunnery.

Ablution: washing of one's body as part of a ritual or religious rite; often for purification.

Abracadabra: magical word spell written triangularly in descending order from the complete word down to the single letter "A"; for protection against a variety of misfortunes; it contains sixty-sixty letters, a magically powerful multiple of three.

Abraxas: magical word referring to the God of the year (the word's seven letters equal 365 according to numerology); used as a symbol to represent totality; depicted on amulets as a composite figure with a rooster's head, human torso and arms, and snake legs.

Actorius: a nonprecious mineral stone found in young, castrated rooster (capon) gizzards used as a magical amulet.

Adjuration: A command by an exorcist or shaman to expel an evil spirit.

Agogós: metal chimes used in Afro-Caribbean religions.

Alchemy: a chemical and philosophical science that pursued the transformation of base metals into gold, the discovery of a universal cure for disease, and the secret to longevity (or immortality).

Almadel: a white wax talisman inscribed with names of angels or spirits to be used in a ritual.

Altar: a structure (often raised) on which offerings or sacrifices are placed and/or incense is burned in worship; a central structure in religious or ritual practices that focuses worship.

Amulet: an object or assemblage of objects used to provide magical protection; sometimes used synonymously with a charm or talisman.

Anathema: an offering, usually hung in a temple, to a deity.

Anchorage: a structure, usually a one- or two-room cell, attached to a church with a mall squint (window) allowing the anchorite to view the altar and a grilled or shuttered window through which confession could be heard.

Anchorite (anchoress): a religious individual who takes a vow of permanent enclosure for an austere life of contemplation and solitude; often viewed as mystics and consulted for their wisdom (visions).

Animatism: the belief in a sentient or intrinsic life force pervading the landscape.

Animic ontologies: belief that all life forms are "people" (e.g., human-people, deer-people, salmon-people) who interact with each other.

Animism: the attribution of souls or spirits to animals, plants, and inanimate objects.

Ankh: an Egyptian tau cross with a looped top; a key-like emblem held by gods or god-kings to symbolize the generative power of life; sometimes called the "key of life."

Anthropomorphic: having human form or characteristics.

Apotheosis: deification of a mortal.

Apotropaic: magically protective.

Apotropaic figures: figurines, statues, or architectural elements intended to repel evil beings and forces; often they are grotesque (e.g., gargoyles) and may be anthropomorphic, theriomorphic, or fantastical.

Arborglyph: also dendroglyph; incised or relief carving on trees.

Aspergillum: a device used to sprinkle holy water in ritual blessing and purification at baptisms, or on corpses at funerals, congregations, candles, palm fronds, and houses. Three distinct forms: a perforated ball (silver, gold, or brass) with a handle of same material or wood; a standing, tapered vessel (silver or brass) with a perforated lid; or a whisk of hair, cloth, or plant fibers and a metal or wooden handle. Usually associated with Catholic and Orthodox Christian rituals but also found in Anglican, Balinese Hindu, and other traditions.

Aspersorium: a small bucket, usually with a bail handle, for holy water and used in conjunction with the aspergillum; sometimes referred to as a situla.

Axis Mundi: see *World Axis*

Baldachin: a symbolic canopy made of fabric (like silk) or an architectural structure (wood) carried over a sacred object or divine personage; in Christian churches it is found over altars, tombs, and statues to symbolically increase the spiritual power of the objects/persons it covers.

Barrow: a human-made mound or hill, usually over a grave.

Beckoning cat (Manoki Neko): a ceramic cat figurine found in Asia set in windows or doorways of homes and businesses to attract good luck, prosperity, and protection; painted or glazed in different colors each of which corresponds to a particular spiritual function.

Beguinage: a house or range of buildings for lay-religious women devoted to charitable work, often in urban areas.

Bottle tree: tree with blue or green bottles suspended or attached to repel evil forces.

Bracteates: thin metal stamped discs often bearing religious imagery and attached to garments or books.

Cairn: a rock pile signifying a burial, a spiritual event, an astronomical alignment, or a cosmologically significant place.

Cartonnage: layers of linen or papyrus covered with plaster to create funerary masks and panels.

Catacomb: a subterranean burial gallery with niches for tombs, often for religious martyrs.

Cenotaph: "empty tomb"; memorial tombs or grave markers without actual human burials.

Cenote: a deep sinkhole in limestone with a pool at the bottom; often used for sacrificial offerings and believed to be portals to the underworld.

Censor: vessel used for burning incense.

Charm: object or written script used to attract good luck or fortune; sometimes used synonymously with amulet.

Cinerarium: a depository for cremation urns.

Circumambulation: a procession in religious/ritual ceremonies in which the sacred space is walked around, often in a prescribed direction (e.g., sunwise/clockwise) to implicate cosmic relationships and a prescribed number of times in accordance with sacred numerology.

Cist grave: stone-built chambers for cremation urns or burials.

Cloister: a rectangular covered walkway found in monasteries, usually connected to the church and encompassing an open garden area (garth), used for meditative silent contemplation.

Clouts: rags or cloths tied to bushes and trees, often near water (holy wells or sacred water bodies) or in sacred groves.

CME (culturally modified ecofact): a natural object intentionally modified (smoothed or texturized, cut, carved, incised, painted, drilled, perforated, knapped, etc.).

CMT (culturally modified tree): trees intentionally bent, carved, pollarded, or otherwise manipulated.

Codex: a bound manuscript of leaves recording religious information.

Colossus: a gigantic statue often representing a deity or divine ruler and expressing supernatural powers.

Columbarium: structure comprised of one or a series of niches for human remains.

Conjuration: rituals to physically manifest spirits or demons in order to control them or utilize their powers.

Contagious magic: the belief that two or more objects/entities that have come into contact retain that connection even when no longer in contact or proximity; this connection makes it possible to use one of the objects to manipulate the other.

Contiguous magic: the belief that a part of someone or animal (e.g., hair, fingernails, measurements, etc.) can be used to magically manipulate that person or animal.

Corno/cornicello/cornetto: a horn-shaped amulet made of gold, silver, or red coral for protection against the evil eye or bad luck and to promote fertility and virility (Italian).

Cosmic wheel: a symbolic representation of the cosmos as a spoked wheel (Hindu, Buddhist, Jain).

Cosmogony: the study of beliefs about the creation/origin of humankind; sometimes also used to refer to the study of the universe's origins.

Cosmology: a culture's set of beliefs about the structure and origins of the cosmos and the relationships among all the elements and entities that make up that cosmos.

Counter-charm: a charm used in retaliation to a maleficent spell.

Cromlech: see *Dolmen*

Cross: one of the oldest and most widespread of religious symbols; while usually having four arms, it can have numerous intersecting branches, which results in hundreds of variations all having numerological significance.

Crossroads: a meeting and crossing of two or more roads. Such intersections are believed in many cultures to concentrate supernatural powers both divine and demonic. They are thought to be liminal places, which makes them especially appropriate locations for shrines, chapels, and holy statues as well as gallows, apotropaic figures, and burial of suicides, criminals, and other social deviants.

Curse: an invocation for harm or misfortune to befall someone or something.

Daisywheel: also hexafoil; a six-petaled flower design usually constructed with a builder's compass; often used as symbol of protection.

Dalle: stone slab or tile incised or otherwise decorated (e.g., sepulcher slabs set in walls or pavement of religious buildings).

Demon: an evil spiritual being.

Dendroglyph: see *Arborglyph*

Dipinti: sketched or painted, rather than incised, inscriptions.

Divination: uses a variety of objects or materials to foresee the future, discover lost or stolen items, determine the most auspicious times for undertakings, or provide guidance for decision-making.

Divining rod (Aaron's rod, Angle rod, Rod of Solomon): a y-shaped branch or two hand-held 90-degree angled rods used for dowsing (finding water or treasure).

Dolmen: also portal-tomb or cromlech; a megalithic single-chambered, free-standing structure comprised of either three or four upright orthostats topped with a large roof-slab or capstone.

Eccentrics: lithic projectile points knapped into complex and fantastic forms for ritualistic rather than practical use.

Ecofact: biological or other natural objects or remains, usually refers to non-living natural elements.

Effigy: a carved or modeled anthropomorphic or theriomorphic image.

Effigy mound: an earthen mound formed in an animal shape.

Elementals or elements: the fundamental structures of the world: air, fire, water, earth. Some cultures also include wood and metal. These elements are often associated with directions, seasons, numbers, spiritual beings, animals, and personality characteristics. Alchemists also included the "philosophical" elements: salt, sulfur, and mercury.

Elf-shot: prehistoric lithic points believed to have been made and used by elves.

Ema: votive tablets made of wood (Shinto).

Enchantment (also bewitchment): to cast a magical spell over someone or thing.

Ensalmo: a spell, charm, or enchantment (Peru); thought to be of Spanish origin.

Entheogen: psychotropic substances used to reveal or induce divine or spiritual experiences.

Entoptics (also phosphenes): abstract visual images produced by the brain (seen when you close your eyes), but that are also produced during the first stage of altered consciousness. Thought to be the source for some rock art imagery.

Eschatology: beliefs pertaining to "last things": death, heaven, hell, the afterlife, etc.

Evil eye (also eye-biting; see also *Fatal look*): a maleficent power cast through glancing, glaring, or staring that causes illness, misfortune, or death; referred to as overlooking, eye-biting, or casting a fatal look.

Execration figures: poppets or anthropomorphic figurines used to curse, vilify, denounce, condemn, decry, or express hatred for an individual.

Fairy (also faerie): creatures of the spirit realm with magical powers who can bring good or ill luck to humans; they are often associated with natural landscape features (e.g., water, caves, hills, etc.) or human domiciles.

Familiar: a spirit companion of a witch that usually took the form of a small animal (cat, bird, mouse, frog, lizard) that did the witch's bidding; also believed the witch could transform into his/her familiar animal form.

Fascination: see *Glamour*

Fasting bed: the structure where a person conducts his/her ritual of isolation, fasting, sleep deprivation, exposure to the elements, and possible physical mutilation and consumption of psychotropic substances in order to receive a divine vision, message, or blessing. These structures often have a semicircle wall of layered stones and evidence of floor cushioning with tree or shrub branches.

Fatal look: a variant of the evil eye in which the caster intentionally wishes the receiver dead or seriously harmed.

Fetish: an object, container, or figurine believed to house a spirit.

Figa (also *mano fico*): Italian amulet in the 3-D shape of a fisted hand worn as a protection against the evil eye.

Figure stones (also eolith): stones naturally occurring, shaped by nature, but resembling anthropomorphic or theriomorphic beings.

Figurine: a carved or modeled 3-D human, animal, or spiritual being.

Foundation rites: ritual sacrifice at the time of a building's construction, renovation, or expansion; meant to protect building from various mishaps, protect the people associated with the building; or appease the land/local spirits on which the building is constructed.

Fuda: inscribed wooden plaque used as a protective amulet (Shinto).

Garth: the open-air garden area encompassed by a cloister.

Glamour: power wielded by faeries to create optical illusions and entrance human victims.

Glyph: a magical symbol representing a person's name and birthday and possessing strong apotropaic power.

Grave goods (mortuary assemblages): objects placed in mortuary contexts with the remains of the deceased.

Gri gri (also *gris-gris*): an amulet (usually a bag filled with a variety of objects) to protect the wearer or bring good luck; originating in Africa, gri gri are usually associated with Vodou.

Grimoire: also receipt book; a book of magical spells, symbols, knowledge, and instructions.

Haint blue: a light blue used to paint the ceilings of porches as a representation of water, which spirits were unable to cross (African/African American tradition).

Hamsa (Arabic) or Hamesh (Hebrew): a flat hand image amulet for protection against the evil eye.

Hearse: metal framework over aristocratic tombs and effigies.

Henge: a usually circular ritual enclosure consisting of wood or stone uprights and possibly a bank and ditch system.

Henotheism: belief in locally residing spirit beings.

Hermatage: an isolated small dwelling of a hermit or a larger religious community seeking solitude and isolation.

Hex: a curse or spell.

Hexafoil: see *Daisywheel*

Hex sign: a geometric design, usually with five, six, eight, or nine points, painted on or embedded in building walls as brick or stonework designs.

Hieratic: some object consecrated by priests for ritual use; also the script used by Egyptian priests.

Hierology: the study of sacred writing, especially ancient Egyptian.

Hoard: an intentionally amassed assemblage of ritual or magical objects.

Holocaust: the complete burning of a sacrifice.

Horse brasses: flat brass objects, usually circular and bearing symbolic images, attached to horse trappings as apotropaic devices; also found in stables and pubs attached to the walls and beams.

Hospital: originally a religious institution offering spiritual and physical care for the poor and ill.

Host: the sacred bread wafer used in Christianity and regarded as the "body" of Christ.

ICO (intentionally concealed object): objects (usually with magical or spiritual intent) buried, secreted under floors, in walls, rafters, hearths and chimneys, in trees or water, etc.

Icon: a pictorial representation of a religious figure.

Image magic: the use of an image (a picture, a poppet, a figurine, etc.) to represent an individual or deity as the sympathetic connection through which magical or spiritual influence can be wielded (see *Sympathetic magic*).

Imitative magic: the use of an object, substance, or behavior to imitate a desired outcome (e.g., loud drumming sounds to imitate thunder to bring on rain showers).

Immolation: a sacrifice or offering to a deity figure.

Impersonal supernatural power: an amoral supernatural force that manifests in people and things; also called mana (Melanesian and Polynesian).

Incantation: the singing or chanting of words of power (magical/religious) in a ceremony or ritual.

Incarnation: to have a physical body and presence.

Initiate: an individual who has successfully undergone an initiation ritual.

Initiation: a magical or religious ceremony of transition or transformation.

Invocation: using the name of an angel or deity to call upon its beneficial power and influence.

Ithyphallic figure: a phallus figure carried in festival processions; fertility/virility figurines/statues with erect and/or oversized or prominent phalluses.

Jetton: medieval metal token or coin-like disc used on a counting board for calculations (similar to an abacus).

Joss stick: an incense stick burned in rituals to appease the gods and banish evil spirits (Chinese).

Ju-Ju: magical rites comprised of secret societies, witch-doctors, amulets, curses, and adjurations (African).

Kabbalah (also Qabalah or Cabala): the mystical aspect of Judaism offering symbolic cosmological and cosmographical explanations.

Kurgans: mounds of earth and/or stones built over graves; usually associated with Russian, Eastern and Northern European, and Central Asian areas.

Labyrinth (see also *Maze*): usually a circular winding path that symbolizes life's trials toward a center point representing salvation. Walking a labyrinth embedded in the tile floors of churches could substitute for religious pilgrimage.

Lapidary: relating to the cutting or inscribing of precious gems.

Lararium: a Roman household shrine.

Larnax: small, closed coffin or ash chest for human remains (Minoan, Ancient Greek).

Leech: a medical practitioner who combines herbalism with magical beliefs and remedies.

Libation: offering of some liquid to the gods or spirits (e.g., wine, milk, honey, blood) usually from a special vessel; see *Patera*, *Phiale*, *Oinochoe*.

Lich (also *lych*) gate: the gate at or near the entrance to a church; funeral services were often held near this gate.

Lithophone: stone that reverberates with a ringing, gonging, or bass-like tone, or that has echoing qualities.

Magic: a supernatural power inherent in particular materials or characteristics (like color, shimmer, or sound) that can be used by people to manipulate or control their worlds through protection, harming, divining, attracting good fortune, and controlling the weather.

Magic square: a square subdivided into equal smaller squares each containing a number. These numbers, when added vertically, horizontally, or diagonally, all produce the same sum.

Magical numbers: numbers associated with deities and believed to have influential powers.

Mana: a generalized force that can be acquired by or transmitted to humans by sacred objects (Polynesia); also the supernatural power wielded by the dead (Melanesia).

Mandala: a circular symbolic image (often complex and colorful) representing the universe.

Manitou: supernatural spirits inhabiting the natural world and possessing great magical power (Algonquin).

Manuport: a natural object transported out of its indigenous environment to a distant place and used or revered as an amulet, talisman, or other sacred or powerful item.

Martyrium or martyria: church, chapel, temple, or shrine built on the site of a martyr's grave or a site associated with Christ's life or Passion.

Mastaba: freestanding rectangular burial structure with inclining sides and entrance shaft leading to subterranean burial and offering chambers.

Maze (see also *Labyrinth*): although often used synonymously, a maze differs from a labyrinth in that the former has multiple dead ends and confusing passageways whereas the latter has one entrance that leads in a direct, albeit winding, path to the center. Mazes can be circular, square, rectangular, or free form.

Medicine bundle/bag: an assemblage of sacred and powerfully animated objects bound in wrappings or a leather or cloth bag; often entrusted to an individual through spiritual visions or clan lineages (Native American).

Medicine wheel: a stone circle, often with radiating spokes, with religious, healing, astronomical, calendrical, and/or territorial power and importance (Native American).

Megalith: large stone monuments like henges, Menhirs, dolmen, etc.

Menhir: a single standing stone.

Menorah: Jewish seven-branched candelabrum.

Mezuzah: small case containing holy text attached to door posts of Jewish homes.

MMC (magical material culture): objects and symbols believed to possess magical power and/or used in the enactment of magical beliefs.

Monolith: single block of stone usually shaped like a pillar or monument.

Monstrance: also ostersorium; a transparent or open container in which the consecrated Host is displayed for veneration in Catholic or other Christian churches.

Necropolis: literally "city of the dead"; a cemetery.

Nimbus: the depiction of the radiating halo or glow surrounding divine or saintly images.

Nkondi/Nkisi (plural *minknodi/minkisi*): a set of materials used in curing rituals among West African groups to manipulate the supernatural world for the benefit of members of a local community.

Numerology: the ascription of powers, meanings, and associations to numbers; also the correlation of numbers and their associated meanings to letters of the alphabet.

Numinous: filled with a sense of the divine, supernatural, sacred, mysterious.

Obelisk: a tall, narrow, four-sided stone pillar that terminates at the top in a pyramid. Often, they were carved with religious images and texts, were associated with the sun god, and were situated in or near temples.

Offering: something sacrificed or given as a token of devotion, appeasement, or propitiation.

Oinochoe: jug made from precious metal, bronze, or clay used in conjunction with the phiale for pouring libations (Greek).

Omamori: amulet tablets of wood or sheaves of paper inscribed with prayers and covered with brocaded silk; offered at Shinto shrines and Buddhist temples or carried to ward off bad luck and bring good fortune (Japanese).

Omen (also portent): a sign giving insight or knowledge concerning a future event.

Omphalos: the world navel; a point representing a culture's perception of the center of the world and the location of the world tree or axis mundi (the communicating conduit between the mundane and spiritual realms of the cosmos).

Oracle: the mediating messenger between supernatural beings and those searching for advice or prophecy.

Orientation: the direction something faces.

***Os resectum*:** finger bone cut off a corpse before cremation to be buried symbolically.

Ossuary: a building or other structure for the deposition of human skeletons; usually a place of secondary deposition where bones of numerous individuals are intermixed either divided by bone type (e.g. skulls, femurs, etc.) or indiscriminately in holes or piles.

Ostersorium: see *Monstrance*

Ouranic: of the heavenly realm.

Palimpsests: a layering of site use/occupation over time; "rewriting" over the top of previous "writing."

Palindrome: words with the same spelling whether forward or reverse; such words deemed especially powerful words for magic word squares.

Papal bullae: lead seals used on papal documents for authentication.

Passage tomb: tomb accessed through a narrow passageway.

Patera: brass bowl with long wooden handle for offering wine libation to the gods (Roman).

***Pawang*:** an Indonesian or Malaysian shaman.

Pax: a tablet or disc made of wood, metal, ivory, or glass used in Christian churches as an intermediating device to transmit the "kiss of peace" from the priest to the congregation.

Perambulation: formally establishing boundaries of parish or other sacred area by ceremoniously walking around them.

Personified supernatural power: the power that resides in deities and spirits.

Phiale: shallow dish (usually silver) for pouring libations (Greek).

Philter: a drink with aphrodisiacal or fertility enhancing powers.

Phylactery: a small leather box containing Hebrew texts; also a general synonym for amulet.

Pilgrim badge: a pin or pendant usually made of ceramic, tin, or paper, acquired as a souvenir and amulet at a pilgrimage site.

Pilgrimage: a spiritual or healing journey to a sacred site or a site believed to have miraculous healing properties.

Pithos: large storage jar used for wine and oil.

Places of power: the physical, spatial areas believed to be inhabited/visited by supernatural beings/forces or that are areas where spiritual/cosmic power is concentrated and accessible.

Poppet: a doll or figure made of cloth, straw, wax, or wood used to harm or manipulate a victim through image magic (see also *Image magic*).

Portable altar: a small, possibly collapsible, altar with associated altar accoutrements meant to bring the benefits of church services to those unable to attend the church due to distance or incapacity.

Portal tomb: see *Dolmen*

Prayer beads (rosaries and paternosters): strings of beads made of amber, coral, glass, jet, precious metals, wood, or bone used to count and somatically engage in the act of devotions—reciting the Hail Mary (rosary) or the Lord's Prayer (paternoster). Beads are strung in groups of ten (decades) and usually in multiples of five or seven. Sometimes a "gaud" or larger bead separates each group of ten. Women generally wore longer strands than men, sometimes as long as 150 beads. Strands may have other objects (drops) attached to the end: medals, figurines, mirrors, tassels, etc. Religions other than Christianity also use prayer beads in a similar fashion.

Prayer wheel: hollow cylinder made of wood, metal, leather, or coarse cotton mounted vertically on a spindle; "Om Mani Padme Hum" often embossed on wheel (Buddhist).

Prie-dieu: a prayer desk for individual devotion consisting of a kneeling platform and an upright with sloping shelf for elbows/hands or books.

Prophesy: a prediction for a significant future event as foretold by divine intercession.

Prophet: person who foretells the future; teacher or chosen one to interpret God's will and intent.

Pyre: a funerary scaffold on which the corpse is placed for cremation.

Pyx: vessel to hold the Eucharist bread.

Relics: objects revered or venerated for their association with saints or martyrs; also the bones of saints or martyrs.

Reliquary: the container for holy relics (chests, boxes, lockets, etc.).

Religion: a structured, culturally shared belief system usually accounting for the creation of the universe and all its elements and including divine beings or forces.

Reredose: the backing to an altar; may be alabaster, painted wood panels, or stone.

Retrospective sanctity: belief by cultural groups that their ancient ancestors held and enacted spiritual/sacred beliefs that they can continue to recognize and interface with.

Rhyta/rhyton: horn-shaped drinking vessel often with animal head or body made of metal, stone, or ceramic.

Rites of passage (initiation): rituals or ceremonies in which an individual (neophyte) undergoes initiation into a new phase of his/her life; usually the neophyte is physically marked in some way that indicates this passage to a new status: tattooing, scarification, tooth filing, etc.

Ritual: a prescribed set of actions carrying and expressing important shared cultural meanings.

Ritual killing: perforating, bending, breaking, or otherwise rendering an object unusable before it is utilized in a religious, magical, or ritualistic context; the "killing" transitions the object into the spirit realm.

Ritual space: an area either specifically designated or marked as dedicated to particular ritual practices.

Rood: a large crucifix on a beam or screen at the entrance of the chancel of a medieval church.

Rood screen: a screen upon which the rood is affixed and that divides the nave from the chancel.

Sacrament: a sacred object or ritual that serves as a visible confirmation of an individual's divine connection or devotion.

Sacred landscape: a topographic and geographic area with natural (e.g., mountains, caves, water bodies, etc.) features and possibly human-made features believed to be imbued with supernatural powers, are the dwelling places of spiritual beings, or indicate places of mythic occurrences.

Sacrifice: objects (including humans and animals) given to deities or other supernatural forces to appease or propitiate; usually were objects highly valued by the culture.

Saint Andrew's Cross (also saltire): an X-shaped cross.

Sarcophagus: stone chest (often an outer vessel for a coffin) used to hold a corpse.

Scrying: gazing into a reflective substance or surface as a form of divination; water, polished metal or stone, or mirrors were most commonly used.

Seal of Solomon: two interlocking or overlain triangles (one pointed up, the other down) that together create a hexagram.

Seer stones: stones (various types) used in divination.

Sequential magic: the belief that when one event follows another, the first must have caused the second (e.g., breaking a mirror causes misfortune).

Sepulcher: tomb cut into rock or constructed of stone or brick.

Shaman: an individual who mediates between the spiritual and human worlds often to discover the cause of illness and misfortune and bring about a resolution.

Shofar: Jewish ritual instrument usually made from a ram's horn.

Shrine: a place or structure dedicated to a sacred object or personage.

Sigil: a symbol, word, or device used in astrology and magic to denote a particular supernatural being.

Signatures: the idea that the attributes of plants (shapes, colors, etc.) are indicative of their function.

Sink or sinkhole: a cavity in the earth into which a stream or other water course disappears.

Sistrum: a ceremonial rattle often used in consort with a drum (Egyptian, Roman, Aztec).

Smudge: a plant burned (e.g., sweetgrass, sage, etc.) to ritually, spiritually purify a space, person, or object.

Songlines: the routes across the landscape marking the path of creator beings (Australia).

Sorcery: using spells and incantations to call upon supernatural powers, usually for malevolent purposes, and/or personal power and gain.

Speculum: any object (but usually something shiny, reflective) used to focus attention in scrying.

Spell: word or words believed to have magical power.

Spiritual midden: an assemblage of objects, usually concealed and often worn or broken, and used as a magically protective device.

Stela: an upright stone (slab or column) carved with funerary, religious, or spiritual reliefs and often used as a grave marker.

Stupa: a Buddhist shrine, either cylindrical or hemispherical in shape; may be a mound, a tower, or a bell-shaped structure; they range in size from small votive statues to large temple-size buildings.

Supernaturalism: belief in forces and beings beyond the laws of the natural world.

Superstition: an obsolete term with derogative connotations referring to cultural beliefs in magic thinking or worldviews.

Swallet: a sink-hole cave; often used to deposit sacrificial victims and offerings.

Sympathetic magic: the belief that objects or entities that share similarities, contact, or connection are integrally related and can be used to influence each other.

Syncretism: the blending of beliefs and practices from two or more belief systems.

Taboo: behaviors forbidden under the proscriptions of a given society.

Talisman: an object believed to possess and generate magical power; sometimes used synonymously with amulet or charm.

Tallit: Jewish ritual garb: tallit katan is a prayer apron; tallit gadal is a prayer shawl.

Tefillin: black boxes and straps containing holy text worn by Jewish men on the head and left arm.

Temenos: sacred enclosure around a temple or other holy area.

Temple: a building dedicated to the worship or reverence of a deity or sacred objects or believed to be the dwelling or manifestation site of a deity.

Thaumaturgy: the working of miracles or magic by calling upon and directing supernatural powers.

Theocracy: the composite intermingling of individual deities or the attributes of such into one being; also the mystical union of a person with God.

Theophagy: the incorporation of or unification with the divine through "eating" the god or some element representative of the flesh and blood of the god (e.g., the Eucharist).

Theophany: the appearance or manifestation of a deity in the presence of humans.

Therianthrope: a composite figure with both human and animal characteristics.

Theriomorphic: having an animal form.

Therurgy: divine or white magic; working miracles or magic through divine intervention.

Tholos: round tomb with rectilinear entrance way.

Thurible: a censor suspended from chains; may be small and handheld or large and suspended from ceilings or rafters.

Ticket: a protective charm, often written (Germanic-American).

Tinkle/jingle cone: a small rectangle or triangle of metal (copper or tin) folded into a cone shape and attached to clothing, horse gear, or personal adornments.

Tjurunga (also Churinga): an oblong polished stone or wood object often marked with sacred symbols and used in various ceremonies as bullroarers or incorporated into ground paintings, poles, headgear, and earth mounds (Australian).

Toponym: place name.

Toran (also Bandanwal): a cotton cloth door valance or hanging usually decorated with marigolds and mango leaves, sometimes including mirrors or sequins to attract wealth and good fortune (Hindu).

Totem: an emblematic animal or plant representing an individual, family, or clan and perceived to share a spiritual connection.

TCP (Traditional cultural property): designated land area sacred to a cultural group or utilized by that group for cultural practices essential to its traditional lifeways. Term usually applied to Native Americans, but it is a concept applicable to any traditional cultural group.

Trick: a spell or amulet (African American).

Tumulus: a human-made mound, usually over a grave.

Tzedahkah: Jewish temple collection box.

Unction: consecrating or healing through the rite of anointment.

Unguent: ointments or salves; in ritual, religion, and magic these are usually psychotropic to produce altered states of consciousness.

Uroboros: serpent (sometimes with a cock's head) coiled in a circle biting its own tail. Sometimes it is depicted as two serpents biting each other's tails. It is a symbol of infinity, the cyclical path of the spirit to the mundane to the spirit again. In alchemy it is the symbol for mutable matter.

Vegetation rites: imitative rituals to influence plant growth.

Vestibular: bodily motion and vibration (rocking, swaying, swinging, bouncing, twirling, etc.).

Viewshed aspect: looking at a ritual feature from an outside point.

Viewshed prospect: looking out from a ritual feature.

Vision quest: a personal ritual involving isolation, fasting, sleep deprivation, exposure to the elements; possible physical mutilation and consumption of psychotropic substances in order to receive a divine vision, message, or blessing.

Vivifact: living elements (e.g., trees and other plants) that are either humanly modified or culturally indicative.

Votive: an offering given as a token of gratitude, devotion, or as a pledge or fulfillment of a vow.

Weapon salve: a salve rubbed on a weapon (knife, sword, etc.) to magically heal the wounds of the victim.

Wheel of Fortune: a twelve-spoke wheel that represents the rising and falling cycles of life and fortune.

Witch: a woman or man possessing the skills, knowledge, and power to control and use magical forces to manipulate, influence, harm, or heal animals, people, or events; usually perceived as a dangerous or malevolent individual.

Witch ball: a hand-blown glass orb with possible inclusions of glass strands, hung in windows or from house eves or tree branches to ward off witches.

Witch bottle: a bottle (phial, case bottle, or stoneware jug [e.g., a Bellarmine/Bartmann jug]) usually containing some combination of urine, bent pins/needles/nails, thorns, and cloth heart, either buried or thrown into a hearth to identify and/or reverse bewitchment from victim onto the suspected witch.

Witchcraft: the use of supernatural power (magic or sorcery), usually for harmful purposes.

World axis (also *Axis mundi*; see also *Omphalos*): the communicating conduit linking the layers of the cosmos (e.g., heaven, earth, and hell). It is often represented by tall, pointed, natural or human-made structures like mountains, trees, columns, spires, poles, staffs, lances, etc.

Ziggurat: step-pyramid temple of Mesopotamia.

Zoanthropy: the belief that humans can transmogrify into animals.

Zodiacal man: the astrological idea that the signs of the zodiac rule particular parts of the human body.

Further Reading

To provide researchers with the quickest and most comprehensive access to references in the area or areas of ritual, religion, or magic they are studying, the following bibliography of sources is divided into specific categories. Some entries are duplicated and placed under all applicable categories, thereby ensuring that no relevant source is missed by researchers. As an example, a reference for an article concerning metal, sound, color, and Mesoamerican peoples will appear under all the following headings:

> Ethnic Studies: Latin American/Mesoamerican
> Artifact Material Types: Metal and Colors
> Sensory and Landscape Studies: Auditory

Categories

Attribute Analysis

Ethnic Studies
  African/African American/African Caribbean
  Arctic/Pacific Northwest Native
  Asian
  Australian/Pacific Islander
  European/Euro-American/Euro-Canadian
  Mediterranean/Classical
  Latin American/Mesoamerican
  Middle Eastern/Indian
  Native American
  Scandinavian

Artifact Material Types and Attributes
  Ceramics
  Colors
  Fauna
  Flora
  Glass
  Metal
  Minerals/Lithics/Soils
  Numbers
  Symbols, Designs, and Images
  Textiles and Clothing

Sensory and Landscape Studies
  General
  Landscape/Seascape
  Affective
  Auditory
  Gustatory (Taste)
  Olfactory
  Tactility/Haptic
  Vestibular
  Visual

Mortuary Studies

Ritual, Religion, and Magic Theory

General Sources

ATTRIBUTE ANALYSIS

Anawalt, Patricia R. 2014. *Shamanic Regalia in the Far North.* London: Thames and Hudson.

Anderson, William. 2004. "An Archaeology of Late Antique Pilgrim Flasks." *Anatolian Studies* 54: 79–93.

Brain, Jeffrey P., and Philip Phillips. 1996. *Shell Gorgets: Styles of Late Prehistoric and Protohistoric Southeast:* Cambridge, MA: Peabody Museum Press.

Cawte, E. Christopher. 1978. *Ritual Animal Disguise: A Historical and Geographical Study of Animal Disguise in the British Isles.* Ipswich: Brewer.

Chapman, John, and Bisserka Gaydarska. 2007. *Parts and Wholes: Fragmentation in Prehistoric Context.* London: Oxbow Books.

Davidson, James M. 2014. "Deconstructing the Myth of the 'Hand Charm': Mundane Clothing Fasteners and Their Curious Transformations into Supernatural Objects." *Historical Archaeology* 48(2): 18–60.

Dubin, Lois Sherr. 2004. *The History of Beads from 30,000 B.C. to the Present.* New York: Harry N. Abrams.

Gilman, Patricia A., and Tammy Stone. 2013. "The Role of Ritual Variability in Social Negotiations of Early Communities: Great Kiva Homogeneity and Heterogeneity in the Mogollon Region of the North American Southwest." *American Antiquity* 78(4): 607–23.

Gilmour, G. H. 1997. "The Nature and Function of Astragalus Bones from Archaeological Contexts in the Levant and Eastern Mediterranean." *Oxford Journal of Archaeology* 16(2): 167–75.

Grinsell, L. V. 1961. "The Breaking of Objects as a Funerary Rite." *Folkore* 72(3): 475–91.

Halperin, Christina T., Katherine A. Faust, Rhonda Taube, and Aurore Giguet, eds. 2009. *Mesoamerican Figurines: Small-Scale Indices of Large-Scale Social Phenomena.* Gainesville: University of Florida Press.

Lipponcott, Kerry. 2015. "A Continent-Wide View of Marine Shell Mask Gorgets." *Archaeology in Montana* 56(1): 31–50.

Mack, John, ed. 1994. *Masks and the Art of Expression.* New York: Harry N. Abrams.

Newall, Venetia. 1971. *An Egg at Easter: A Folklore Study*. Bloomington: Indiana University Press.

Schroedl, Alan. 1977. "The Grand Canyon Figurine Complex." *American Antiquity* 42(2): 254–65.

Smith, Marvin T., and Julie Barnes Smith. 1989. "Engraved Shell Masks in North America." *Southeastern Archaeology* 8(1): 9–18.

Wallis, Neill J. 2013. "The Materiality of Signs: Enchainment and Animacy in Woodland Southeastern North American Pottery." *American Antiquity* 78(2): 207–26.

Wehmeyer, Stephen C. 2017. "From the Back of the Mirror: 'Quicksilver,' Tinfoil, and the Shimmer of Sorcery in African-American Vernacular Magic." *Magic, Ritual, and Witchcraft* 12(2): 163–85.

Weightman, Barbara A. 1996. "Sacred Landscapes and the Phenomenon of Light." *Geographical Review* 86(1): 59–71.

Whalen, Michael E. 2013. "Wealth, Status, Ritual, and Marine Shell at Casas Grandes, Chihuahua, Mexico." *American Antiquity* 78(4): 624–39.

ETHNIC STUDIES

African/African American/African Caribbean

Bacon, A. M. 1896. "Conjuring and Conjure-Doctors in the Southern United States." *The Journal of American Folklore* 9(33): 143–47.

Bankoff, H. Arthur, Christopher Ricciardi, and Alyssa Loorya. 2001. "Remembering Africa Under the Eaves." *Archaeology* 54(3): 36–40.

Brown, Kenneth. 2001. "Interwoven Traditions: Archaeology of the Conjurer's Cabins and the African American Cemetery." In *Places of Cultural Memory: African Reflections on the American Landscape*. Conference Proceedings, 9–12 May, Atlanta, 99–104. Washington DC: Department of the Interior, National Park Service.

———. 2008. "Africans in American Material Culture: Does a Pot Hanger Only Function When It Is Used for Cooking?" *Bulletin of the Texas Archaeological Society* 79: 3–18.

Cochran, Matthew David. 1999. "Hoodoo's Fire: Interpreting Nineteenth Century African-American Material Culture at the Brice House, Annapolis, Maryland." *Archaeology* 35(1): 25–33.

Davidson, James M. 2004. "Rituals Captured in Context and Time: Charm Use in North Dallas Freedman's Town (1869–1907), Dallas, Texas." *Historical Archaeology* 38(2): 22–54.

———. 2014. "Deconstructing the Myth of the 'Hand Charm': Mundane Clothing Fasteners and Their Curious Transformations into Supernatural Objects." *Historical Archaeology* 48(2): 18–60.

Davis, Rod. 1998. *American Voudou: Journey into a Hidden World*. Denton: University of North Texas Press.

Douny, Laurence. 2017. "Connecting Worlds through Silk: The Cosmological Significance of Sheen in West African Talismanic Magic." *Magic, Ritual, and Witchcraft* 12(2): 186–209.

Ferguson, Leland. 1992. *Uncommon Ground: Archaeology and Early African America: 1650–1800*. Washington, DC: Smithsonian Institution Press.

———. 1999. "'The Cross as a Magic Sign': Marks on Eighteenth-Century Bowls from South Carolina." In *"I, Too, Am American": Archaeological Studies of African American Life*, ed. T. A. Singleton, 116–31. Charlottesville: University of Virginia Press.

Fernández Olmos, Margarite, and Lizabeth Paravisini-Gebert. 2011. *Creole Religions of the Caribbean: An Introduction from Vodou and Santeria to Obeah and Espiritismo.* New York: New York University Press.

Galke, L. J. 1996. "Did the Gods of Africa Die? A Re-examination of a Carroll House Crystal Assemblage." *North American Archaeologist* 21(1): 19–33.

Gremillion, Kristen J. 2002. "Archaeology at Old Mobile." *Historical Archaeology* 36(1): 117–28.

Horton, Robert. 1994. *Patterns of Thought in Africa and the West: Essays on Magic, Religion and Science.* Cambridge: Cambridge University Press.

Johnson, A. 1996. "'Pray's House Spirit': The Institutional Structure and Spiritual Core of an African American Folk Tradition." In *"Ain't Gonna Lay My 'Ligion Down": African American Religion in the South*, ed. A. Johnson and P. Jersild, 8–38. Columbia: University of South Carolina Press.

Joseph, J. W., Charles R. Ewan, Christopher C. Fennell, Lelang G. Ferguson, Carl Steen, Grey Gundaker, Andrew Agha, and Nicole M. Isenbarger. 2011. "Forum: Crosses to Bear: Cross Marks as African Symbols in Southern Pottery." *Historical Archaeology* 45(2): 132–88.

Klingelhofer, Eric. 1987. "Aspects of Early Afro-American Material Culture: Artifacts from the Slave Quarters at Garrison Plantation, Maryland." *Historical Archaeology* 21(2): 112–19.

Leone, Mark P., and Gladys-Marie Fry. 1999. "Conjuring in the Big House: An Interpretation of African American Belief Systems Based on the Uses of Archaeology and Folklore Sources." *Journal of American Folklore* 112(445): 272–403.

Leone, Mark P., Gladys-Marie Fry, and Timothy Ruppel. 2001. "Spirit Management among Americans of African Descent." In *Race and the Archaeology of Identity*, ed. Charles E. Orser, 143–57. Salt Lake City: University of Utah Press.

Lewis-Williams, J. David, and Thomas A. Dowson. 1990. "Through the Veil: San Rock Paintings and the Rock Face." *South African Archaeological Bulletin* 45: 5–16.

Lucas, Michael T. 2014. "Empowered Objects: Material Expressions of Spiritual Beliefs in the Colonial Chesapeake Region." *Historical Archaeology* 48(3): 106–24.

Mercier, Jacques. 1979. *Ethiopian Magic Scrolls.* New York: George Braziller.

Ogundiran, Akinwumi, and Paula Saunders, eds. 2014. *Materialities of Ritual in the Black Atlantic.* Bloomington: Indiana University Press.

Phaup, N. A. 2001. "Cultural Modification of Buttons at the Levi Jordan Plantation, Brazoria County, Texas." Master's thesis, University of Houston.

Raboteau, A. J. 1978. *Slave Religion: The "Invisible Institution" in the Antebellum South.* Oxford: Oxford University Press.

Ruppel, T., J. Neuwirth, Mark P. Leone, and Gladys-Marie Fry. 2003. "Hidden in View: African Spiritual Spaces in North American Landscapes." *Antiquity* 77: 321–35.

Russell, A. E. 1997. "Material Culture and African American Spirituality at the Hermitage." *Historical Archaeology* 31(2): 63–80.

Samford, Patricia. 1996. "The Archaeology of African-American Slavery and Material Culture." *The William and Mary Quarterly* 53(1): 87–114.

Spence, K. 1999. "Red, White and Black: Colour in Building Stone in Ancient Egypt." *Cambridge Archaeological Journal* 9: 114–17.

Springate, Megan E. 2014. "Double Consciousness and the Intersections of Beliefs in an African American Home in Northern New Jersey." *Historical Archaeology* 48(3): 125–43.

Steiner, Roland. 1901. "Observations on the Practice of Conjuring in Georgia." *The Journal of American Folklore* 14(54): 173–80.

Stine, Linda France, Melanie A. Cabak, and Mark D. Groover. 1996. "Blue Beads as African-American Culture Symbols." *Historical Archaeology* 30(3): 49–75.

Thompson, R. F. 1983. *Flash of the Spirit: African and Afro-American Art and Philosophy*. New York: Random House.

———. 1993. *Face of the Gods: Art and Altars of Africa and the African Americas*. The Museum of African Art, New York. Munich: Prestal Publishing.

Wahlman, M. S. 2001. *Signs and Symbols: African Images in African American Quilts*. Rev. ed. Atlanta: Tinwood Books.

Walton, James. 1980. "Art and Magic in the Southern Bantu Vernacular Architecture." In *Shelter, Sign & Symbol*, ed. Paul Oliver, 115–34. Woodstock: The Overlook Press.

Wehmeyer, Stephen C. 2017. "From the Back of the Mirror: 'Quicksilver,' Tinfoil, and the Shimmer of Sorcery in African-American Vernacular Magic." *Magic, Ritual, and Witchcraft* 12(2): 163–85.

Whitten, Jr., Norman E. 1962. "Contemporary Patterns of Malign Occultism among Negroes in North Carolina." *The Journal of American Folklore* 75(298): 311–25.

Wilkie, Laurie A. 1997. "Secret and Sacred: Contextualizing the Artifacts of African-American Magic and Religion." *Historical Archaeology* 31(4): 81–106.

———. 2003. *The Archaeology of Mothering: An African-American Midwife's Tale*. New York: Routledge.

Willis, W. B. 1998. *The Adrinka Dictionary: A Visual Primer on the Language of Adrinka*. Washington, DC: Pyramid Complex.

Young, A. L. 1997. "Risk Management Strategies among African American Slaves at Locust Grove Plantation." *International Journal of Historical Archaeology* 1(1): 5–37.

Arctic/Pacific Northwest Native

Anawalt, Patricia R. 2014. *Shamanic Regalia in the Far North*. London: Thames and Hudson.

Barbeau, Marius. 1950. *Totem Poles I: According to Crests and Topics*. Ottawa: National Museum of Canada.

———. 1950. *Totem Poles II: According to Location*. Ottawa: National Museum of Canada.

Jonaitis, A. 1999. *The Yuquot Whalers' Shrine*. Seattle: University of Washington Press.

Lee, Molly, ed. 1999. *Not Just a Pretty Face: Dolls and Human Figurines in Alaska Native Cultures*. Fairbanks: University of Alaska Museum.

Sabo, G., and Sabo, D. 1985. "Belief Systems and the Ecology of Sea Mammal Hunting among the Baffinland Eskimo." *Arctic Anthropology* 22(2): 77–86.

Stewart, Andrew M., Darren Keith, and Joan Scottie. 2004. "Caribou Crossings and Cultural Meanings: Placing Traditional Knowledge and Archaeology in Context in an Inuit Landscape." *Journal of Archaeological Method and Theory* 11(2): 183–211.

Whitridge, P. 2004. "Landscapes, Houses, Bodies, Things: 'Place' and the Archaeology of Inuit Imaginaries." *Journal of Archaeological Method and Theory* 11(2): 213–50.

Asian

Bohak, G. 1995. "Traditions of Magic in Late Antiquity: Protective Magic Babylonian Demon Bowls." Retrieved May 2009 from http:www.lib.umich.edu/pap/magic/def2.html.

Critchlow, Keith. 1980. "Nikke: The Siting of a Japanese Rural House." In *Shelter, Sign & Symbol*, ed. Paul Oliver, 219–26. Woodstock: The Overlook Press.

Fogelin, Lars. 2006. *Archaeology of Early Buddhism*. Walnut Creek: AltaMira Press.

Fowler, C. T. 2002. "Altar Rituals in Thirdspace." In *Ethnobiology and Biocultural Diversity: Proceedings of the Seventh International Congress of Ethnobiology*, ed. John R. Stepp, Felice S. Wyndham, and Rebecca K. Zarger, 152–70. Athens, GA: International Society of Ethnobiology.

Hakansson, Tore. 1980. "House Decoration Among South Asian Peoples." In *Shelter, Sign & Symbol*, ed. Paul Oliver, 84–94. Woodstock: The Overlook Press.

Levene, Dan. 2002. *A Corpus of Magic Bowls*. London: Routledge.

Mack, Alexandra. 2004. "One Landscape, Many Experiences: Differing Perspectives of the Temple Districts of Vijayanagara." *Journal of Archaeological Method and Theory* 11(1): 59–81.

Naquin, S., and Chün-fang Yü, eds. 1992. *Pilgrims and Sacred Sites in China*. Berkeley: University of California Press.

Peterson, John A. 2005. "Liminal Objects, Sacred Places: Epistemological and Archaeological Investigations at the Aleonar Site in Cebu, Philippines." *Philippine Quarterly of Culture and Society* 33(3–4): 218–40.

Ray, Himansha Prabha. 1994. "Kanheri: The Archaeology of an Early Buddhist Pilgrimage Centre in Western India." *World Archaeology* 26(1): 35–46.

Vu, Hông Thuâ. 2008. "Amulets and the Marketplace." *Asian Ethnology: Popular Religion and the Sacred Life of Material Goods* 67(2): 237–55.

Australian/Pacific Islander

Burke, Heather, Susan Arthure, and Cherrie de Leiuen. 2016. "A Context for Concealment: The Historical Archaeology of Folk Ritual and Superstition in Australia." *International Journal of Historical Archaeology* 20: 45–72.

David, Bruno, Max Pivoru, William Pivoru, Michael Green, Bryce Barker, James F. Weiner, Douglas Simala, Thomas Kokents, Lisa Araho, and John Dop. 2008. "Living Landscapes of the Dead: Archaeology of the Afterworld among the Rumu of Papua New Guinea." In *Handbook of Landscape Archaeology*, ed. Bruno David and Julian Thomas, 158–66. Walnut Creek: Left Coast Press.

David, Bruno, and Mura Badulgal Committee. 2006. "What Happened in Torres Strait 400 Years Ago? Ritual Transformations in an Island Seascape." *Journal of Island and Coastal Archaeology* 1: 123–43.

Evans, Ian. 2011. "Touching Magic: Deliberately Concealed Objects in Old Australian Houses and Buildings." PhD diss., University of Newcastle.

———. 2015. "These Walls Can Talk: Australian History Preserved by Folk Magic." *The Conversation: Academic Rigor, Journalistic Flair*. Retrieved September 2015 from http://theconversation.com/these-walls-can-talk-australian-history-preserved-by-folk-magic-47636.

———. 2018. "Tasmanian Magic Research Project: Report of the Second Field Season, January 6–27, 2018." Retrieved June 2021 from http://academia.edu/36996265/Tasmanian_Magic_Research_Project_Second_Field_Season.

Evans, Ian, M. Chris Manning, and Owen Davies. 2015. "The Wider Picture: Parallel Evidence in America and Australia." In *Physical Evidence for Ritual Acts, Sorcery and Witchcraft in Christian Britain: A Feeling for Magic*, ed. Ronald Hutton, 232–54. New York: Palgrave Macmillan.

Gourlay, K. A. 1975. *Sound Producing Instruments in Traditional Society: A Study of Esoteric Instruments and Their Role in Male-Female Relations*. Canberra: Australian National University Press.

Keen, Ian. 2006. "Ancestors, Magic, and Exchange in Yolngu Doctrines: Extensions of the Person in Time and Place." *Journal of the Royal Anthropological Institute (N.S.)* 12: 515–30.

McNiven, Ian J. 2003. "Saltwater People: Spiritscapes, Maritime Rituals and the Archaeology of Australian Indigenous Seascapes." *World Archaeology* 35: 329–49.

———. 2008. "Sentient Sea: Seascapes as Spiritscapes." In *Handbook of Landscape Archaeology*, ed. Bruno David and Julian Thomas, 149–57. Walnut Creek: Left Coast Press.

———. 2010. "Navigating the Human-Animal Divide: Marine Mammal Hunters and Rituals of Sensory Allurement." *World Archaeology* 42(2): 215–30.

———. 2013. "Between the Living and the Dead: Relational Ontologies and the Ritual Dimensions of Dugong Hunting across Torres Strait." In *Relational Archaeologies: Humans, Animals, Things*, ed. Christopher Watts, 97–116. London: Routledge.

McNiven, Ian J., and R. Feldman. 2003. "Ritual Orchestration of Seascapes: Hunting Magic and Dugong Bone Mounds in Torres Strait, NE Australia." *Cambridge Archaeological Journal* 13(2): 169–94.

Morwood, M. J. 2002. *Visions from the Past: The Archaeology of Australian Aboriginal Art*. Washington, DC: Smithsonian Institution Scholarly Press.

Munn, Nancy D. 2003. "Excluded Spaces: The Figure in the Australian Aboriginal Landscape." In *The Anthropology of Space and Place: Locating Culture*, ed. Setha M. Low and Denise Lawrence-Zúñiga, 92–109. Malden: Blackwell Publishing.

Taçon, Paul S. C. 1991. "The Power of Stone: Symbolic Aspects of Stone Use and Development in Western Arnhem Land, Australia." *Antiquity* 65: 192–207.

———. 1999. "Identifying Ancient Sacred Landscapes in Australia: From Physical to Social." In *Archaeologies of Landscape: Contemporary Perspectives*, ed. Wendy Ashmore and A. B. Knapp, 33–57. Oxford: Blackwell.

———. 2004. "Ochre, Clay, Stone and Art: The Symbolic Importance of Minerals as Life Force among Aboriginal Peoples of Nnorthern and Central Australia." In *Soils, Stones and Symbols: Cultural Perceptions of the Mineral World*, ed. N. Boivin and M. A. Owoc, 31–42. London: UCL Press.

European/Euro-American/Euro-Canadian

Aldhouse-Green, Miranda. 2002. *Dying for the Gods: Human Sacrifice in Iron Age and Roman Europe*. London: Tempus Publishing.

———. 2004. *An Archaeology of Images: Iconology and Cosmology in Iron Age and Roman Europe*. London: Routledge.

———. 2005. *The Quest for the Shaman: Shapeshifters, Sorcerers, and Spirit-Healers of Ancient Europe*. London: Thames and Hudson.

Alexandrowicz, J. Stephen. 1986. "The Market Street Witch Bottle, Pittsburgh, Pennsylvania." *Proceedings of the Symposium on Ohio Valley Urban and Historic Archaeology IV*: 117–32.

Augé, C. Riley. 2013. "Silent Sentinels: Archaeology, Magic, and the Gendered Control of Domestic Boundaries in New England, 1620–1725." PhD diss., University of Montana.

———. 2014. "Embedded Implication of Cultural Worldviews in the Use and Pattern of Magical Material Culture." *Historical Archaeology* 48(3): 166–78.

———. 2020. *The Archaeology of Magic: Gender and Domestic Protection in Seventeenth-Century New England*. Gainesville: University Press of Florida.

Becker, Marshall Joseph. 1978. "An Eighteenth-Century Witch Bottle in Delaware County, Pennsylvania." *Pennsylvania Archaeologist* 48(1–2): 1–11.

———. 1980. "An American Witch Bottle: 'White Magic' among Pennsylvania Colonists." *Archaeology* 33: 18–23.

———. 2005. "An Update on Colonial Witch Bottles." *Pennsylvania Archaeologist* 75(2): 12–23.

Billingsley, John. 1992. "Archaic Head Carving in West Yorkshire and Beyond." Master's thesis, University of Sheffield.

———. 2015. "Instances and Contexts of the Head Motif in Britain." In *Physical Evidence for Ritual Acts, Sorcery and Witchcraft in Christian Britain: A Feeling for Magic*, ed. Ronald Hutton, 68–90. New York: Palgrave Macmillan.

Bishop, Louise M. 2007. *Words, Stones, & Herbs: The Healing Word in Medieval and Early Modern England*. New York: Syracuse University Press.

Bradley, Richard. 1990. *The Passage of Arms: An Archaeological Analysis of Prehistoric Hoards and Votive Deposits*. Cambridge: Cambridge University Press.

Bradley, Richard, and K. Gordon. 1988. "Human Skulls from the River Thames, Their Dating and Significance." *Antiquity* 62: 503–9.

Brennan, Martin. 1994. *The Stones of Time: Calendars, Sundials, and Stone Chambers of Ancient Ireland*. Rochester, VT: Inner Traditions International.

Briggs, Katharine. 1957. "The English Fairies." *Folklore* 68(1): 270–87.

———. (1967) 2003. *The Fairies in Tradition and Literature*. 2nd ed. London: Routledge.

———. 1976. *An Encyclopedia of Fairies: Hobgoblins, Brownies, Bogies, and Other Supernatural Creatures*. New York: Pantheon Books.

———. 1978. *The Vanishing People: Fairy Lore and Legends*. New York: Pantheon Books.

Butler, Jon. 1979. "Magic, Astrology, and the Early American Religious Heritage." *The American Historical Review* 84(2): 317–46.

Caple, Chris. 2012. "The Apotropaic Symbolled Threshold to Nevern Castle: Castell Nanhyfer." *Archaeological Journal* 169: 422–52.

Carver, Martin, Sarah Semple, and Alex Sanmark, eds. 2010. *Signals of Belief in Early England: Anglo-Saxon Paganism Revisited*. Oxford: Oxbow Books.

Cawte, E. Christopher. 1978. *Ritual Animal Disguise: A Historical and Geographical Study of Animal Disguise in the British Isles*. Ipswich: Brewer.

Champion, Matthew. 2014. "Ill Wishing on the Walls: The Medieval Graffiti Curses of Norwich Cathedral." *Norfolk Archaeology* XLVI: 61–66.

Cheape, Hugh. 2008. "Charms against Witchcraft: Magic and Mischief in Museum Collections." In *Witchcraft and Belief in Early Modern Scotland*, ed. Julian Goodare, Lauren Martin, and Joyce Miller, 227–48. New York: Palgrave Macmillan.

Choyke, Alice. 2010. "The Bone Is the Beast: Animal Amulets and Ornaments in Power and Magic." In *Anthropological Approaches to Zooarchaeology: Complexity, Colonialism, and Animal Transformations*, ed. Douglas Campana, Pam Crabtree, Susan deFrance, Justin Lev-Tov, and Alice Choyke, 197–209. Oxford: Oxbow Books.

Corbin, Alain. 1998. *Village Bells: Sound and Meaning in the Nineteenth-Century French Countryside*. New York: Columbia University Press.

Costello, Jessica. 2014. "Tracing the Footsteps of Ritual: Concealed Footwear in America." *Historical Archaeology* 48(3): 35–51.

Crawford-Mowday, Imogen. 2008. "Caul: A Sailor's Charm." In *England: The Other Within: Analysing the English Collections at the Pitt Rivers Museum*. Retrieved March 2012 from http://england.prm.ox.ac.uk/englishness-sailors-charm.html.

Davies, Owen. 1999. *Witchcraft, Magic, and Culture, 1736–1951*. Manchester, UK: Manchester University Press.

———. 2007. *Popular Magic: Cunning Folk in English History*. London: Hambledon.

———. 2013. *America Bewitched: The Story of Witchcraft After Salem*. Oxford: Oxford University Press.

———. 2018. *A Supernatural War: Magic, Divination, and Faith during the First World War*. Oxford: Oxford University Press.

Davies, Owen, and Ceri Houlbrook, eds. 2021. *Building Magic: Ritual and Re-enchantment in Post-Medieval Structures*. Cham, Switzerland: Palgrave Macmillan.

De Cunzo, Lu Ann. 1995. "Reform, Respite, Ritual: An Archaeology of Institutions: Ihe Magdalen Society of Philadelphia, 1800–1850." *Historical Archaeology* 29(3): 1–168.

Dickinson, Tania M. 2005. "Symbols of Protection: The Significance of Animal-Ornamental Shields in Early Anglo-Saxon England." *Medieval Archaeology* 49: 109–63.

Dowd, Marion. 2015. *The Archaeology of Caves in Ireland*. Oxford: Oxbow Books.

Dronfield, Jeremy. 1995. "Subjective Vision and the Source of Irish Megalithic Art." *Antiquity* 69: 539–49.

Duffy, Eamon. 1992. *The Stripping of the Altars: Traditional Religion in England 1400–1580*. New Haven: Yale University Press.

Easton, Timothy. 2012. "Burning Issues." *SPAB* Winter 2012: 44–47.

———. 2013. "Plumbing a Spiritual World." *SPAB* Winter 2013: 41–45.

———. 2014. "Four Spiritual Middens in Mid Suffolk, England, ca. 1650 to 1850." *Historical Archaeology* 48(3): 10–34.

Easton, Timothy, and Jeremy Hodgkinson. 2013. "Apotropaic Symbols on Cast-Iron Firebacks." *Journal of the Antique Metalware Society* 21: 15–33.

Edwards, Eric. 2008. "A Fisherman's 'Lucky stone' from Newbiggin-by-the-Sea, Northumberland." In *England: The Other Within: Analysing the English Collections at the Pitt Rivers Museum*. Retrieved March 2012 from http://england.prm.ox.ac.uk/englishness-Lucky-Newbiggin-stone.html.

Edwards, Kathryn, ed. 2016. *Everyday Magic in Early Modern Europe*. New York: Routledge.

Evans, George Ewart. 1971. *The Pattern under the Plough: Aspects of the Folk-Life of East Anglia*. London: Faber and Faber.

Evans, Ian, M. Chris Manning, and Owen Davies. 2015. "The Wider Picture: Parallel Evidence in America and Australia." In *Physical Evidence for Ritual Acts, Sorcery and Witchcraft in Christian Britain: A Feeling for Magic*, ed. Ronald Hutton, 232–34. New York: Palgrave Macmillan.

Evans-Wentz, W. Y. (1911) 1994. *The Fairy Faith in Celtic Countries: The Classic Study of Leprechauns, Pixies and Other Fairy Spirits*. New York: Citadel Press.

Fitzpatrick, Martin. 2010. "Pilgrimage to Santiago de Compostela." *Archaeology Ireland* 24(4): 14–17.

Gardner, Gerald Brosseau. 1942. "British Charms, Amulets, and Talismans." *Folklore* 53(2): 95–103.

Gilchrist, Roberta. 1994. *Gender and Material Culture: The Archaeology of Religious Women*. London: Routledge.

———. 2012. *Medieval Life: Archaeology and the Life Course*. Woodbridge: Boydell Press.

Gruia, Ana Maria. 2007. "Magic in the House: Functions of Images on Medieval Stove Tiles from Transylvania, Moldavia and Walachia." *Studia Patzinaka* 5: 7–46.

Hamerow, Helena. 2006. "'Special Deposits' in Anglo-Saxon Settlements." *Medieval Archaeology* 50: 1–30.

Hand, Wayland D. 1980. *Magical Medicine: The Folkloric Component of Medicine in the Folk Belief, Custom, and Ritual of the Peoples of Europe and America*. Berkeley: University of California Press.

———. 1981. "European Fairy Lore in the New World." *Folklore* 92(2): 141–48.

Hill, J. D. 1996. "The Identification of Ritual Deposits of Animals: A General Perspective from a Specific Study of 'Special Animal Deposits' from the Southern English Iron Age." In *Ritual Treatment of Human and Animal Remains: Proceedings of the First meeting of the Osteological Research Group*, ed. S. Anderson and K. Boyle, 17–32. Oxford: Oxbow Books.

Hoggard, Brian. 2004. "The Archaeology of Counter-Witchcraft and Popular Magic." In *Beyond the Witch Trials: Witchcraft and Magic in Enlightenment Europe*, ed. Owen Davies and Willem de Blécourt, 167–86. Manchester, UK: Manchester University Press.

———. 2019. *Magical House Protection: The Archaeology of Counter-Witchcraft*. New York: Berghahn Books.

Hohman, John George. 1820. *Pow-Wows or Long-Lost Friend: A Collection of Mysterious and Invaluable Arts and Remedies*. Pomeroy: Health Research Books.

Houlbrook, Ceri. 2013. "Ritual, Recycling and Recontextualization: Putting the Concealed Shoe in Context." *Cambridge Archaeological Journal* 23(1): 99–112.

———. 2016. "The Other Shoe: Fragmentation in the Post-Medieval Home." *Cambridge Archaeological Journal* 27(2): 261–74.

Hulubas, Sonja. 2017. "A Psychology Function of Sacrifices in Romanian Construction Rites." *Bulletin of Integrated Psychiatry* 3(74): 88–97.

Hutton, Ronald, ed. 2016. *Physical Evidence for Ritual Acts, Sorcery and Witchcraft in Christian Britain: A Feeling for Magic*. London: Palgrave Macmillan.

Incenti, Manuela. 2002. "Solar Geometry in Italian Cistercian Architecture." *Archeoastronomy: The Journal of Astronomy in Culture* 16: 3–23.

———. 2013. "Astronomical Knowledge in the Sacred Architecture of the Middle Ages in Italy." *Nexus Netw J* 15(3): 503–26.

Johnson, D. F. 2006. "The Crux Usualis as Apotropaic Weapon in Anglo-Saxon England." In *The Place of the Cross in Anglo-Saxon England*, ed. Catherine E. Karkov, Sarah L. Keefer, and Karen L. Jolly, 80. Woodbridge: Boydell Press.

Jolly, Karen L. 1996. *Popular Religion in Late Saxon England: Elf Charms in Context*. Chapel Hill: University of North Carolina Press.

Jones, A., and R. Bradley. 1999. "The Significance of Colour in European Archaeology." *Cambridge Archaeological Journal* 9: 112–14.

Jones, Lawrence E. 1973. *The Observer's Book of Old English Churches*. London: Frederick Warne & Co.

King, Chris, and Duncan Sayer, eds. 2011. *The Archaeology of Post-Medieval Religion*. Woodbridge: Boydell Press.

Kittredge, George Lyman. 1972. *Witchcraft in Old and New England*. New York: Atheneum.

Knight, Stephanie. 2001. "Beasts and Burial in the Interpretation of Ritual Space: A Case Study from Danebury." In *Holy Ground: Theoretical Issues Relating to the Landscape and Material Culture of Ritual Space*, ed. A. T. Smith and A. Brookes, 49–59. Cardiff: BAR International Series 956.

Kruczek-Aaron, Hadley. 2015. *Everyday Religion: An Archaeology of Protestant Belief and Practice in the Nineteenth Century*. Gainesville: University Press of Florida.

Ladurie, Emmanuel LeRoy. 1979. *Montaillou: The Promised Land of Error*. Translated by Barbara Bray. New York: Vintage Books.

Lane, Belden C. 1988. *Landscapes of the Sacred: Geography and Narrative in American Spirituality*. New York: Paulist Press.

Lecouteux, Claude. 2000. *The Tradition of Household Spirits: Ancestral Lore and Practices*. Rochester, VT: Inner Traditions.

———. 2015. *Demons and Spirits of the Land: Ancestral Lore and Practices*. Rochester, VT: Inner Traditions.

Lee, Christina. 2007. *Feasting the Dead: Food and Drink in Anglo-Saxon Burial Rituals*. Woodbridge: Boydell Press.

Linn, Meredith B. 2014. "Irish Immigrant Healing Magic in Nineteenth-Century New York City." *Historical Archaeology* 48(3): 144–65.

Loren, Diana Di Paolo. 2011. *The Archaeology of Clothing and Bodily Adornment in Colonial America*. Gainesville: University of Florida Press.

Lucas, Michael T. 2014. "Empowered Objects: Material Expressions of Spiritual Beliefs in the Colonial Chesapeake Region." *Historical Archaeology* 48(3): 106–24.

Mahoney-Swales, Diana, Richard O'Neill, and Hugh Willmott. 2011. "The Hidden Material Culture of Death: Coffins and Grave Goods in Late 18th and Early 19th Century Sheffield." In *The Archaeology of Post-Medieval Religion*, ed. Chris King and Duncan Sayer, 215–32. Woodbridge: Boydell Press.

Manning, M. Chris. 2012. "Homemade Magic: Concealed Deposits in Architectural Contexts in the Eastern United States." Master's thesis, Ball State University.

———. 2014. "The Material Culture of Ritual Concealments in the United States." *Historical Archaeology* 48(3): 52–83.

Mason, Austin. 1990. Buried Buckets: Rethinking Ritual Behavior before England's Conversion. *Haskins Society Journal* 20: 3–18.

McDannell, Colleen. 1998. *Material Christianity: Religion and Popular Culture in America*. New Haven: Yale University Press.

McKitrick, Patrick. 2009. "The Material Culture of Magic and Popular Belief in the Colonial Mid-Atlantic." *Journal of Middle Atlantic Archaeology* 25: 59–72.

McNally, Kenneth. 1988. *Standing Stones and Other Monuments of Early Ireland*. Belfast: Appletree Press.

Meaney, Audrey L. 1981. *Anglo-Saxon Amulets and Curing Stones*. Oxford: British Archaeological Report.

Mellinkoff, Ruth. 2004. *Averting Demons: The Protective Power of Medieval Visual Motifs and Themes*. Two volumes. Los Angeles: Ruth Mellinkoff Publications.

Merrifield, Ralph. 1955. "Witch Bottles and Magical Jugs." *Folklore* 66(1): 195–207.

Milnes, Gerald C. 2007. *Signs, Cures, & Witchery: German Appalachian Folklore*. Knoxville: University of Tennessee Press.

Morehouse, Rebecca. 2009. "Witch Bottle." Jefferson Patterson Park & Museum, Maryland Department of Planning. Retrieved June 2012 from http://www.jefpat.org/CuratorsChoiceArchive/2009CuratorsChoice/Aug2009WitchBottle.html.

Morris, Rosie. 2011. "Maidens' Garlands: A Funeral Custom of Post-Reformation England." In *The Archaeology of Post-Medieval Religion*, ed. Chris King and Duncan Sayer, 271–82. Woodbridge: Boydell Press.

Nelson, Louis P. 2007. "Sensing the Sacred: Anglican Material Religion in Early South Carolina." *Winterthur Portfolio* 41(4): 203–38.

Nickolai, Carol A. 2003. "The Relevance of Nineteenth-Century Religion to the Archaeological Record: An Example from the Home of Ellen White, Prophetess of Seventh-Day Adventism." *International Journal of Historical Archaeology* 7(2): 145–59.

Painter, Floyd. 1980. "An Early 18th Century Witch Bottle." *Chesopiean* 18(6): 62–71.

Parman, Susan. 1977. "Curing Beliefs and Practices in the Outer Hebrides." *Folklore* 88(1): 107–9.

Petch, Alison. 2008. "A Dorset Hag Stone." In *England: The Other Within: Analysing the English Collections at the Pitt Rivers Museum*. Retrieved March 2012 from http://england.prm.ox.ac.uk/englishness-Dorset-hag-stone.html.

Pluskowski, Aleksander. 2005. "Narwhals or Unicorns? Exotic Animals as Material Culture in Medieval Europe." *European Journal of Archaeology* 7(3): 291–313.

———, ed. 2012. *The Ritual Killing and Burial of Animals: European Perspectives*. Oxford: Oxbow Books.

Quinn, D. Michael. 1987. *Early Mormonism and the Magic World View*. Salt Lake City: Signature Books.

Reynolds, Andrew J. 2009. *Anglo-Saxon Deviant Burial Customs*. Oxford: Oxford University Press.

Rivers Cofield, Sara. 2010. "Why Keep a Crooked Sixpence: Religion and Magic at a Jesuit Plantation in St. Inigoes, Maryland." *Maryland Archaeology* 46(1 & 2): 60–70.

———. 2014. "Keeping a Crooked Sixpence: Coin Magic and Religion in the Colonial Chesapeake." *Historical Archaeology* 48(3): 84–105.

Rodwell, Warwick. 1981. *Archaeology of the English Church: The Study of Historic Churches and Churchyards*. London: B.T. Batsford.

———. 1989. *Church Archaeology*. London: English Heritage.

Roud, Steve. 2003. *Superstitions of Britain and Ireland*. London: Penguin Books.

Ruhmann, Christiane, and Vera Brieska, eds. 2015. *Dying Gods—Religious Beliefs in Northern and Eastern Europe in the Time of Christianisation*. Hanover: Niedersachsisches Landesmuseum.

Saunders, Nicholas J. 2003. "Crucifix, Calvary, and Cross: Materiality and Spirituality in Great War Landscapes." *World Archaeology* 35(1): 7–21.

Scholl, Michael. 1998. "'In Delaware the Millennium Has Begun': 19th-Century Farmstead Archaeology and the Methodist Discipline." *Northeast Historical Archaeology* 27: 12–32.

St. George, Robert Blair. 1998. *Conversing by Signs: Poetics of Implication in Colonial New England Culture*. Chapel Hill: University of North Carolina Press.

Stoodley, Nick. 1999. *The Spindle and the Spear: A Critical Enquiry into the Construction and Meaning of Gender in the Early Anglo-Saxon Burial Rite*. Oxford: BAR British Series 288.

Szczepanik, Pawet, and Stawomir Wadyl. 2014. "A Comparative Analysis of Early Medieval North-West Slavonic and West Baltic Sacred Landscapes: An Introduction to the Problems." *Networks and Neighbours* 2(1): 1–19.

Viegas, Jennifer. 2009. "17th Century Urine-Filled 'Witch Bottle' Found." Retrieved June 2009 from http://msnbc.msn.com.

Williams, Howard. 2007. "The Emotive Force of Early Medieval Mortuary Practices." *Archaeological Review from Cambridge* 22(1): 107–23.

Willmott, Hugh, and Adam Daubney. 2020. "Of Saints, Sows or Smiths? Copper-Brazed Iron Handbells in Early Medieval England." *Archaeological Journal* 177(1): 63–82.

Wilson, Stephen. 2001. *The Magical Universe: Everyday Ritual and Magic in Pre-Modern Europe*. London: Hambledon.

Wingfield, Chris. 2008. "Tylor's Onion: A Curious Case of Bewitched Onions from Somerset." In *England: The Other Within: Analysing the English Collections at the Pitt Rivers Museum*. Retrieved March 2012 from http://england.prm.ox.ac.uk/englishness-tylors-onion.html.

Wyse Jackson, P. N., and M. Connolly. 2002. "Fossils as Neolithic Funereal Adornments in County Kerry, South-west Ireland." *Geology Today* 18(4): 139–43.

Mediterranean/Classical

Aldhouse-Green, Miranda. 2002. *Dying for the Gods: Human Sacrifice in Iron Age and Roman Europe*. London: Tempus Publishing.

———. 2004. *An Archaeology of Images: Iconology and Cosmology in Iron Age and Roman Europe*. London: Routledge.

Anderson, William. 2004. "An Archaeology of Late Antique Pilgrim Flasks." *Anatolian Studies* 54: 79–93.

Bartosiewicz, L. 1998. "A Systematic Review of Astragalus Finds from Archaeological Sites." *Anthaeus* 24: 37–44.

Boschung, Dietrich, and Jan N. Bremmer, eds. 2015. *The Materiality of Magic*. Paderborn: Wilhelm Fink.

Boutsikas, Efrosyni, and Clive Ruggles. 2011. "Temples, Stars, and Ritual Landscapes: The Potential for Archaeoastronomy in Ancient Greece." *American Journal of Archaeology* 115(1): 55–68.

Curbera, Jaime. 2015. "From the Magician's Workshop: Notes on the Materiality of Greek Curse Tablets." In *The Materiality of Magic*, ed. Dietrich Boschung and Jan N. Bremmer, 97–122. Paderborn: Wilhelm Fink.

De Grossi Mazzorin, Jacopo, and Claudia Minniti. 2013. "Ancient Use of the Knuckle-Bone for Rituals and Gaming Piece." *Anthropozoologica* 48(2): 371–80.

Derrick, Thomas. 2018. "Little Bottles of Power: Roman Glass Unguentaria in Magic, Ritual, and Poisoning." In *Material Approaches to Roman Magic: Occult Objects and Supernatural Substances*, ed. Adam Parker and Stuart Mckie, 33–44. Oxford: Oxbow Books.

Eckhardt, Hella, Peter Brewer, Sophie Hay, and Sarah Poppy. 2009. "Roman Barrows and Their Landscape Context: a GIS Case Study at Bartlow, Cambridgeshire." *Britannia* XL: 65–98.

Gilmour, G. H. 1997. "The Nature and Function of Astragalus Bones from Archaeological Contexts in the Levant and Eastern Mediterranean." *Oxford Journal of Archaeology* 16(2): 167–75.

Incenti, Manuela. 2002. "Solar Geometry in Italian Cistercian Architecture." *Archeoastronomy: The Journal of Astronomy in Culture* 16: 3–23.

———. 2013. "Astronomical Knowledge in the Sacred Architecture of the Middle Ages in Italy." *Nexus Netw J* 15(3): 503–26.

Nagy, Árpád M. 2015. "Engineering Ancient Amulets: Magical Gems of the Roman Imperial Period." In *The Materiality of Magic*, ed. Dietrich Boschung and Jan N. Bremmer, 205–40. Paderborn: Wilhelm Fink.

Parker, Adam. 2018. "'The Bells! The Bells!' Approaching *Tintinnabula* in Roman Britain and Beyond." In *Material Approaches to Roman Magic: Occult Objects and Supernatural Substances*, ed. Adam Parker and Stuart Mckie, 57–68. Oxford: Oxbow Books.

Parker, Adam, and Stuart Mckie, eds. 2018. *Material Approaches to Roman Magic: Occult Objects and Supernatural Substances*. Oxford: Oxbow Books.

Pettegrew, David K., William R. Caraher, and Thomas W. Davis, eds. 2019. *The Oxford Handbook of Early Christian Archaeology*. New York: Oxford University Press.

Sagiv, Idit. 2018. "Victory of Good over Evil? Amuletic Animal Images on Roman Engraved Gems." In *Material Approaches to Roman Magic: Occult Objects and Supernatural Substances*, ed. Adam Parker and Stuart Mckie, 45–56. Oxford: Oxbow Books.

Wilburn, Andrew T. 2013. *Materia Magica: The Archaeology of Magic in Roman Egypt, Cyprus, and Spain*. Ann Arbor: University of Michigan Press.

Latin American/Mesoamerican

Bauer, Brian S. 1998. *The Sacred Landscape of the Inca: The Cusco Ceque System*. Austin: University of Texas Press.

Brady, James E. 1992. "Function and Meaning of Lowland Maya Shoe-Pots." *Ceramica de Cultura Maya* 16: 1–10.

Brady, James E., and Andrea Stone. 1986. "Naj Tunich: Entrance to the Maya Underworld." *Archaeology* 39(6): 18–25.

Brady, James, George Hasemann, and John H. Fogarty. 1995. "Harvest of Bones: Ritual Cave Burial in Honduras." *Archaeology* 48(3): 36–41.

Brady, James E., and Polly Peterson. 2008. "Re-envisioning Ancient Maya Ritual Assemblages." In *Religion, Archaeology, and the Material World*, ed. Lars Fogelin, 78–96. Carbondale: Center for Archaeological Investigations, Southern Illinois University.

Brady, James E., and Keith M. Prufer, eds. 2005. *In the Maw of the Earth Monster: Mesoamerican Ritual Cave Use*. Austin: University of Texas Press.

———. 2005. *Stone Houses and Earth Lords: Maya Religion in the Cave Context*. Boulder: University Press of Colorado.

Brown, Linda A. 2004. "Dangerous Places and Wild Spaces: Creating Meaning with Materials and Spaces at Contemporary Maya Shrines on El Duende Mountain." *Journal of Archaeological Method and Theory* 11: 31–58.

Brown, Linda A., and Kitty Emery. 2008. "Negotiations with the Animal Forest: Hunting Shrines in the Guatemalan Highlands." *Journal of Archaeological Method and Theory* 15: 300–37.

Bruchez, Margaret Sabom. 2007. "Artifacts that Speak for Themselves: Sounds Underfoot in Mesoamerica." *Journal of Anthropological Archaeology* 26: 47–64.

Coltman, Jeremy D., and John M. D. Pohl, eds. 2021. *Sorcery in Mesoamerica*. Louisville: University Press of Colorado.

Emery, Kitty F. 2005. "Animals and Ritual in the Copán Acropolis: Zooarchaeology of Special Deposits." Los Angeles: FAMSI.

Geller, Pamela. 2004. "Transforming Bodies, Transforming Identities: A Consideration of Pre-Columbian Maya Corporeal Beliefs and Practices." PhD diss., University of Pennsylvania.

Halperin, Christina T., Katherine A. Faust, Rhonda Taube, and Aurore Giguet, eds. 2009. *Mesoamerican Figurines: Small-Scale Indices of Large-Scale Social Phenomena.* Gainesville: University of Florida Press.

Hosler, Dorothy. 1995. "Sound, Color and Meaning in the Metallurgy of Ancient West Mexico." *World Archaeology* 27(1): 100–15.

Houston, Stephen, Claudia Brittenham, Cassandra Mesick, Alexandre Tokovinine, and Christina Warinner. 2009. *Veiled Brightness: A History of Ancient Maya Color.* Austin: University of Texas Press.

Landau, Kristin. 2015. "Spatial Logic and Maya City Planning: The Case for Cosmology." *Cambridge Archaeological Journal* 25(1): 275–92.

Moore, Jerry D. 2004. "The Social Basis of Sacred Spaces in the Prehispanic Andes: Ritual Landscapes of the Dead in Chimú and Inka Societies." *Journal of Archaeological Method and Theory* 11(1): 83–124.

Moyes, Holley. 2001. "The Cave as Cosmogram: The Use of GIS in an Intrasite Spatial Analysis of the Main Chamber of Actun Tunichil Muknal, a Maya Ceremonial Cave in Western Belize." Master's thesis, Florida Atlantic University.

Pitt-Rivers, Julian. 1970. "Spiritual Power in Central America: The Naguals of Chiapas." In *Witchcraft Confessions and Accusations*, ed. Mary Douglas, 183–206. London: Tavistock Publications.

Racoviteanu, Adina E. 2004. "Sacred Mountains and Glacier Archaeology in the Andes." Master's thesis, University of Colorado.

Racoviteanu, Adina, Todd Ackerman, Mark Williams, and William Manley. 2002. "High Altitude Ceremonial Sites in the Peruvian Andes: GIS Modeling." Boulder: Carbon Climate and Society Initiative and Long-Term Ecological Research.

Russell, Andrew, and Elizabeth Rahman, eds. 2015. *The Master Plant: Tobacco in Lowland South America.* London: Bloomsbury Academic.

Suhler, Charles, and David Friedel. 2005. "Life and Death in a Maya War Zone." In *The Archaeology of War*, ed. Mark Rose, 17–22. New York: Hatherleigh Press.

Sullivan, Kelsey Jean. 2017. "Caching It In: Local Patterns in Ancient Maya Ritual Caches of Eccentric Lithics within the Belize Valley." Master's thesis, Northern Arizona University.

Tiesler, Vera, and Andrea Cucina, eds. 2007. *New Perspectives on Human Sacrifice and Ritual Body Treatment in Ancient Maya Society.* New York: Springer.

Zucchi, Alberta. 1997. "Tombs and Testaments: Mortuary Practices during the Seventeenth to Nineteenth Centuries in the Spanish-Venezuelan Catholic Tradition." *Historical Archaeology* 31(2): 31–42.

Middle Eastern/Indian

Beck, Brenda E. F. 1969. "Colour and Heat in South Indian Ritual." *Man* 4(4): 553–72.

Dafni, Amots. 2007. 'Rituals, Ceremonies and Customs Related to Sacred Trees with Special Reference to the Middle East." *Journal of Ethnobiology and Ethnomedicine* 3(28). Retrieved February 2021 from https://doi.org/10.11861746-42693-28.

Huyler, Stephen. 1995. *Painted Prayers: Women's Art in Village India.* New York. Rizzoli.

Layard, John. 1937. "Labyrinth Ritual in South India: Threshold and Tattoo Designs." *Folklore* 48(2): 115–82.

Levene, Dan. 2002. *A Corpus of Magic Bowls.* London: Routledge.

Lymer, Kenneth. 2004. "Rags and Rock Art: The Landscapes of Holy Site Pilgrimage in the Republic of Kazakhstan." *World Archaeology* 36(1): 158–72.

Minniti, Claudia, and L. Peyronel. 2005. "Symbolic or Functional Astragals from Tell Mardikh-Ebla (Syria)." *Archaeofauna* 14: 7–26.

Mohan, Urmila. 2017. "Clothing as a Technology of Enchantment: Gaze and Glaze in Hindu Garments." *Magic, Ritual, and Witchcraft* 12(2): 225–44.

Naidu, Maheshvari. 2011. "Animated Environment: Animism and the Environment Revisited." *Journal of Dharma* 36(3): 257–73.

Ray, Himansha Prabha. 1994. "Kanheri: The Archaeology of an Early Buddhist Pilgrimage Centre in Western India." *World Archaeology* 26(1): 35–46.

Regourd, Anne. 2007. "A Magic Mirror in the Louvre and Additional Observations on the Use of Magic Mirrors in Contemporary Yemen." In *Word of God, Art of Man: The Qur'an and Its Creative Expressions*, ed. Fahmida Suleman, 135–55. Oxford: Oxford University Press.

Native American

Brain, Jeffrey P., and Philip Phillips. 1996. *Shell Gorgets: Styles of Late Prehistoric and Protohistoric Southeast*. Cambridge, MA: Peabody Museum Press.

Branson, Oscar T. 1976. *Fetishes and Carvings of the Southwest*. Tucson: Treasure Chest Publications.

Brown, Joseph Epes. 1997. *Animals of the Soul: Sacred Animals of the Oglala Sioux*. Rockport: Element.

Browner, Tara. 2002. *Heartbeat of the People: Music and Dance of the Northern Pow-wow*. Urbana: University of Illinois Press.

Burley, David V., J. Scott Hamilton, and Knut R. Fladmark. 1996. *Prophecy of the Swan: The Upper Peace River Fur Trade of 1794–1823*. Vancouver: University of British Columbia Press.

Chacon, Richard, and Rubén G. Mendoza. 2007. *Native American Indigenous Warfare and Ritual Violence*. Phoenix: University of Arizona.

Crosby, Harry W. 1997. *The Cave Paintings of Baja California: Discovering the Great Murals of an Unknown People*. San Diego: Sunbelt Publications.

Fergusson, Erna. 1931. *Dancing Gods: Indian Ceremonials of New Mexico & Arizona*. Albuquerque: University of New Mexico Press.

Fowles, Severin M. 2013. *An Archaeology of Doings: Secularism and the Study of Pueblo Religion*. Sante Fe: School for Advanced Research Press.

Fox, William A. 1991. "The Serpent's Copper Scales." *Wanikan* 91(3): 3–15.

———. 1992. "Dragon Side Plates from York Factory: A New Twist on an Old Tail." *Manitoba Archaeological Journal* 2(2): 21–35.

Gill, Sam D. 1975. "The Color of Navajo Ritual Symbolism: An Evaluation of Methods." *Journal of Anthropological Research* 31(4): 350–63.

Greer, John, and Mavis Greer. 1998. "Dark Zone Rock Art in North America." In *Rock Art Papers, Vol. 13*, ed. Ken Hedges, 135–44. San Diego: San Diego Museum Papers 35.

———. 1999. "Handprints in Montana Rock Art." *Plains Anthropologist* 44(167): 59–71.

Gulliford, Andrew. 2000. *Sacred Objects and Sacred Places: Preserving Tribal Traditions*. Boulder: University Press of Colorado.

Hall, Robert L. 1976. "Ghosts, Water Barriers, Corn, and Sacred Enclosures in the Eastern Woodlands." *American Antiquity* 41: 353–59.

———. 1997. *An Archaeology of the Soul: North American Indian Belief and Ritual.* Urbana: University of Illinois Press.

Houston, Stephen, Claudia Brittenham, Cassandra Mesick, Alexandre Tokovinine, and Christina Warinner. 2009. *Veiled Brightness: A History of Ancient Maya Color.* Austin: University of Texas Press.

Howey, Meghan C. L. 2011. "Colonial Encounters, European Kettles, and the Magic of Mimesis in the Late Sixteenth and Early Seventeenth Century Indigenous Northeast and Great Lakes." *International Journal of Historical Archaeology* 15: 329–57.

Kicking Woman, Kevin Dale. 2014. "Blackfoot Ceremony through the Power of Song." Master's thesis, University of Montana.

Lander, Herbert J., Susan M. Ervin, and Arnold E. Horowitz. 1960. "Navaho Color Categories." *Language* 36(3): 368–82.

Lee, Molly, ed. 1999. *Not Just a Pretty Face: Dolls and Human Figurines in Alaska Native Cultures.* Fairbanks: University of Alaska Museum.

Lindauer, O. 1996. *Historical Archaeology of the United States Industrial Indian School at Phoenix.* Anthropological Field Studies. Tempe: Arizona State University, Office of Cultural Resource Management.

Lipponcott, Kerry. 2015. "A Continent-Wide View of Marine Shell Mask Gorgets." *Archaeology in Montana* 56(1): 31–50.

Lucas, Michael T. 2014. "Empowered Objects: Material Expressions of Spiritual Beliefs in the Colonial Chesapeake Region." *Historical Archaeology* 48(3): 106–24.

McCleary, Timothy P. 2015. *Crow Indian Rock Art: Indigenous Perspectives and Interpretations.* New York: Routledge.

McManis, Kent. 1998. *A Guide to Zuni Fetishes & Carvings: Vol. I, The Animals & The Carvers.* Tucson: Treasure Chest Books.

———. 1998. *A Guide to Zuni Fetishes & Carvings: Vol. II, The Materials & The Carvers.* Tucson: Treasure Chest Books.

Mills, Barbara J., and T. J. Ferguson. 2008. "Animate Objects: Shell Trumpets and Ritual Networks in the Greater Southwest." *Journal of Archaeological Method and Theory* 15: 338–61.

Milne, Courtney. 1995. *Sacred Places in North America: A Journey into the Medicine Wheel.* New York: Stewart, Tabori & Chang.

Monroe, Jean Guard, and Ray A. Williamson. 1993. *First Houses: Native American Homes and Sacred Structures.* Boston: Houghton Mifflin.

Nettl, Bruno. 1989. *Blackfoot Musical Thought.* Kent: Kent State University Press.

Patterson, Alex. 1992. *A Field Guide to Rock Art Symbols of the Greater Southwest.* Boulder: Johnson Books.

Reid, C. S. (Paddy). 1992. "Here Be Dragons: The Indian Trade Gun Side Plates from the Ballynacree site (DKKp-8) Kenora." *KEWA* (Newsletter of the Ontario Archaeological Society London Chapter) 8: 15–20.

Rockwell, David. 1991. *Giving Voice to Bear: North American Indian Myths, Rituals, and Images of the Bear.* Niwot: Roberts Rinehart Publishers.

Romain, William F. 2015. *An Archaeology of the Sacred: Adena-Hopewell Astronomy and Landscape Archaeology.* Olmsted Township: The Ancient Earthworks Project.

Schroedl, Alan. 1977. "The Grand Canyon Figurine Complex." *American Antiquity* 42(2): 254–65.

Smith, Marvin T., and Julie Barnes Smith. 1989. "Engraved Shell Masks in North America." *Southeastern Archaeology* 8(1): 9–18.

Stokes, William Michael, and William Lee Stokes. 1980. *Messages on Stone: Selections of Native Western Rock Art*. Salt Lake City: Starstone Publishing.

Sundstrom, Linea. 2003. "Sacred Islands: An Exploration of Religion and Landscape in the Northern Great Plain." In *Islands on the Plains: Ecological, Social, and Ritual Use of Landscapes*, ed. Marcel Kornfeld and Alan J. Osborn, 258–300. Salt Lake City: University of Utah Press.

Turpin, Solveg A., ed. 1994. *Shamanism and Rock Art in North America*. Special Publication 1. San Antonio: Rock Art Foundation, Inc.

VanPool, Christine S., and Elizabeth Newsome. 2012. "The Spirit in the Material: A Case Study of Animism in the American Southwest." *American Antiquity* 77: 243–62.

Zedeño, Maria Nieves. 2008. "Bundled Worlds: The Roles and Interactions of Complex Objects from the North American Plains." *Journal of Archaeological Method and Theory* 15: 362–78.

Scandinavian

Andrén, Anders. 1993. "Doors to Other Worlds: Scandinavian Death Rituals in Gotlandic Perspective." *Journal of European Archaeology* 1: 33–56.

Brink, Stefan, and Saebjorg W. Nordeide, eds. 2013. *Sacred Sites and Holy Places: Exploring the Sacralization of Landscape through Time and Space*. Turnhout, Belgium: Brepols.

Carlie, Anne. 2006. "Ancient Building Cults: Aspects of Ritual Traditions in Southern Scandinavia." In *Old Norse Religion in Long-Term Perspectives*, ed. Anders Andrén, Kristina Jennbert, and Catharina Raudvere, 206–11. Lund: Nordic Academic Press.

Eriksen, Marianne Hem. 2013. "Doors to the Dead. The Power of Doorways and Thresholds in Viking Age Scandinavia." *Archaeological Dialogues* 20(2): 187–214.

———. 2015. "Portals to the Past: An Archaeology of Doorways, Dwellings, and Ritual Practice in Late Iron Age Scandinavia." PhD diss., University of Oslo.

Horn, Christian, Johan Ling, Ulf Bertilsson, and Rich Potter. 2018. "By All Means Necessary—2.5D and 3D Recording of Surfaces in the Study of Southern Scandinavian Rock Art." *Open Archaeology* 4: 81–96.

Hukantaival, Sonja. 2009. "Horse Skulls and 'Alder Horse': The Horse as Depositional Sacrifice in Buildings." *Archaeoligica Baltica* 11: 350–55.

———. 2015. "Frogs in Miniature Coffins from Churches in Finland: Folk Magic in Holy Christian Places." *Mirator* 16(1): 192–220.

———. 2016. *"For a Witch Cannot Cross Such a Threshold!" Building Concealment Traditions in Finland c. 1200–1950*. Turku: The Society for Medieval Archaeology in Finland.

———. 2017. "Finding Folk Religion: An Archaeology of 'Strange' Behavior." *Folklore* 55: 99–124. Retrieved February 2021 from www.folklore.ee/folklore.

Jenson, Bo. 2010. *Viking Age Amulets in Scandinavia and Western Europe*. Oxford: BAR.

Jonsson, Kristina. 2007. "Burial Rods and Charcoal Graves: New Light on Old Burial Practices." In *Viking and Medieval Scandinavia*, ed. Stefan Brink, Judy Quinn, and John Hines, 43–73. Belgium: Brepol.

———. 2009. "Dangerous Death and Dangerous Dead: Examples from Scandinavian Burial Practices from the Middle Ages to the Early Modern Period." In *On the Threshold: Burial Archaeology in the Twenty-first Century*, 173–86. Stockholm: Stockholm University.

Kirkinen, Tuija. 2017."'Burning Pelts': Brown Bear Skins in the Iron Age and Early Medieval (1–1300 AD) Burials in South-Eastern Fennoscandia." *Estonian Journal of Archaeology* 21(1): 3–29.

Kristoffersen, Siv. 2010. "Half Beast—Half Man: Hybrid Figures in Animal Art." *World Archaeology* 12(2): 261–72.

Lucas, Gavin, and Thomas H. McGovern. 2007. "Bloody Slaughter: Ritual Decapitation and Display at the Viking Settlement of Hofstaðir, Iceland." *European Journal of Archaeology* 10(1): 7–30.

Lund, Julie. 2008. "Banks, Borders, and Bodies of Water in a Viking Age Mentality." *Journal of Wetland Archaeology* 8: 51–70.

Olofsson, Camilla. 2010. "Making New Antlers: Depositions of Animal Skulls and Antlers as a Message of Regeneration in South Sami Grave Contexts." *Norwegian Archaeological Review* 43(2): 97–114.

Price, Neil. 2019. *The Viking Way: Magic and Mind in Late Iron Age Scandinavia*. 2nd ed. Oxford: Oxbow Books.

Smith, Kevin P. 2016. "The Colour of Belief: Objects of Jasper, Opal, Chalcedony, and Obsidian from the Reykholt Churches." In *Reykholt: The Church Excavations*, ed. Guðrún Sveibjarnardóttir, 230–42. Snorrastofa: The National Museum of Iceland and University of Iceland Press.

Svanberg, Fredrik. 2003. *Death Rituals in South-east Scandinavia, AD 800–1000*. Stockholm: Almqvist and Wicksell.

Thilderkvist, Johan. 2013. *Ritual Bones or Common Waste: A Study of Early Medieval Bone Deposits in Northern Europe*. Netherlands: Barkhaus and University of Groningen.

Williams, Howard. 2016. "Citations in Stone: The Material World of Hogbacks." *European Journal of Archaeology* 19(3): 497–518.

ARTIFACT MATERIAL TYPES AND ATTRIBUTES

Ceramics

Alexandrowicz, J. Stephen. 1986. "The Market Street Witch Bottle, Pittsburgh, Pennsylvania." *Proceedings of the Symposium on Ohio Valley Urban and Historic Archaeology IV*: 117–32.

Becker, Marshall Joseph. 1978. "An Eighteenth-Century Witch Bottle in Delaware County, Pennsylvania." *Pennsylvania Archaeologist* 48(1–2): 1–11.

———. 1980. "An American Witch Bottle: 'White Magic' among Pennsylvania Colonists." *Archaeology* 33: 18–23.

———. 2005. "An Update on Colonial Witch Bottles." *Pennsylvania Archaeologist* 75(2): 12–23.

Brady, James E. 1992. "Function and Meaning of Lowland Maya Shoe-Pots." *Ceramica de Cultura Maya* 16: 1–10.

Fremmer, Ray. 1973. "Dishes in Colonial Graves: Evidence from Jamaica." *Historical Archaeology* 7: 58–62.

Halperin, Christina T., Katherine A. Faust, Rhonda Taube, and Aurore Giguet, eds. 2009. *Mesoamerican Figurines: Small-Scale Indices of Large-Scale Social Phenomena*. Gainesville: University of Florida Press.

Levene, Dan. 2002. *A Corpus of Magic Bowls*. London: Routledge.

Merrifield, Ralph. 1955. "Witch Bottles and Magical Jugs." *Folklore* 66(1): 195–207.

Morehouse, Rebecca. 2009. "Witch Bottle." Jefferson Patterson Park & Museum, Maryland Department of Planning. Retrieved June 2012 from http://www.jefpat.org/Curatorsrs ChoiceArchive/2009CuratorsChoice/Aug2009WitchBottle.html.

Painter, Floyd. 1980. "An Early 18th Century Witch Bottle." *Chesopiean* 18(6): 62–71.

Viegas, Jennifer. 2009. "17th Century Urine-Filled 'Witch Bottle' Found." Retrieved June 2009 from http://msnbc.msn.com.

Colors

Antonvic, Dragana, Selena Vitezovic, and Vidan Dimic. 2016. "Life in White: Symbolism and the Importance of the White Colour in the Neolithic in the Balkans." *Acta Musei Tiberiopolitani* 2: 26–37.

Beck, Brenda E. F. 1969. "Colour and Heat in South Indian Ritual." *Man* 4(4): 553–72.

DeBoer, Warren R. 2005. "Colors for a North American Past." *World Archaeology* 37(1): 66–91.

Gage, John. 1999. *Color and Culture: Practice and Meaning from Antiquity to Abstraction*. Berkeley: University of California Press.

———. 1999. "What Meaning Had Colour in Early Societies?" *Cambridge Archaeological Journal* 9(1): 109–26.

———. 2000. *Color and Meaning: Art, Science, and Symbolism*. Berkeley: University of California Press.

Gerharz, Rudolf Richard, Renate Lantermann, and Dirk R. Spennemann. 1988. "Munsell Color Charts: A Necessity for Archaeologists?" *Australian Journal of Historical Archaeology: Australia 1788–1988: Bicentennial Edition* 6: 88–95.

Gill, Sam D. 1975. "The Color of Navajo Ritual Symbolism: An Evaluation of Methods." *Journal of Anthropological Research* 31(4): 350–63.

Greenfield, Amy Butler. 2006. *A Perfect Red: Empire, Espionage, and the Quest for the Color of Desire*. New York: Harper Perennial.

Hosler, Dorothy. 1995. "Sound, Color and Meaning in the Metallurgy of Ancient West Mexico." *World Archaeology* 27(1): 100–15.

Houston, Stephen, Claudia Brittenham, Cassandra Mesick, Alexandre Tokovinine, and Christina Warinner. 2009. *Veiled Brightness: A History of Ancient Maya Color*. Austin: University of Texas Press.

Jones, A., and R. Bradley. 1999. "The Significance of Colour in European Archaeology." *Cambridge Archaeological Journal* 9: 112–14.

Jones, A., and G. McGregor, eds. 2002. *Colouring the Past: The Significance of Colour in Archaeological Research*. Oxford: Berg.

Lander, Herbert J., Susan M. Ervin, and Arnold E. Horowitz. 1960. "Navaho Color Categories." *Language* 36(3): 368–82.

McKinley, Catherine. 2011. *Indigo: In Search of the Color that Seduced the World*. New York: Bloomsbury.

Meloy, Ellen. 2002. *The Anthropology of Turquoise: Reflections on Desert, Sea, Stone, and Sky*. New York: Vintage Books.

Pastoureau, Michael. 2008. *Black: The History of a Color*. Princeton: Princeton University Press.

Smith, Kevin P. 2016. "The Colour of Belief: Objects of Jasper, Opal, Chalcedony, and Obsidian from the Reykholt Churches." In *Reykholt: The Church Excavations*, ed. Guðrún Sveibjarnardóttir, 230–42. Snorrastofa: The National Museum of Iceland and University of Iceland Press.

Spence, K. 1999. "Red, White and Black: Colour in Building Stone in Ancient Egypt." *Cambridge Archaeological Journal* 9: 114–17.

Sterman, Baruch. 2012. *The Rarest Blue: The Remarkable Story of an Ancient Color Lost to History and Rediscovered*. Guilford: Lyons Press.

Taussig, Michael T. 2009. *What Color Is the Sacred?* Chicago: University of Chicago Press.

Varichon, Anne. 2007. *Colors: What They Mean and How to Make Them*. New York: Harry N. Abrams.

Fauna

Bartosiewicz, L. 1998. "A Systematic Review of Astragalus Finds from Archaeological Sites." *Anthaeus* 24: 37–44.

Bond, Julie. 1996. "Burnt Offerings: Animal Bone in Anglo-Saxon Cremations." *World Archaeology* 28(1): 76–88.

Brady, James, George Hasemann, and John H. Fogarty. 1995. "Harvest of Bones: Ritual Cave Burial in Honduras." *Archaeology* 48(3): 36–41.

Brain, Jeffrey P., and Philip Phillips. 1996. *Shell Gorgets: Styles of Late Prehistoric and Protohistoric Southeast*. Cambridge, MA: Peabody Museum Press.

Brown, Joseph Epes. 1997. *Animals of the Soul: Sacred Animals of the Oglala Sioux*. Rockport: Element.

Campana, Douglas, Pam Crabtree, Susan deFrance, Justin Lev-Tov, and Alice Choyke, eds. 2010. *Anthropological Approaches to Zooarchaeology: Complexity, Colonialism, and Animal Transformations*. Oxford: Oxbow Books.

Choyke, Alice. 2010. "The Bone Is the Beast: Animal Amulets and Ornaments in Power and Magic." In *Anthropological Approaches to Zooarchaeology: Complexity, Colonialism, and Animal Transformations*, ed. Douglas Campana, Pam Crabtree, Susan deFrance, Justin Lev-Tov, and Alice Choyke, 197–209. Oxford: Oxbow Books.

Davis, S. J. M. 1987. *The Archaeology of Animals*. London: Batsford.

De Grossi Mazzorin, Jacopo, and Claudia Minniti. 2013. "Ancient Use of the Knuckle-Bone for Rituals and Gaming Piece." *Anthropozoologica* 48(2): 371–80.

Dickinson, Tania M. 2005. "Symbols of Protection: The Significance of Animal-Ornamental Shields in Early Anglo-Saxon England." *Medieval Archaeology* 49: 109–63.

Ellis, Bill. 2002. "Why Is a Lucky Rabbit's Foot Lucky? Body Parts as Fetishes." *Journal of Folklore Research* 39(1): 51–84.

Emery, Kitty F. 2005. "Animals and Ritual in the Copán Acropolis: Zooarchaeology of Special Deposits." Los Angeles: FAMSI.

Gilmour, G. H. 1997. "The Nature and Function of Astragalus Bones from Archaeological Contexts in the Levant and Eastern Mediterranean." *Oxford Journal of Archaeology* 16(2): 167–75.

Hamerow, Helena. 2006. "'Special Deposits' in Anglo-Saxon Settlements." *Medieval Archaeology* 50: 1–30.

Hill, J. D. 1996. "The Identification of Ritual Deposits of Animals: A General Perspective from a Specific Study of 'Special Animal Deposits' from the Southern English Iron Age."

In *Ritual Treatment of Human and Animal Remains: Proceedings of the First Meeting of the Osteological Research Group*, ed. S. Anderson and K. Boyle, 17–32. Oxford: Oxbow Books.

Hukantaival, Sonja. 2009. "Horse Skulls and 'Alder Horse': The Horse as Depositional Sacrifice in Buildings." *Archaeoligica Baltica* 11: 350–55.

———. 2015. "Frogs in Miniature Coffins from Churches in Finland: Folk Magic in Holy Christian Places." *Mirator* 16(1): 192–220.

Kirkinen, Tuija. 2017. "'Burning Pelts': Brown Bear Skins in the Iron Age and Early Medieval (1–1300 AD) Burials in South-Eastern Fennoscandia." *Estonian Journal of Archaeology* 21(1): 3–29.

Knight, Stephanie. 2001. "Beasts and Burial in the Interpretation of Ritual Space: A Case Study from Danebury." In *Holy Ground: Theoretical Issues Relating to the Landscape and Material Culture of Ritual Space*, ed. A. T. Smith and A. Brookes, 49–59. Cardiff: BAR International Series 956.

Kristoffersen, Siv. 2010. "Half Beast—Half Man: Hybrid Figures in Animal Art." *World Archaeology* 12(2): 261–72.

Lipponcott, Kerry. 2015. "A Continent-Wide View of Marine Shell Mask Gorgets." *Archaeology in Montana* 56(1): 31–50.

Luckenbach, Al. 2004. "Fowl Play at London Town?" *Maryland Archaeology* 40(2): 8.

McNiven, Ian J. 2010. "Navigating the Human-Animal Divide: Marine Mammal Hunters and Rituals of Sensory Allurement." *World Archaeology* 42(2): 215–30.

———. 2013. "Between the Living and the Dead: Relational Ontologies and the Ritual Dimensions of Dugong Hunting across Torres Strait." In *Relational Archaeologies: Humans, Animals, Things*, ed. Christopher Watts, 97–116. London: Routledge.

Mercier, Jacques. 1979. *Ethiopian Magic Scrolls*. New York: George Braziller.

Mills, Barbara J., and T. J. Ferguson. 2008. "Animate Objects: Shell Trumpets and Ritual Networks in the Greater Southwest." *Journal of Archaeological Method and Theory* 15: 338–61.

Minniti, Claudia, and L. Peyronel. 2005. "Symbolic or Functional Astragals from Tell Mardikh-Ebla (Syria)." *Archaeofauna* 14: 7–26.

Morris, J. 2011. *Investigating Animal Burials: Ritual, Mundane and Beyond*. Oxford: Archaeopress BAR 535.

Newall, Venetia. 1971. *An Egg at Easter: A Folklore Study*. Bloomington: Indiana University Press.

Oakley, K. P. 1978. "Animal Fossils as Charms." In *Animals in Folklore*, ed. J. R. Porter and W. M. S. Russell, 208–40. Ipswich: D. S. Brewer Ltd and Rowman and Littlefield.

O'Day, Sharyn Jones, Wim Van Neer, and Anton Ervynck, eds. 2004. *Behavior Behind Bones: The Zooarchaeology of Ritual, Religion, Status, and Identity*. Oxford: Oxbow Books.

Olofsson, Camilla. 2010. "Making New Antlers: Depositions of Aanimal Skulls and Antlers as a Message of Regeneration in South Sami Grave Contexts." *Norwegian Archaeological Review* 43(2): 97–114.

Perri, Angela. 2017. "A Typology of Dog Deposition in Archaeological Contexts." In *Economic Zooarchaeology: Studies in Hunting, Herding, and Early Agriculture*, ed. Peter Rowley-Conwy, Paul Halstead, and Dale Serjeantson, 1–18. Oxford: Oxbow Books.

Pluskowski, Aleksander. 2005. "Narwhals or Unicorns? Exotic Animals as Material Culture in Medieval Europe." *European Journal of Archaeology* 7(3): 291–313.

———, ed. 2012. *The Ritual Killing and Burial of Animals: European Perspectives*. Oxford: Oxbow Books.

Rockwell, David. 1991. *Giving Voice to Bear: North American Indian Myths, Rituals, and Images of the Bear*. Niwot: Roberts Rinehart Publishers.

Russell, Nerissa. 2012. *Social Zooarchaeology: Humans and Animals in Prehistory*. Cambridge: Cambridge University Press.

Sabo, G., and Sabo, D. 1985. "Belief Systems and the Ecology of Sea Mammal Hunting among the Baffinland Eskimo." *Arctic Anthropology* 22(2): 77–86.

Smith, Marvin T., and Julie Barnes Smith. 1989. "Engraved Shell Masks in North America." *Southeastern Archaeology* 8(1): 9–18.

Thilderkvist, Johan. 2013. *Ritual Bones or Common Waste: A Study of Early Medieval Bone Deposits in Northern Europe*. Netherlands: Barkhaus and University of Groningen.

Watts, Christopher, ed. 2013. *Relational Archaeologies: Humans, Animals, Things*. London: Routledge.

Wilson, B. 1992. "Considerations for the Identification of Ritual Deposits of Animal Bones in Iron Age Pits." *International Journal of Osteoarchaeology* 2: 331–49.

———. 1999. "Displayed or Concealed? Cross Cultural Evidence for Symbolic and Ritual Activity Depositing Iron Age Animal Bones." *Oxford Journal of Archaeology* 18(3): 297–305.

Wyse Jackson, P. N., and M. Connolly. 2002. "Fossils as Neolithic Funereal Adornments in County Kerry, South-west Ireland." *Geology Today* 18(4): 139–43.

Flora

Arrowsmith, Nancy. 2009. *Essential Herbal Wisdom: A Complete Exploration of 50 Remarkable Herbs*. Woodbury: Llewellyn Publications.

Bown, Deni. 1995. *The Herb Society of America Encyclopedia of Herbs & Their Uses*. London: Dorling Kindersley.

Cunningham, Scott. 1985. *Cunningham's Encyclopedia of Magical Herbs*. St. Paul: Llewellyn Worldwide.

Dafni, Amots. 2007. "Rituals, Ceremonies and Customs Related to Sacred Trees with Special Reference to the Middle East." *Journal of Ethnobiology and Ethnomedicine* 3(28). Retrieved February 2021 from https://doi.org/10.11861746-42693-28.

Erichsen-Brown, Charlotte. 1979. *Use of Plants for the Past 500 Years*. Ontario: Breezy Creeks Press.

Gifford, Jane. 2000. *The Wisdom of Trees: Mysteries, Magic, and Medicine*. New York: Sterling Publishing Company.

Hageneder, Fred. 2001. *The Heritage of Trees: History, Culture and Symbolism*. Edinburgh: Floris Books.

Hansson, Ann-Marie, and Andreas G. Heiss. 2014. "Plants Used in Ritual Offerings and in Festive Contexts." In *Plants and People: Choices and Diversity through Time*, ed. Alexandre Chevalier, Elena Marinova, and Leonor Peña-Chocarro, 311–34. Oxford: Oxbow Books.

Hatfield, Gabrielle. 2003. *Encyclopedia of Folk Medicine: Old World and New World Traditions*. Santa Barbara: ABC-CLIO, Inc.

Lipp, Frank J. 1996. *Herbalism: Healing and Harmony; Symbolism, Ritual, and Folklore; Traditions of East and West*. Boston: Little, Brown, and Company.

———. 2006. *Healing Herbs*. New York: Barnes & Noble.

Merlin, M. 2003. "Archaeological Evidence for the Tradition of Psychoactive Plant Use in the Old World." *Economic Botany* 57(3): 295–323.

Morris, Rosie. 2011. "Maidens' Garlands: A Funeral Custom of Post-Reformation England." In *The Archaeology of Post-Medieval Religion*, ed. Chris King and Duncan Sayer, 271–82. Woodbridge: Boydell Press.

Paterson, Jacqueline M. 1996. *Tree Wisdom: The Definitive Guidebook to the Myth, Folklore and Healing Power of Trees*. San Francisco: Thorsons.

Picton, Margaret. 2000. *The Book of Magical Herbs: Herbal History, Mystery, and Folklore*. New York: Barron's Hauppauge.

Rätch, Christian. 1992. *The Dictionary of Sacred and Magical Plants*. Santa Barbara: ABC-CLIO.

———. 1994. "The Mead of Inspiration and Magical Plants of the Ancient Germans." In *The Well of Remembrance: Rediscovering the Early Wisdom Myths of Northern Europe*, ed. R. Metzner, 279–323. Boston: Shambhala.

Russell, Andrew, and Elizabeth Rahman, eds. 2015. *The Master Plant: Tobacco in Lowland South America*. London: Bloomsbury Academic.

Schultes, Richard Evans, and Albert Hofmann. 1992. *Plants of the Gods: Their Sacred, Healing, and Hallucinogenic Powers*. Rochester, VT: Healing Arts Press.

Wingfield, Chris. 2008. "Tylor's Onion: A Curious Case of Bewitched Onions from Somerset." In *England: The Other Within: Analysing the English Collections at the Pitt Rivers Museum*. Retrieved March 2012 from http://england.prm.ox.ac.uk/englishness-tylors-onion.html.

Glass

Derrick, Thomas. 2018. "Little Bottles of Power: Roman Glass Unguentaria in Magic, Ritual, and Poisoning." In *Material Approaches to Roman Magic: Occult Objects and Supernatural Substances*, ed. Adam Parker and Stuart Mckie, 33–44. Oxford: Oxbow Books.

Melchior-Bonnet, Sabine. 1994. *The Mirror: A History*. New York: Routledge.

Pendergrast, Mark. 2003. *Mirror, Mirror: A History of the Human Love Affair with Reflection*. New York: Basic Books.

Metal

Anonymous. 1909. "The Good Luck Horseshoe." *The William and Mary Quarterly* 17(4): 247–48.

Budd, P., and T. Taylor. 1995. "The Faerie Smith Meets the Bronze Industry: Magic versus Science in the Interpretation of Prehistoric Metal-Making." *World Archaeology* 27(1): 133–43.

Corbin, Alain. 1998. *Village Bells: Sound and Meaning in the Nineteenth-Century French Countryside*. New York: Columbia University Press.

Cowie, T. G. 1988. *Magic Metal: Early Metalworkers in the North East*. Aberdeen: University of Aberdeen.

Cressy, David. (1989) 2004. *Bonfires and Bells: National Memory and the Protestant Calendar in Elizabethan and Stuart England*. Phoenix Mill: Sutton Publishing.

Davidson, James M. 2014. "Deconstructing the Myth of the 'Hand Charm': Mundane Clothing Fasteners and Their Curious Transformations into Supernatural Objects." *Historical Archaeology* 48(2): 18–60.

Easton, Timothy. 2013. "Plumbing a Spiritual World." *SPAB* Winter 2013: 41–45.

Easton, Timothy, and Jeremy Hodgkinson. 2013. "Apotropaic Symbols on Cast-Iron Firebacks." *Journal of the Antique Metalware Society* 21: 15–33.

Fox, William A. 1991. "The Serpent's Copper Scales." *Wanikan* 91(3): 3–15.

———. 1992. "Dragon Side Plates from York Factory: A New Twist on an Old Tail." *Manitoba Archaeological Journal* 2(2): 21–35.

Gerish, W. B. 1893. "Key Magic." *Folklore* 4(3): 391–92.

Hosler, Dorothy. 1995. "Sound, Color and Meaning in the Metallurgy of Ancient West Mexico." *World Archaeology* 27(1): 100–15.

Howey, Meghan C. L. 2011. "Colonial Encounters, European Kettles, and the Magic of Mimesis in the Late Sixteenth and Early Seventeenth Century Indigenous Northeast and Great Lakes." *International Journal of Historical Archaeology* 15: 329–57.

Lawrence, Robert Means. 1898. "The Magic of the Horseshoe: With Other Folklore Notes." Retrieved December 2012 from http:www.sacred-texts.com/etc/mhs/mhs04.htm.

Linn, Meredith B. 2014. "Irish Immigrant Healing Magic in Nineteenth-Century New York City." *Historical Archaeology* 48(3) 144–65.

Mitchiner, Michael. 1986. *Medieval Pilgrim and Secular Badges*. London: Hawkins Publications.

Parker, Adam. 2018. "'The Bells! The Bells!' Approaching *Tintinnabula* in Roman Britain and Beyond." In *Material Approaches to Roman Magic: Occult Objects and Supernatural Substances*, ed. Adam Parker and Stuart Mckie, 57–68. Oxford: Oxbow Books.

Raffield, B. 2014. "'A River of Knives and Swords': Ritually Deposited Weapons in English Watercourses and Wetlands during the Viking Age." *European Journal of Archaeology* 17(4): 634–55.

Reid, C. S. (Paddy). 1992. "Here Be Dragons: The Indian Trade Gun Side Plates from the Ballynacree Site (DKKp-8) Kenora." *KEWA* (Newsletter of the Ontario Archaeological Society London Chapter) 8: 15–20.

Rivers Cofield, Sara. 2010. "Why Keep a Crooked Sixpence: Religion and Magic at a Jesuit Plantation in St. Inigoes, Maryland. *Maryland Archaeology* 46(1 & 2): 60–70.

———. 2014. "Keeping a Crooked Sixpence: Coin Magic and Religion in the Colonial Chesapeake." *Historical Archaeology* 48(3): 84–105.

Saunders, Nicholas J. 2003. "Crucifix, Calvary, and Cross: Materiality and Spirituality in Great War Landscapes." *World Archaeology* 35(1): 7–21.

Spencer, Ann. 2003. *And Round Me Rings: Bell Tales and Folklore*. Toronto: Tundra Books.

Wehmeyer, Stephen C. 2017. "From the Back of the Mirror: 'Quicksilver,' Tinfoil, and the Shimmer of Sorcery in African-American Vernacular Magic." *Magic, Ritual, and Witchcraft* 12(2): 163–85.

Willmott, Hugh, and Adam Daubney. 2020. "Of Saints, Sows or Smiths? Copper-Brazed Iron Handbells in Early Medieval England." *Archaeological Journal* 177(1): 63–82.

Minerals/Lithics/Soils

Boivin, N., and M. A. Owoc, eds. 2004. *Soils, Stones and Symbols: Cultural Perceptions of the Mineral World*. London: UCL Press.

Brennan, Martin. 1994. *The Stones of Time: Calendars, Sundials, and Stone Chambers of Ancient Ireland*. Rochester, VT: Inner Traditions International.

Callahan, Kevin L. 2000. "Pica, Geophagy, and Rock Art: Ingestion of Rock Powder and Clay by Humans and Its Implications for the Production of Some Rock Art on a Global Basis." Society for American Archaeology Conference, Philadelphia, PA, 8 April 2000.

Dowd, Marion. 2018. "Bewitched by an Elf Dart: Fairy Archaeology, Folk Magic and Traditional Medicine in Ireland." *Cambridge Archaeological Journal* 28(3): 451–73.

Duffin, Christopher J., and Jane P. Davidson. 2011. "Geology and the Dark Side." *Proceedings of the Geologists' Association* 122(1): 7–15.

Evans, Joan. (1922) 2004. *Magical Jewels of the Middle Ages and Renaissance*. London: Constable.

Landa, Edward R., and Christian Feller. 2009. *Soil and Culture*. Netherlands: Springer.

Lecouteux, Claude. 2011. *A Lapidary of Sacred Stones*. Rochester, VT: Inner Traditions.

Naidu, Maheshvari. 2011. "Animated Environment: Animism and the Environment Revisited." *Journal of Dharma* 36(3): 257–73.

Sagiv, Idit. 2018. "Victory of Good over Evil? Amuletic Animal Images on Roman Engraved Gems." In *Material Approaches to Roman Magic: Occult Objects and Supernatural Substances*, ed. Adam Parker and Stuart Mckie, 45–56. Oxford: Oxbow Books.

Smith, Kevin P. 2016. "The Colour of Belief: Objects of Jasper, Opal, Chalcedony, and Obsidian from the Reykholt Churches." In *Reykholt: The Church Excavations*, ed. Guðrún Sveibjarnardóttir, 230–42. Snorrastofa: The National Museum of Iceland and University of Iceland Press.

Spence, K. 1999. "Red, White and Black: Colour in Building Stone in Ancient Egypt." *Cambridge Archaeological Journal* 9: 114–17.

Sullivan, Kelsey Jean. 2017. "Caching It In: Local Patterns in Ancient Maya Ritual Caches of Eccentric Lithics within the Belize Valley." Master's thesis, Northern Arizona University.

Taçon, Paul S. C. 1991. "The Power of Stone: Symbolic Aspects of Stone Use and Development in Western Arnhem Land, Australia." *Antiquity* 65: 192–207.

———. 2004. "Ochre, Clay, Stone and Art: The Symbolic Importance of Minerals as Life Force among Aboriginal Peoples of Northern and Central Australia." In *Soils, Stones and Symbols: Cultural Perceptions of the Mineral World*, ed. N. Boivin and M. A. Owoc, 31–42. London: UCL Press.

Williams, Howard. 2016. "Citations in Stone: The Material World of Hogbacks." *European Journal of Archaeology* 19(3): 497–518.

Numbers

Aldhouse-Green, Miranda. 2004. "Paths of Perception: Ways of Seeing, Ways of Telling." In *An Archaeology of Images: Iconology and Cosmology in Iron Age and Roman Europe*, 174–214. London: Routledge.

Augé, C. Riley. 2014. "Embedded Implication of Cultural Worldviews in the Use and Pattern of Magical Material Culture." *Historical Archaeology* 48(3): 166–78.

Crump, Thomas. 1992. *The Anthropology of Numbers*. Cambridge: Cambridge University Press.

Hemenway, Priya. 2005. *Divine Proportion: Phi in Art, Nature, and Science*. New York: Sterling Publishing.

Incenti, Manuela. 2002. "Solar Geometry in Italian Cistercian Architecture." *Archeoastronomy: The Journal of Astronomy in Culture* 16: 3–23.

———. 2013. "Astronomical Knowledge in the Sacred Architecture of the Middle Ages in Italy." *Nexus Netw J* 15(3): 503–26.

Lawlor, Robert. 1982. *Sacred Geometry: Philosophy and Practice*. London: Thames and Hudson.

Morley, Iain, and Colin Renfrew, eds. 2010. *The Archaeology of Measurement: Comprehending Heaven, Earth and Time in Ancient Societies*. Cambridge: Cambridge University Press.

Schimmel, Annemarie. 1993. *The Mystery of Numbers*. Oxford: Oxford University Press.

Symbols, Designs, and Images

Aldhouse-Green, Miranda. 2004. *An Archaeology of Images: Iconology and Cosmology in Iron Age and Roman Europe*. London: Routledge.

Barbeau, Marius. 1950. *Totem Poles I: According to Crests and Topics*. Ottawa: National Museum of Canada.

———. 1950. *Totem Poles II: According to Location*. Ottawa: National Museum of Canada.

Baugher, Sherene, and Frederick Winter. 1983. "Early American Gravestones: Archaeological Perspectives on Three Cemeteries of Old New York." *Archaeology* 36(5): 46–53.

Benes, Peter, ed. 1976. *Puritan Gravestone Art*. The Dublin Seminar for New England Folklife Annual Proceedings 1976. Boston: Boston University.

———. 1978. *Puritan Gravestone Art II*. The Dublin Seminar for New England Folklife Annual Proceedings 1978. Boston: Boston University.

———. 1992. *Wonders of the Invisible World: 1600–1900*. The Dublin Seminar for New England Folklife Annual Proceedings 1992. Boston: Boston University.

Binder, Pearl. 1972. *Magic Symbols of the World*. London: Hamlyn.

Branson, Oscar T. 1976. *Fetishes and Carvings of the Southwest*. Tucson: Treasure Chest Publications.

Brennan, Martin. 1994. *The Stones of Time: Calendars, Sundials, and Stone Chambers of Ancient Ireland*. Rochester, VT: Inner Traditions International.

Callahan, Kevin L. 2000. "Pica, Geophagy, and Rock Art: Ingestion of Rock Powder and Clay by Humans and Its Implications for the Production of Some Rock Art on a Global Basis." Society for American Archaeology Conference, Philadelphia, PA, 8 April 2000.

Caple, Chris. 2012. "The Apotropaic Symbolled Threshold to Nevern Castle: Castell Nanhyfer." *Archaeological Journal* 169: 422–52.

Champion, Matthew. 2014. "Ill Wishing on the Walls: The Medieval Graffiti Curses of Norwich Cathedral." *Norfolk Archaeology* XLVI: 61–66.

Chippindale, Christopher, and Paul S. C. Taçon, eds. 1998. *The Archaeology of Rock Art*. Cambridge: Cambridge University Press.

Crosby, Harry W. 1997. *The Cave Paintings of Baja California: Discovering the Great Murals of an Unknown People*. San Diego: Sunbelt Publications.

Davide, Bruno, and Ian J. McNiven, eds. 2018. *The Oxford Handbook of the Archaeology and Anthropology of Rock Art*. Oxford: Oxford University Press.

Davidson, Hilda Ellis. 1989. "Myths and Symbols in Religion and Folklore." *Folklore* 100(2): 131–42.

Dickinson, Tania M. 2005. "Symbols of Protection: The Significance of Animal-Ornamental Shields in Early Anglo-Saxon England." *Medieval Archaeology* 49: 109–63.

Dronfield, Jeremy. 1995. "Subjective Vision and the Source of Irish Megalithic Art." *Antiquity* 69: 539–49.

Duval, Francis Y., and Ivan B. Rigby. 1978. *Early American Gravestone Art in Photographs*. New York: Dover Publications.

Easton, Timothy. 1988. "Apotropaic Marks, Scribed and Scratched in Barns and Houses." *Newsletter*, Bury St. Edmonds, Suffolk: Suffolk Institute of Archaeology, 7–8.

———. 1999. "Scribed and Painted Symbols." In *Vernacular Architecture of the World*, 1997/8, four vols, ed. Paul Oliver, 533–34. Cambridge: Cambridge University Press.

———. 1999. "Ritual Marks on Historic Timber." *Weald and Downland Open Air Museum Magazine* Spring: 22–30.

———. 2011. "Candle Power." *Cornerstone* 32(4): 56–60.

———. 2012. "Burning Issues." *SPAB* Winter 2012: 44–47.

———. 2013. "Plumbing a Spiritual World." *SPAB* Winter 2013: 41–45.

———. 2015. "Like the Circles that You Find." *SPAB* Winter 2015: 51–57.

Easton, Timothy, and Jeremy Hodgkinson. 2013. "Apotropaic Symbols on Cast-Iron Firebacks." *Journal of the Antique Metalware Society* 21: 15–33.

Farbridge, Maurice H. 1970. *Studies in Biblical and Semitic Symbolism*. The Library of Biblical Studies. New York: KTAV Publishing House.

Forbes, Harriette M. (1927) 1967. *Gravestones of Early New England and the Men Who Made Them, 1653–1800*. New York: Da Capo Press.

Fox, William A. 1991. "The Serpent's Copper Scales." *Wanikan* 91(3): 3–15.

———. 1992. "Dragon Side Plates from York Factory: A New Twist on an Old Tail." *Manitoba Archaeological Journal* 2(2): 21–35.

Gage, Mary Elaine, and James E. Gage. 2003. *Stories Carved in Stone: The Story of the Dummer Family, the Merrimac Valley Gravestone Carvers, and the Newbury Carved Stones, 1636–1735*. Amesbury: Powwow River Books.

Gell, Alfred. 1992. "The Technology of Enchantment and the Enchantment of Technology." In *Anthropology, Art, and Aesthetics*, ed. Jeremy Coote and Anthony Shelton, 40–63. Oxford: Clarendon Press.

———. 1998. *Art and Agency: An Anthropological Theory*. Oxford: Clarendon Press.

Gheorghiu, Dragos, and Ann Cyphers, eds. 2010. *Anthropomorphic and Zoomorphic Miniature Figures in Eurasia, Africa and Meso-America: Morphology, Materiality, Technology, Function and Context*. Bar International Series 2138. Oxford: Archaeopress.

Gibson, Claire. 2001. *Signs & Symbols: An Illustrated Guide to Their Meaning and Origins*. New York: Barnes & Noble.

Greer, John, and Mavis Greer. 1998. "Dark Zone Rock Art in North America." In *Rock Art Papers, Vol. 13*, ed. Ken Hedges, 135–44. San Diego: San Diego Museum Papers 35.

———. 1999. "Handprints in Montana Rock Art." *Plains Anthropologist* 44(167): 59–71.

Gruia, Ana Maria. 2007. "Magic in the House: Functions of Images on Medieval Stove Tiles from Transylvania, Moldavia and Walachia." *Studia Patzinaka* 5: 7–46.

Halperin, Christina T., Katherine A. Faust, Rhonda Taube, and Aurore Giguet, eds. 2009. *Mesoamerican Figurines: Small-Scale Indices of Large-Scale Phenomena*. Gainesville: University Press of Florida.

Horn, Christian, Johan Ling, Ulf Bertilsson, and Rich Potter. 2018. "By All Means Necessary—2.5D and 3D Recording of Surfaces in the Study of Southern Scandinavian Rock Art." *Open Archaeology* 4: 81–96.

Huyler, Stephen. 1995. *Painted Prayers: Women's Art in Village India*. New York. Rizzoli.

Insoll, Timothy, ed. 2017. *The Oxford Handbook of Prehistoric Figurines*. Oxford: Oxford University Press.

Keister, Douglas. 2004. *Stories in Stone: A Field Guide to Cemetery Symbolism and Iconography*. New York: MJF Books.

Keyser, James D., and David S. Whitley. 2006. "Sympathetic Magic in Western North American Rock Art." *American Antiquity* 71(1): 3–26.

Kimball, Jane A. 2004. *Trench Art: An Illustrated History*. London: Silverpenny Press.

Kristoffersen, Siv. 2010. "Half Beast—Half Man: Hybrid Figures in Animal Art." *World Archaeology* 12(2): 261–72.

Layard, John. 1937. "Labyrinth Ritual in South India: Threshold and Tattoo Designs." *Folklore* 48(2): 115–82.

Lee, Molly, ed. 1999. *Not Just a Pretty Face: Dolls and Human Figurines in Alaska Native Cultures*. Fairbanks: University of Alaska Museum.

Lewis-Williams, J. David, and Thomas A. Dowson. 1990. "Through the Veil: San Rock Paintings and the Rock Face." *South African Archaeological Bulletin* 45: 5–16.

Lipponcott, Kerry. 2015. "A Continent-Wide View of Marine Shell Mask Gorgets." *Archaeology in Montana* 56(1): 31–50.

Lloyd, Virgina, John Dean, and Jennifer Westwood. 2001. "Burn Marks as Evidence of Apotropaic Practices in Houses, Farm Buildings and Churches in Post-Medieval East Anglia." In *A Permeability of Boundaries? New Approaches to the Archaeology of Art, Religion and Folklore*, ed. Robert J. Wallis and Kenneth Lymer, 57–70. Oxford: John and Erica Hedges, Ltd.

Ludwig, Allan I. 1966. *Graven Images: New England Stonecarving and Its Symbols, 1650–1815*. Middletown: Wesleyan University Press.

Mack, John, ed. 1994. *Masks and the Art of Expression*. New York: Harry N. Abrams.

MacLeod, Mindy, and Bernard Mees. 2006. *Runic Amulets and Magic Objects*. Suffolk: Boydell Press.

McCleary, Timothy P. 2015. *Crow Indian Rock Art: Indigenous Perspectives and Interpretations*. New York: Routledge.

McManis, Kent. 1998. *A Guide to Zuni Fetishes & Carvings: Vol. I, The Animals & The Carvers*. Tucson: Treasure Chest Books.

———. 1998. *A Guide to Zuni Fetishes & Carvings: Vol. II, The Materials & The Carvers*. Tucson: Treasure Chest Books.

Meeson, B. 2005. "Ritual Marks and Graffiti: Curiosities or Meaningful Symbols?" *Vernacular Architecture* 36: 41–48.

Mellinkoff, Ruth. 2004. *Averting Demons: The Protective Power of Medieval Visual Motifs and Themes*. Two volumes. Los Angeles: Ruth Mellinkoff Publications.

Mendel-Geberovich, Anat, Arie Shaus, Shira Faigenbaum-Golovin, Barak Sober, Michael Cordonsky, Eli Piasetzky, and Israel Finkestein. 2017. "A Brand New Old Inscription: Arad Ostracon 16 Rediscovered via Multispectral Imaging." *BASOR* 378: 113–25.

Mercier, Jacques. 1979. *Ethiopian Magic Scrolls*. New York: George Braziller.

Mitchiner, Michael. 1986. *Medieval Pilgrim and Secular Badges*. London: Hawkins Publications.

Morwood, M. J. 2002. *Visions from the Past: The Archaeology of Australian Aboriginal Art*. Washington, DC: Smithsonian Institution Scholarly Press.

Murray, M. A. 1946. "Wax or Clay Images." *Folklore* 57(2): 93.

O'Connell, Mark, and Raje Airey. 2005. *The Complete Encyclopedia of Signs & Symbols*. London: Hermes House.

Oliver, Paul, ed. 1980. *Shelter, Sign & Symbol*. Woodstock: The Overlook Press.

Pastoureau, Michael. 2003. *The Devil's Cloth: A History of Stripes*. Princeton: Princeton University Press.

Patterson, Alex. 1992. *A Field Guide to Rock Art Symbols of the Greater Southwest*. Boulder: Johnson Books.

Reid, C. S. (Paddy). 1992. "Here Be Dragons: The Indian Trade Gun Side Plates from the Ballynacree site (DKKp-8) Kenora." *KEWA* (Newsletter of the Ontario Archaeological Society London Chapter) 8: 15–20.

Robb, John E. 1998. "The Archaeology of Symbols." *Annual Review of Anthropology* 27: 329–46.

Ryan, Kathleen, and Pam J. Crabtree, eds. 1995. *The Symbolic Role of Animals in Archaeology*. Philadelphia: MASCA, University of Pennsylvania Museum of Archaeology and Anthropology.

Ryken, Leland, James C. Wilhoit, and Tremper Longman III, eds. 1998. *Dictionary of Biblical Imagery*. Downers Grove: International Press.

Sagiv, Idit. 2018. "Victory of Good over Evil? Amuletic Animal Images on Roman Engraved Gems." In *Material Approaches to Roman Magic: Occult Objects and Supernatural Substances*, ed. Adam Parker and Stuart Mckie, 45–56. Oxford: Oxbow Books.

Saunders, Nicholas J. 2003. "Crucifix, Calvary, and Cross: Materiality and Spirituality in Great War Landscapes." *World Archaeology* 35(1): 7–21.

———. 2003. *Trench Art: Materialities and Memories of War*. London: Berg.

Saunders, Nicholas J., and Mark J. R. Dennis. 2003. *Craft and Conflict: Masonic Trench Art and Military Memorabilia*. London: Savannah Publications.

Schroedl, Alan. 1977. "The Grand Canyon Figurine Complex." *American Antiquity* 42(2): 254–65.

Smith, Marvin T., and Julie Barnes Smith. 1989. "Engraved Shell Masks in North America." *Southeastern Archaeology* 8(1): 9–18.

Stokes, William Michael, and William Lee Stokes. 1980. *Messages on Stone: Selections of Native Western Rock Art*. Salt Lake City: Starstone Publishing.

Turpin, Solveg A., ed. 1994. *Shamanism and Rock Art in North America*. Special Publication 1. San Antonio: Rock Art Foundation, Inc.

VanPool, Christine S., and Todd VanPool. 2007. *Signs of the Casas Grandes Shamans*. Salt Lake City: University of Utah Press.

Wahlman, M. S. 2001. *Signs and Symbols: African Images in African American Quilts*. Rev. ed. Atlanta: Tinwood Books.

Whitley, David S. 2005. *Introduction to Rock Art Research*. Walnut Creek: Left Coast Press.

Textiles and Clothing

Costello, Jessica. 2014. "Tracing the Footsteps of Ritual: Concealed Footwear in America." *Historical Archaeology* 48(3): 35–51.

Douny, Laurence. 2017. "Connecting Worlds through Silk: The Cosmological Significance of Sheen in West African Talismanic Magic." *Magic, Ritual, and Witchcraft* 12(2): 186–209.

Eastop, Dinah. 2001. "Garments Deliberately Concealed in Buildings." In *A Permeability of Boundaries? New Approaches to the Archaeology of Art, Religion and Folklore*, ed. Robert J. Wallis and Kenneth Lymer, 79–83. Oxford: John and Erica Hedges, British Archaeology Reports.

———. 2006. "Outside In: Making Sense of the Deliberate Concealment of Garments within Buildings." *Textile* 3: 238–55.

Geisler, Jessica W. 2003. "Tracing the Footsteps of Ritual: Concealed Footwear in Quincy, Massachusetts." Master's thesis, University of Massachusetts.

Goubitz, Olaf. 1984. "The Drawing and Registration of Archaeological Footwear." *Studies in Conservation* 29(4): 187–96.

Hauser-Schäublin, Brigitta, Marie-Louise Nabholz-Kartaschoff, and Urs Ramseyer. 1991. *Balinese Textiles*. Basel: Periplus Editions (HK) Ltd.

Houlbrook, Ceri. 2013. "Ritual, Recycling and Recontextualization: Putting the Concealed Shoe in Context." *Cambridge Archaeological Journal* 23(1): 99–112.

———. 2016. "The Other Shoe: Fragmentation in the Post-Medieval Home." *Cambridge Archaeological Journal* 27(2): 261–74.

Loren, Diana Di Paolo. 2011. *The Archaeology of Clothing and Bodily Adornment in Colonial America*. Gainesville: University of Florida Press.

Lymer, Kenneth. 2004. "Rags and Rock Art: The Landscapes of Holy Site Pilgrimage in the Republic of Kazakhstan." *World Archaeology* 36(1): 158–72.

Mohan, Urmila. 2017. "Clothing as a Technology of Enchantment: Gaze and Glaze in Hindu Garments." *Magic, Ritual, and Witchcraft* 12(2): 225–44.

Paine, Sheila. 2008. *Embroidered Textiles: Traditional Patterns from Five Continents*. London: Thames and Hudson.

Pastoureau, Michael. 2003. *The Devil's Cloth: A History of Stripes*. Princeton: Princeton University Press.

Swann, June. 1996. "Shoes Concealed in Buildings." *Costume* 30: 56–69.

Textile Society of America. 1996. *Sacred and Ceremonial Textiles*. Chicago: Proceeding of the Fifth Biennial Symposium of the Textile Society of America.

Veres, Maya. 2005. "Introduction to the Analysis of Archaeological Footwear." *Australian Historical Archaeology* 23: 89–66.

Welters, Linda, ed. 1999. *Folk Dress in Europe and Anatolia: Beliefs about Protection and Fertility*. Oxford: Berg.

SENSORY AND LANDSCAPE STUDIES

General

Abram, David. 1996. *The Spell of the Sensuous: Perception and Language in a More-Than-Human World*. New York: Vintage Books.

Ackerman, Diane. 1991. *A Natural History of the Senses*. New York: Vintage Books.

Árnason, Arnar, Nicolas Ellison, Jo Vergunst, and Andrew Whitehouse, eds. 2012. *Landscapes Beyond Land: Routes, Aesthetics, Narratives*. New York: Berghahn Books.

Bodenhamer, David J., John Corrigan, and Trevor M. Harris, eds. 2015. *Deep Maps and Spatial Narratives*. Bloomington: Indiana University Press.

Bull, Michael, and Jon P. Mitchell, eds. 2015. *Ritual, Performance, and the Senses*. London: Bloomsbury Academic.

Classen, Constance. 1993. *Worlds of Sense: Exploring the Senses in History and Across Cultures*. London: Routledge.

Coones, P. 1985. "One Landscape or Many? A Geographical Perspective." *Landscape History* 25: 5–12.

Evans, Christopher. 1985. "Tradition and the Cultural Landscape: An Archaeology of Place." *Archaeological Review from Cambridge* 4(1): 80–94.

Fahlander, Fredrik, and Anna Kjellström, eds. 2010. *Making Sense of Things: Archaeologies of Sensory Perception*. Stockholm: Stockholm University.

Faycurry, J. 2013. "Approaches to Sensory Landscape Archaeology." *Spectrum Online Journal* 67: 67–77.

Gray, Madeleine. 2001. "The Pilgrimage as Ritual Space." In *Holy Ground: Theoretical Issues Relating to the Landscape and Material Culture of Ritual Space*, ed. A. T. Smith and A. Brookes, 91–97. Cardiff: BAR International Series 956.

Hamilakis, Yannis. 2013. *Archaeology and the Senses: Human Experience, Memory, and Affect*. New York: Cambridge University Press.

Hamilton, Sue, Edward Herring, Mike Seager Thomas, Ruth Whitehouse, Keri Brown, and Pamela Combs. 2006. "Phenomenology in Practice: Towards a Methodology for a Subjective Approach." *European Journal of Archaeology* 9(1): 31–71.

Harmansah, Ömür, ed. 2014. *Of Rocks and Water: Towards an Archaeology of Place*. Oxford: Oxbow Books.

Herring, Peter Charles. 2009. "Framing Perceptions of the Historic Landscape." *Scottish Geographical Journal* 125(1): 61–67.

Hoffer, P. C. 2003. *Sensory Worlds in Early America*. Baltimore: Johns Hopkins University Press.

Howard, Phil. 2007. *Archaeological Surveying and Mapping: Recording and Depicting the Landscape*. London: Routledge.

Howes, David, ed. 1994. *The Varieties of Sensory Experience: A Sourcebook in the Anthropology of the Senses*. Toronto: University of Toronto Press.

———. 2003. *Sensual Relations: Engaging the Senses in Culture and Social Theory*. Ann Arbor: Michigan University Press.

———. 2005. *Empire of the Senses: The Sensual Culture Reader*. Oxford: Berg.

Howes, David, and Constance Classen. 1994. "Sounding Sensory Profiles." In *The Varieties of Sensory Experience: A Sourcebook in the Anthropology of the Senses*, ed. David Howes, 257–88. Toronto: University of Toronto Press.

———. 2013. *Ways of Sensing: Understanding the Senses in Society*. London: Routledge.

Hume, L. 2007. *Portals: Opening Doorways to Other Realities through the Senses*. Oxford: Berg.

Hurcombe, Linda. 2007. "A Sense of Materials and Sensory Perception in Concepts of Materiality." *World Archaeology* 39(4): 532–45.

Llobera, Marcos. 1996. "Exploring the Topography of Mind: GIS, Social Space, and Archaeology." *Antiquity* 70: 612–22.

Nelson, Louis P. 2007. "Sensing the Sacred: Anglican Material Religion in Early South Carolina." *Winterthur Portfolio* 41(4): 203–38.

Pink, Sarah. 2015. *Doing Sensory Ethnography*. 2nd ed. London: SAGE Publishing.

Rainbird, Paul. 2008. "The Body and the Senses: Implications for Landscape Archaeology." In *Handbook of Landscape Archaeology*, ed. Bruno David and Julian Thomas, 263–70. Walnut Creek: Left Coast Press.

Ryden, Kent C. 1993. *Mapping the Invisible Landscape: Folklore, Writing, and the Sense of Place*. Iowa City: University of Iowa Press.

Stoller, Paul. 1989. *The Taste of Ethnographic Things: The Senses in Anthropology*. Philadelphia: University of Pennsylvania Press.

Tilley, Christopher. 1994. *A Phenomenology of Landscape: Places, Paths, and Monuments*. Oxford: Berg.

Landscape/Seascape

Anderson, William. 2004. "An Archaeology of Late Antique Pilgrim Flasks." *Anatolian Studies* 54: 79–93.

Ashmore, Wendy. 2008. "Visions of the Cosmos: Ceremonial Landscapes and Civic Plans." In *Handbook of Landscape Archaeology*, ed. Bruno David and Julian Thomas, 167–75. Walnut Creek: Left Coast Press.

Bauer, Brian S. 1998. *The Sacred Landscape of the Inca: The Cusco Ceque System*. Austin: University of Texas Press.

Boutsikas, Efrosyni, and Clive Ruggles. 2011. "Temples, Stars, and Ritual Landscapes: The Potential for Archaeoastronomy in Ancient Greece." *American Journal of Archaeology* 115(1): 55–68.

Bradley, Richard. 2000. *An Archaeology of Natural Places*. London: Routledge.

Brady, James E., and Andrea Stone. 1986. "Naj Tunich: Entrance to the Maya Underworld." *Archaeology* 39(6): 18–25.

Brady, James E., and Wendy Ashmore. 1999. "Mountains, Caves, Water: Ideational Landscapes of the Ancient Maya." In *Archaeologies of Landscape: Contemporary Perspectives*, ed. Wendy Ashmore and A. Bernard Knapp, 124–45. Malden: Blackwell Publishers.

Brady, James E., and Keith M. Prufer, eds. 2005. *In the Maw of the Earth Monster: Mesoamerican Ritual Cave Use*. Austin: University of Texas Press.

———. 2005. *Stone Houses and Earth Lords: Maya Religion in the Cave Context*. Boulder: University Press of Colorado.

Brennan, Martin. 1994. *The Stones of Time: Calendars, Sundials, and Stone Chambers of Ancient Ireland*. Rochester, VT: Inner Traditions International.

Brink, Stefan, and Saebjorg W. Nordeide, eds. 2013. *Sacred Sites and Holy Places: Exploring the Sacralization of Landscape through Time and Space*. Turnhout, Belgium: Brepols.

Brody, Hugh. 1988. *Maps and Dreams: Indians and the British Columbian Frontier*. Vancouver: Douglas & McIntyre.

Brown, Linda A. 2004. "Dangerous Places and Wild Spaces: Creating Meaning with Materials and Spaces at Contemporary Maya Shrines on El Duende Mountain." *Journal of Archaeological Method and Theory* 11: 31–58.

Brown, Linda A., and Kitty Emery. 2008. "Negotiations with the Animal Forest: Hunting Shrines in the Guatemalan Highlands." *Journal of Archaeological Method and Theory* 15: 300–37.

Candy, Julie. 2005. "Landscape and Perception: The Medieval Pilgrimage to Santiago de Compostela from an Archaeological Perspective." *eSharp* 4: 1–18.

Carroll, Alex K., Maria Nieves Zedeño, and Richard W. Stoffle. 2004. "Landscapes of the Ghost Dance: A Cartography of Numic Ritual." *Journal of Archaeological Method and Theory* 11(2): 127–56.

David, Bruno, Max Pivoru, William Pivoru, Michael Green, Bryce Barker, James F. Weiner, Douglas Simala, Thomas Kokents, Lisa Araho, and John Dop. 2008. "Living Landscapes of the Dead: Archaeology of the Afterworld among the Rumu of Papua New Guinea." In *Handbook of Landscape Archaeology*, ed. Bruno David and Julian Thomas, 158–66. Walnut Creek: Left Coast Press.

Dowd, Marion. 2015. *The Archaeology of Caves in Ireland*. Oxford: Oxbow.

Eckhardt, Hella, Peter Brewer, Sophie Hay, and Sarah Poppy. 2009. "Roman Barrows and Their Landscape Context: a GIS Case Study at Bartlow, Cambridgeshire." *Britannia* XL: 65–98.

Fontijn, D. 2007. "The Significance of 'Invisible' Places." *World Archaeology* 39(1): 70–83.

Fowler, C. T. 2002. "Altar Rituals in Thirdspace." In *Ethnobiology and Biocultural Diversity: Proceedings of the Seventh International Congress of Ethnobiology*, ed. John R. Stepp, Felice S. Wyndham, and Rebecca K. Zarger, 152–70. Athens, GA: International Society of Ethnobiology.

Gulliford, Andrew. 2000. *Sacred Objects and Sacred Places: Preserving Tribal Traditions*. Boulder: University Press of Colorado.

Harmansah, Ömür. 2015. *Place, Memory, and Healing: An Archaeology of Anatolian Rock Monuments*. London: Routledge.

Harrison-Buck, Eleanor. 2012. "Architecture as Animate Landscape: Circular Shrines in the Ancient Maya Lowlands." *American Anthropologist* 114: 64–80.

Higuchi, Tadahiko. 1983. *The Visual and Spatial Structure of Landscapes*. Cambridge, MA: MIT Press.

Incenti, Manuela. 2002. "Solar Geometry in Italian Cistercian Architecture." *Archeoastronomy: The Journal of Astronomy in Culture* 16: 3–23.

———. 2013. "Astronomical Knowledge in the Sacred Architecture of the Middle Ages in Italy." *Nexus Netw J* 15(3): 503–26.

Landau, Kristin. 2015. "Spatial Logic and Maya City Planning: The Case for Cosmology." *Cambridge Archaeological Journal* 25(1): 275–92.

Lane, Belden C. 1988. *Landscapes of the Sacred: Geography and Narrative in American Spirituality*. New York: Paulist Press.

Lecouteux, Claude. 2015. *Demons and Spirits of the Land: Ancestral Lore and Practices*. Rochester, VT: Inner Traditions.

Lund, Julie. 2008. "Banks, Borders, and Bodies of Water in a Viking Age Mentality." *Journal of Wetland Archaeology* 8: 51–70.

Lymer, Kenneth. 2004. "Rags and Rock Art: The Landscapes of Holy Site Pilgrimage in the Republic of Kazakhstan." *World Archaeology* 36(1): 158–72.

Mackian, Sara. 2004. "Mapping Reflexive Communities: Visualizing the Geographies of Emotion." *Social and Cultural Geography* 5(4): 615–33.

McNiven, Ian J. 2008. "Sentient Sea: Seascapes as Spiritscapes." In *Handbook of Landscape Archaeology*, ed. Bruno David and Julian Thomas, 149–57. Walnut Creek: Left Coast Press.

Milne, Courtney. 1995. *Sacred Places in North America: A Journey into the Medicine Wheel*. New York: Stewart, Tabori & Chang.

Moore, Jerry D. 2004. "The Social Basis of Sacred Spaces in the Prehispanic Andes: Ritual Landscapes of the Dead in Chimú and Inka Societies." *Journal of Archaeological Method and Theory* 11(1): 83–124.

Moyes, Holley. 2001. "The Cave as Cosmogram: The Use of GIS in an Intrasite Spatial Analysis of the Main Chamber of Actun Tunichil Muknal, a Maya Ceremonial Cave in Western Belize." Master's thesis, Florida Atlantic University.

———, ed. 2013. *Sacred Darkness: A Global Perspective on the Ritual Use of Caves*. Boulder: University Press of Colorado.

Munn, Nancy D. 2003. "Excluded Spaces: The Figure in the Australian Aboriginal Landscape." In *The Anthropology of Space and Place: Locating Culture*, ed. Setha M. Low and Denise Lawrence-Zúñiga, 92–109. Malden: Blackwell Publishing.

Naidu, Maheshvari. 2011. "Animated Environment: Animism and the Environment Revisited." *Journal of Dharma* 36(3): 257–73.

Racoviteanu, Adina E. 2004. "Sacred Mountains and Glacier Archaeology in the Andes." Master's thesis, University of Colorado.

Racoviteanu, Adina, Todd Ackerman, Mark Williams, and William Manley. 2002. "High Altitude Ceremonial Sites in the Peruvian Andes: GIS Modeling." Boulder Carbon Climate and Society Initiative and Long-Term Ecological Research.

Ray, Himansha Prabha. 1994. "Kanheri: The Archaeology of an Early Buddhist Pilgrimage Centre in Western India." *World Archaeology* 26(1): 35–46.

Rodwell, Warwick. 1981. *Archaeology of the English Church: The Study of Historic Churches and Churchyards*. London: B.T. Batsford.

———. 1989. *Church Archaeology*. London: English Heritage.

Romain, William F. 2015. *An Archaeology of the Sacred: Adena-Hopewell Astronomy and Landscape Archaeology*. Olmsted Township: The Ancient Earthworks Project.

Stewart, Andrew M., Darren Keith, and Joan Scottie. 2004. "Caribou Crossings and Cultural Meanings: Placing Traditional Knowledge and Archaeology in Context in an Inuit Landscape." *Journal of Archaeological Method and Theory* 11(2): 183–211.

Stopford, J. 1994. "Some Approaches to the Archaeology of Christian Pilgrimage." *World Archaeology* 26(1): 57–72.

Sundstrom, Linea. 2003. "Sacred Islands: An Exploration of Religion and Landscape in the Northern Great Plain." In *Islands on the Plains: Ecological, Social, and Ritual Use of Landscapes*, ed. Marcel Kornfeld and Alan J. Osborn, 258–300. Salt Lake City: University of Utah Press.

Szczepanik, Pawet, and Stawomir Wadyl. 2014. "A Comparative Analysis of Early Medieval North-West Slavonic and West Baltic Sacred Landscapes: An Introduction to the Problems." *Networks and Neighbours* 2(1): 1–19.

Taçon, Paul S. C. 1999. "Identifying Ancient Sacred Landscapes in Australia: From Physical to Social." In *Archaeologies of Landscape: Contemporary Perspectives*, ed. Wendy Ashmore and A. B. Knapp, 33–57. Oxford: Blackwell.

Tilley, Christopher, and W. Bennett. 2001. "An Archaeology of Supernatural Places: The Case of West Penwith." *The Journal of the Royal Anthropological Institute* 7(2): 335–62.

Tuan, Yi-Fu. 1979. *Landscapes of Fear*. New York: Pantheon Books.

Veit, Richard F., Sherene B. Baugher, and Gerard P. Scharfenberger. 2009. "Historical Archaeology of Religious Sites and Cemeteries." *Historical Archaeology* 43(1): 1–11.

Weightman, Barbara A. 1996. "Sacred Landscapes and the Phenomenon of Light." *Geographical Review* 86(1): 59–71.

Westerdahl, C. 2005. "Seal on Land, Elk at Sea: Notes on and Applications of the Ritual Landscape at the Seaboard." *The International Journal of Nautical Archaeology* 34(1): 2–23.

Willsher, Betty. 1985. *Understanding Scottish Graveyards: An Interpretive Approach*. Edinburgh: Council for British Archaeology Scotland.

Zucchi, Alberta. 1997. "Tombs and Testaments: Mortuary Practices during the Seventeenth to Nineteenth Centuries in the Spanish-Venezuelan Catholic Tradition." *Historical Archaeology* 31(2): 31–42.

Affective

Fleisher, Jeffrey, and Neil Norman, eds. 2016. *The Archaeology of Anxiety: The Materiality of Anxiousness, Worry, and Fear*. New York: Springer.

Pink, Sarah. 2015. *Doing Sensory Ethnography*. 2nd ed. London: SAGE Publishing.

Tuan, Yi-Fu. 1979. *Landscapes of Fear*. New York: Pantheon Books.

Williams, Howard. 2007. "The Emotive Force of Early Medieval Mortuary Practices." *Archaeological Review from Cambridge* 22(1): 107–23.

Auditory

Bruchez, Margaret Sabom. 2007. "Artifacts that Speak for Themselves: Sounds Underfoot in Mesoamerica." *Journal of Anthropological Archaeology* 26: 47–64.

Bull, Michael, ed. 2003. *The Auditory Culture Reader*. Oxford: Berg.

Corbin, Alain. 1998. *Village Bells: Sound and Meaning in the Nineteenth-Century French Countryside*. New York: Columbia University Press.

Drobnick, J., ed. 2004. *Aural Cultures*. Toronto: YYZ Books.

Gourlay, K. A. 1975. *Sound Producing Instruments in Traditional Society: A Study of Esoteric Instruments and Their Role in Male-Female Relations*. Canberra: Australian National University Press.

Hendy, David. 2013. *Noise: A Human History of Sound and Listening*. New York: ECCO, HarperCollins.

Hosler, Dorothy. 1995. "Sound, Color and Meaning in the Metallurgy of Ancient West Mexico." *World Archaeology* 27(1): 100–15.

Howey, Meghan C. L. 2011. "Colonial Encounters, European Kettles, and the Magic of Mimesis in the Late Sixteenth and Early Seventeenth Century Indigenous Northeast and Great Lakes." *International Journal of Historical Archaeology* 15: 329–57.

Kicking Woman, Kevin Dale. 2014. "Blackfoot Ceremony through the Power of Song." Master's thesis, University of Montana.

Lawson, Graeme, and Chris Scarre, eds. 2006. *Archaeoacoustics*. Cambridge, UK: McDonald Institute for Archaeological Research.

Mills, Barbara J., and T. J. Ferguson. 2008. "Animate Objects: Shell Trumpets and Ritual Networks in the Greater Southwest." *Journal of Archaeological Method and Theory* 15: 338–61.

Nettl, Bruno. 1989. *Blackfoot Musical Thought*. Kent: Kent State University Press.

Parker, Adam. 2018. "'The Bells! The Bells!' Approaching *Tintinnabula* in Roman Britain and Beyond." In *Material Approaches to Roman Magic: Occult Objects and Supernatural Substances*, ed. Adam Parker and Stuart Mckie, 57–68. Oxford: Oxbow Books.

Price, Percival. 1983. *Bells and Man*. Oxford: Oxford University Press.

Rath, Richard Cullen. 2003. *How Early America Sounded*. Ithaca: Cornell University Press.

Rouget, Gilbert. 1985. *Music and Trance: A Theory of the Relations between Music and Possession*. Chicago: University of Chicago Press.

Spencer, Ann. 2003. *And Round Me Rings: Bell Tales and Folklore*. Toronto: Tundra Books.

Taussig, Michael T. 2009. *What Color Is the Sacred?* Chicago: University of Chicago Press.

Watson, Aaron. 2001. "The Sounds of Transformation: Acoustics, Monuments and Ritual in the British Neolithic." In *The Archaeology of Shamanism*, ed. Neil Price, 178–92. London: Routledge.

Willmott, Hugh, and Adam Daubney. 2020. "Of Saints, Sows or Smiths? Copper-Brazed Iron Handbells in Early Medieval England." *Archaeological Journal* 177(1): 63–82.

Gustatory (Taste)

Callahan, Kevin L. 2000. "Pica, Geophagy, and Rock Art: Ingestion of Rock Powder and Clay by Humans and Its Implications for the Production of Some Rock Art on a Global Basis." Society for American Archaeology Conference, Philadelphia, PA, 8 April 2000.

Detienne, M., and J. Vernant, eds. 1989. *The Cuisine of Sacrifice among the Greeks.* Chicago: University of Chicago Press.

Korsmeyer, C., ed. 2005. *The Taste Culture Reader.* Oxford: Berg.

Sutton, D. 2001. "Food and the Senses." *Annual Review of Anthropology* 39: 209–23.

Olfactory

Bartosiewicz, László. 2003. "There's Something Rotten in the State . . . Bad Smells in Antiquity." *European Journal of Archaeology* 6: 175–95.

Classen, Constance, David Howes, and Anthony Synnott, eds. 1994. *Aroma: The Cultural History of Smell.* New York: Routledge.

Drobnick, J., ed. 2006. *The Smell Culture Reader.* Oxford: Berg.

Green, Deborah A. 2011. *The Aroma of Righteousness.* University Park: Penn State University Press.

Harvey, Susan Ashbrook. 2006. *Scents of Salvation: Ancient Christianity and the Olfactory Imagination.* Los Angeles: University of California Press.

Howes, David. 1987. "Olfaction and Transition: An Essay on the Ritual Uses of Smell." *Canadian Review of Anthropology and Sociology* 24(3): 398–416.

Tactility/Haptic

Classen, Constance, ed. 2005. *The Book of Touch.* Oxford: Berg.

Tilley, Christopher. 2004. *The Materiality of Stone Explorations in Landscape Phenomenology.* Oxford: Berg.

Vestibular

Browner, Tara. 2002. *Heartbeat of the People: Music and Dance of the Northern Pow-wow.* Urbana: University of Illinois Press.

Bruchez, Margaret Sabom. 2007. "Artifacts that Speak for Themselves: Sounds Underfoot in Mesoamerica." *Journal of Anthropological Archaeology* 26: 47–64.

Fergusson, Erna. 1931. *Dancing Gods: Indian Ceremonials of New Mexico & Arizona.* Albuquerque: University of New Mexico Press.

Visual

Bakeless, John. (1950) 1961. *America as Seen by Its First Explorers: The Eyes of Discovery.* New York: Dover Publications.

Dronfield, Jeremy. 1995. "Subjective Vision and the Source of Irish Megalithic Art." *Antiquity* 69: 539–49.

Higuchi, Tadahiko. 1983. *The Visual and Spatial Structure of Landscapes*. Cambridge, MA: MIT Press.

Kay, Stephen, and Timothy Sly. 2001. "An Application of Cumulative Viewshed Analysis to a Medieval Archaeological Study: The Beacon System of the Isle of Wight, United Kingdom." *Archaeologia e Calcolatori* 25: 167–79.

Lake, M. W., P. E. Woodman, and S. J. Mithen. 1998. "Tailoring GIS Software for Archaeological Applications: An Example Concerning Viewshed Analysis." *Journal of Archaeological Science* 25: 27–38.

Lock, Gary R., ed. 2000. *Beyond the Map: Archaeology and Spatial Technologies*. Amsterdam: IOS Press.

Lock, Gary R., and Zoran Stančič, eds. 1995. *Archaeology and GIS: A European Perspective*. London: Routledge.

Morgan, David. 1998. *Visual Piety: A History and Theory of Popular Religious Images*. Berkeley: University of California Press.

Nutsford, Daniel, Femke Reitsma, Amber L. Pearson, and Simon Kingham. 2015. "Personalizing the Viewshed: Visibility Analysis from Human Perspective." *Applied Geography* 62: 1–7.

Tilley, Christopher. 1994. *A Phenomenology of Landscape Places, Paths, and Monuments*. Oxford: Berg.

Weightman, Barbara A. 1996. "Sacred Landscapes and the Phenomenon of Light." *Geographical Review* 86(1): 59–71.

Wheatley, David, and Mark Gillings. 2000. "Vision, Perception and GIS: Developing Enriched Approaches to the Study of Archaeological Visibility." In *Beyond the Map: Archaeology and Spatial Technologies*, ed. Gary R. Lock, 1–27. Amsterdam: IOS Press.

MORTUARY STUDIES

Aldhouse-Green, Miranda. 2002. *Dying for the Gods: Human Sacrifice in Iron Age and Roman Europe*. London: Tempus Publishing.

Andrén, Anders. 1993. "Doors to Other Worlds: Scandinavian Death Rituals in Gotlandic Perspective." *Journal of European Archaeology* 1: 33–56.

Arnold, Bettina. 2006. "Gender and Archaeological Mortuary Analysis." In *Handbook of Gender in Archaeology*, ed. Sarah Nelson, 137–70. Lanham: Alta Mira Press.

Arnold, Bettina, and Nancy L. Wicker, eds. 2001. *Gender and the Archaeology of Death*. Walnut Creek: Alta Mira Press.

Baugher, Sherene, and Frederick Winter. 1983. "Early American Gravestones: Archaeological Perspectives on Three Cemeteries of Old New York." *Archaeology* 36(5): 46–53.

Bell, Edward. 1994. *Vestiges of Mortality and Remembrance: A Bibliography on the Historical Archaeology of Cemeteries*. Metuchen: The Scarecrow Press.

Benes, Peter, ed. 1976. *Puritan Gravestone Art*. The Dublin Seminar for New England Folklife Annual Proceedings 1976. Boston: Boston University.

———. 1978. *Puritan Gravestone Art II*. The Dublin Seminar for New England Folklife Annual Proceedings 1978. Boston: Boston University.

———. 1992. Wonders of the Invisible World: 1600–1900. The Dublin Seminar for New England Folklife Annual Proceedings 1992. Boston: Boston University.

Betsinger, Tracy K., Amy B. Scott, and Anatasia Tsaliki, eds. 2020. *The Odd, the Unusual, and the Strange: Bioarchaeological Explorations of Atypical Burials*. Gainesville: University Press of Florida.

Bond, Julie. 1996. "Burnt Offerings: Animal Bone in Anglo-Saxon Cremations." *World Archaeology* 28(1): 76–88.

Brady, James, George Hasemann, and John H. Fogarty. 1995. "Harvest of Bones: Ritual Cave Burial in Honduras." *Archaeology* 48(3): 36–41.

Carr, Christopher. 1995. "Mortuary Practices: Their Social, Philosophical-Religious, Circumstantial, and Physical Determinates." *Journal of Archaeological Method and Theory* 2(2): 105–200.

Crowell, Elizabeth A. 1981. "Philadelphia Gravestones, 1760–1820." *Northeast Historical Archaeology* 10: 23–26.

David, Bruno, Max Pivoru, William Pivoru, Michael Green, Bryce Barker, James F. Weiner, Douglas Simala, Thomas Kokents, Lisa Araho, and John Dop. 2008. "Living Landscapes of the Dead: Archaeology of the Afterworld among the Rumu of Papua New Guinea." In *Handbook of Landscape Archaeology*, ed. Bruno David and Julian Thomas, 158–66. Walnut Creek: Left Coast Press.

Duval, Francis Y., and Ivan B. Rigby. 1978. *Early American Gravestone Art in Photographs*. New York: Dover Publications.

Eriksen, Marianne Hem. 2013. "Doors to the Dead. The Power of Doorways and Thresholds in Viking Age Scandinavia." *Archaeological Dialogues* 20(2): 187–214.

———. 2015. "Portals to the Past: An Archaeology of Doorways, Dwellings, and Ritual Practice in Late Iron Age Scandinavia." PhD diss., University of Oslo.

Forbes, Harriette M. (1927) 1967. *Gravestones of Early New England and the Men Who Made Them, 1653–1800*. New York: Da Capo Press.

Gage, Mary Elaine, and James E. Gage. 2003. *Stories Carved in Stone: The Story of the Dummer Family, the Merrimac Valley Gravestone Carvers, and the Newbury Carved Stones, 1636–1735*. Amesbury: Powwow River Books.

Gilchrist, Roberta. 2008. "Magic for the Dead? The Archaeology of Magic in Later Medieval Burials." *Medieval Archaeology* 52: 119–59.

———. 2012. *Medieval Life: Archaeology and the Life Course*. Woodbridge: Boydell Press.

Gradwohl, David Meyer. 1998. "'Benditcha Sea Vuestra Memoria': Sephardic Jewish Cemeteries in the Caribbean and Eastern North America." *Journal of the Association for Gravestone Studies Markers* 15(vi): 1–29.

Greene, Meg. 2008. *Rest in Peace: A History of American Cemeteries*. Minneapolis: Twenty-First Century Books.

Grinsell, L. V. 1961. "The Breaking of Objects as a Funerary Rite." *Folkore* 72(3): 475–91.

Jones, Jeremy. 1984. *How to Record Graveyards*. London: The Council for British Archaeology and RESCUE.

Jonsson, Kristina. 2007. "Burial Rods and Charcoal Graves: New Light on Old Burial Practices." In *Viking and Medieval Scandinavia*, ed. Stefan Brink, Judy Quinn, and John Hines, 43–73. Belgium: Brepol.

———. 2009. "Dangerous Death and Dangerous Dead: Examples from Scandinavian Burial Practices from the Middle Ages to the Early Modern Period." In *On the Threshold: Burial Archaeology in the Twenty-first Century*, 173–86. Stockholm: Stockholm University.

Keister, Douglas. 2004. *Stories in Stone: A Field Guide to Cemetery Symbolism and Iconography*. New York: MJF Books.

King, Heather A. 1985. "Irish Wayside and Churchyard Crosses, 1600–1700." *Post-Medieval Archaeology* 19: 13–34.

Kirkinen, Tuija. 2017. "'Burning Pelts': Brown Bear Skins in the Iron Age and Early Medieval (1–1300 AD) Burials in South-Eastern Fennoscandia." *Estonian Journal of Archaeology* 21(1): 3–29.

Lee, Christina. 2007. *Feasting the Dead: Food and Drink in Anglo-Saxon Burial Rituals.* Woodbridge: Boydell Press.

Ludwig, Allan I. 1966. *Graven Images: New England Stonecarving and Its Symbols, 1650–1815.* Middletown: Wesleyan University Press.

Mahoney-Swales, Diana, Richard O'Neill, and Hugh Willmott. 2011. "The Hidden Material Culture of Death: Coffins and Grave Goods in Late 18th and Early 19th Century Sheffield." In *The Archaeology of Post-Medieval Religion*, ed. Chris King and Duncan Sayer, 215–32. Woodbridge: Boydell Press.

Moore, Jerry D. 2004. "The Social Basis of Sacred Spaces in the Prehispanic Andes: Ritual Landscapes of the Dead in Chimú and Inka Societies." *Journal of Archaeological Method and Theory* 11(1): 83–124.

Morris, Rosie. 2011. "Maidens' Garlands: A Funeral Custom of Post-Reformation England." In *The Archaeology of Post-Medieval Religion*, ed. Chris King and Duncan Sayer, 271–82. Woodbridge: Boydell Press.

Murphy, Eileen M. 2008. *Deviant Burial in the Archaeological Record.* Oxford: Oxbow Books.

Olofsson, Camilla. 2010. "Making New Antlers: Depositions of Animal Skulls and Antlers as a Message of Regeneration in South Sami Grave Contexts." *Norwegian Archaeological Review* 43(2): 97–114.

Pearson, Mike Parker. 2000. *The Archaeology of Death and Burial.* College Station: Texas A&M University Press.

Ralph Lewis, Brenda. 2001. *Ritual Sacrifice: Blood and Redemption.* London: Sutton Publishing.

Reynolds, Andrew J. 2009. *Anglo-Saxon Deviant Burial Customs.* Oxford: Oxford University Press.

Rutherford, Sarah. 2009. *The Victorian Cemetery.* New York: Doubleday.

Shay, Talia. 1985. "Differential Treatment of Deviancy at Death as Revealed in Anthropological and Archaeological Material." *Journal of Anthropological Archaeology* 4: 221–41.

———. 1999. *The Spindle and the Spear: A Critical Enquiry into the Construction and Meaning of Gender in the Early Anglo-Saxon Burial Rite.* Oxford: BAR British Series 288.

Soren, David. 2016. "The Children's Cemetery of Lugnano in Teverina, Umbria: Hierarchy, Magic, and Malaria." In *The Archaeology of Childhood*, ed. Güner Coskunsu, 235–50. Albany: State University of New York Press.

Sprague, Roderick. 2005. *Burial Terminology: A Guide for Researchers.* Lanham: AltaMira.

Svanberg, Fredrik. 2003. *Death Rituals in South-east Scandinavia, AD 800–1000.* Stockholm: Almqvist and Wicksell.

Tarlow, Sarah, and Liv Nilsson Stutz, eds. 2013. *The Oxford Handbook of the Archaeology of Death and Burial.* Oxford: Oxford University Press.

Taylor, Timothy. 2002. *The Buried Soul: How Humans Invented Death.* Boston: Beacon Press.

Thompson, Tim, ed. 2015. *The Archaeology of Cremation: Burned Human Remains in Funerary Studies.* Oxford: Oxbow Books.

Tiesler, Vera, and Andrea Cucina, eds. 2007. *New Perspectives on Human Sacrifice and Ritual Body Treatment in Ancient Maya Society*. New York: Springer.

Veit, Richard F., Sherene B. Baugher, and Gerard P. Scharfenberger. 2009. "Historical Archaeology of Religious Sites and Cemeteries." *Historical Archaeology* 43(1): 1–11.

Williams, Howard. 2007. "The Emotive Force of Early Medieval Mortuary Practices." *Archaeological Review from Cambridge* 22(1): 107–23.

———. 2016. "Citations in Stone: The Material World of Hogbacks." *European Journal of Archaeology* 19(3): 497–518.

Willsher, Betty. 1985. *Understanding Scottish Graveyards: An Interpretive Approach*. Edinburgh: Council for British Archaeology Scotland.

Wyse Jackson, P. N., and M. Connolly. 2002. "Fossils as Neolithic Funereal Adornments in County Kerry, South-west Ireland." *Geology Today* 18(4): 139–43.

Yalom, Marilyn. 2008. *The American Resting Place: Four Hundred Years of History through Our Cemeteries and Burial Grounds*. Boston: Houghton Mifflin Company.

Zucchi, Alberta. 1997. "Tombs and Testaments: Mortuary Practices during the Seventeenth to Nineteenth Centuries in the Spanish-Venezuelan Catholic Tradition." *Historical Archaeology* 31(2): 31–42.

RITUAL, RELIGION, AND MAGIC THEORY

Aldenderfer, M. 2011. "Envisioning a Pragmatic Approach to the Archaeology of Religion." *Archaeological Papers of the American Anthropological Association* 21(1): 23–36.

Barrett, Justin L. 1996. "Anthropomorphism, Intentional Agents, and Conceptualizing God." PhD diss., Cornell University.

Berggren, Åsa, and Liv Nilsson Stutz. 2010. "From Spectator to Critic and Participant: New Role for Archaeology in Ritual Studies." *Journal of Social Archaeology* 10: 171–97.

Brown, Linda A., and William H. Walker. 2008. "Prologue: Archaeology, Animism, and Non-Human Agents." *Journal of Archaeological Method and Theory* 15: 297–99.

Brown, P. W. F. 1954. "Comments on Instances of Sympathetic Magic." *Folklore* 65(2): 115.

Brück, J. 1999. "Ritual and Rationality: Some Problems of Interpretation in European Archaeology." *European Journal of Archaeology* 2(3): 313–44.

Buchowski, Michal. 1988. "The Rationality of Magic." *Philosophy of the Social Sciences* 18: 509–18.

Budd, P., and T. Taylor. 1995. "The Faerie Smith Meets the Bronze Industry: Magic versus Science in the Interpretation of Prehistoric Metal-Making." *World Archaeology* 27(1): 133–43.

Burdick, Lewis Dayton. 1901. *Foundation Rites with Some Kindred Ceremonies: A Contribution to the Study of Beliefs, Customs, and Legends Connected with Buildings, Locations, Landmarks, etc., etc.* New York: Abbey Press.

Burton, Dan, and David Grandy. 2004. *Magic, Mystery, and Science: The Occult in Western Civilization*. Bloomington: Indiana University Press.

Chadwick, Adrian M. 2012. "Routine Magic, Mundane Ritual: Towards a Unified Notion of Depositional Practice." *Oxford Journal of Archaeology* 31(3): 283–315.

Chenoweth, John M. 2009. "Social Identity, Material Culture and the Archaeology of Religion." *Journal of Social Archaeology* 9: 319–40.

Cunningham, Graham. 1999. *Religion and Magic: Approaches and Theories*. New York: New York University Press.

Czachesz, István. 2007. "Magic and Mind: Toward a New Cognitive Theory of Magic, with Special Attention to the Canonical and Apocryphal Acts of the Apostles." In *Neues Testament und Magie: Verhältnisbestimmungen*, special issue, *Annali di Storia dell'Esegesi* 24: 295–321.

Davies, Owen. 2012. *Magic: A Very Short Introduction*. Oxford: Oxford University Press.

Dennett, D. C. 1971. "Intentional Systems." *Journal of Philosophy* 68(4): 87–106.

Droogan, Julian. 2013. *Religion, Material Culture and Archaeology*. London: Bloomsbury.

Felson, Richard B., and George Gmelch. 1979. "Uncertainty and the Use of Magic." *Current Anthropology* 20(3): 587–89.

Fennell, Christopher C. 2000. "Conjuring Boundaries: Inferring Past Identities from Religious Artifacts." *International Journal of Historical Archaeology* 4(4): 281–313.

———. 2007. *Crossroads & Cosmologies: Diasporas and Ethnogenesis in the New World*. Gainesville: University Press of Florida.

Fogelin, Lars. 2007. "The Archaeology of Religious Ritual." *Annual Review of Anthropology* 36: 55–71.

———, ed. 2008. *Religion, Archaeology, and the Material World*. Carbondale: Center for Archaeological Investigations, Southern Illinois University.

Garwood, P., D. Jennings, R. Skeates, and J. Toms. 1991. *Sacred and Profane: Proceedings of a Conference on Archaeology, Ritual and Religion*. Oxford: Oxbow Books.

Gazin-Schwartz, Amy. 2001. "Archaeology and Folklore of Material Culture, Ritual, and Everyday Life." *International Journal of Historical Archaeology* 5(4): 263–80.

Gazin-Schwartz, Amy, and Cornelius Holtorf, eds. 1999. *Archaeology and Folklore*. London: Routledge.

Gilchrist, Roberta. 1994. *Gender and Material Culture: The Archaeology of Religious Women*. London: Routledge.

Guthrie, Stewart. 1993. *Faces in the Clouds: A New Theory of Religion*. Oxford: Oxford University Press.

Habbe, P. 2006. "How to Sort Out Ritual from Context of Practice." In *Old Norse Religion in Long-Term Perspectives: Origins, Changes, and Interactions; An International Conference in Lund, Sweden, June 3–7, 2004*, ed. A. Andren, K. Jennbert, and C. Raudvere, 92–94. Nordic Lund: Academic Press.

Halliday, W. R. 1910. "The Force of Initiative in Magical Conflict." *Folklore* 21(2): 147–67.

Hays-Gilpin, Kelley. 2008. "Archaeology and Women's Ritual Business." In *Belief in the Past: Theoretical Approaches to the Archaeology of Religion*, ed. David S. Whitley and Kelley Hays-Gilpin, 247–58. Walnut Creek: Left Coast Press.

Hodder, Ian, ed. 1987. *The Archaeology of Contextual Meanings*. Cambridge: Cambridge University Press.

Houlbrook, Ceri, and Natalie Armitage, eds. 2015. *The Materiality of Magic*. Oxford: Oxbow Books.

Insoll, Timothy. 2001. *Archaeology and World Religion*. London: Routledge.

———. 2004. *Archaeology, Ritual, Religion*. London: Routledge.

———. 2011. *The Oxford Handbook of the Archaeology of Ritual and Religion*. Oxford: Oxford University Press.

Kyriakidis, Evangelos, ed. 2007. *The Archaeology of Ritual*. Los Angeles: Cotsen Institute of Archaeology, University of California.

Manning, M. Chris. 2014. "Magic, Religion, and Ritual in Historical Archaeology." *Historical Archaeology* 48(3): 1–9.

McNiven, Ian J. 2012. "Ritualized Middening Practices." *Journal of Archaeological Method and Theory* 19(4): 1–36.

Merrifield, Ralph. 1988. *The Archaeology of Ritual and Magic*. New York: New Amsterdam Books.

Moyes, Holley, ed. 2013. *Sacred Darkness: A Global Perspective on the Ritual Use of Caves*. Boulder: University Press of Colorado.

Needham, Rodney, ed. 1973. *Right and Left: Essays on Dual Symbolic Classification*. Chicago: University of Chicago Press.

Osborne, R. 2004. "Hoards, Votives, Offerings: The Archaeology of the Dedicated Object." *World Archaeology* 36(1): 1–10.

Price, Neil, ed. 1999. *The Archaeology of Shamanism*. London: Routledge.

Ralph Lewis, Brenda. 2001. *Ritual Sacrifice: Blood and Redemption*. London: Sutton Publishing.

Renfrew, Colin. 1994. "The Archaeology of Religion." In *The Ancient Mind: Elements of Cognitive Archaeology*, ed. Colin Renfrew and Ezra B. W. Zubrow, 47–54. Cambridge: Cambridge University Press.

Renfrew, Colin, and Ezra B. W. Zubrow, eds. 1994. *The Ancient Mind: Elements of Cognitive Archaeology*. Cambridge: Cambridge University Press.

Renfrew, Colin, and Paul Bahn. 2004. *Archaeology: Theory, Method and Practice*. 4th ed. London: Thames and Hudson.

Rodwell, Warwick. 1989. *Church Archaeology*. London: English Heritage.

Rountree, Kathryn, Christine Morris, and Alan A. D. Peatfield, eds. 2013. *Archaeology of Spiritualities*. New York: Springer.

Rozin, P., and C. Nemeroff. 1990. "The Laws of Sympathetic Magic: A Psychological Analysis of Similarity and Contagion." In *Cultural Psychology: Essays on Comparative Human Development*, ed. J. W. Stigler, R. A. Shweder, and G. Herdt, 205–32. Cambridge: Cambridge University Press.

Rozin, P., C. Nemeroff, M. Horowtiz, B. Gordon, and W. Voet. 1995. "The Borders of the Self: Contamination Sensitivity and Potency of the Mouth, Other Apertures and Body Parts." *Journal of Research in Personality* 22(14): 1081–92.

Smith, Alexander T., and Alison Brookes, eds. 2001. *Holy Ground: Theoretical Issues Relating to the Landscape and Material Culture of Ritual Space*. Theoretical Archaeology Group Conference, Cardiff, Wales 1999. Cardiff: BAR International Series 956.

Sørensen, Jesper. 2007. *A Cognitive Theory of Magic*. Lanham: Alta Mira Press.

Steadman, Sharon R. 2009. *The Archaeology of Religion: Cultures and Their Beliefs in Worldwide Context*. Walnut Creek: Left Coast Press.

Subbotsky, Eugene. 2010. *Magic and the Mind: Mechanisms, Functions, and Development of Magical Thinking and Behaviour*. New York: Oxford University Press.

Tambiah, Stanley Jeyaraja. 1990. *Magic, Science, Religion, and the Scope of Rationality*. Cambridge: Cambridge University Press.

Timbers, Frances. 2007. "Liminal Language: Boundaries of Magic and Honor in Early Modern Essex." *Magic, Ritual, and Witchcraft* 2(2): 174–92.

VanPool, Christine S. 2009. "The Signs of the Sacred: Identifying Shamans using Archaeological Evidence." *Journal of Anthropological Archaeology* 28(2): 177–90.

Walker, William H., and Lisa J. Lucero. 2000. "The Depositional History of Ritual and Power." In *Agency in Archaeology*, ed. Marcia-Anne Dobres and John Robb, 130–47. London: Routledge.

Whitehouse, Harvey, and James Laidlaw, eds. 2004. *Ritual and Memory: Toward a Comparative Anthropology of Religion*. Walnut Creek: Altamira Press.

Whitley, David S., and Kelley Hays-Gilpin, eds. 2008. *Belief in the Past: Theoretical Approaches to the Archaeology of Religion*. Walnut Creek: Left Coast Press.

Whitson, Jennifer A., and Adam D. Galinsky. 2008. "Lacking Control Increases Illusory Pattern Perception." *Science* 322(115): 116–17.

Wilburn, Andrew T. 2013. *Materia Magica: The Archaeology of Magic in Roman Egypt, Cyprus, and Spain*. Ann Arbor: University of Michigan Press.

Wile, Ira S. 1934. *Handedness: Right and Left*. Boston: Lothrop, Lee and Shepard Company.

Wilson, Stephen. 2001. *The Magical Universe: Everyday Ritual and Magic in Pre-Modern Europe*. London: Hambledon.

Winkelman, Michael, Kate Ware Ankenbrandt, Agehananda Bharati, Erika Bourguignon, Marlene Dobkin de Rios, Alan Dundes, Jule Eisenbud, Felicitas D. Goodman, C. R. Hallpike, Åke Hultkrantz, I. C. Jarvie, Barbara W. Lex, Joseph K. Long, Leonard W. Moss, Richard J. Preston, Lola Romanucci-Ross, Hans Sebald, Dean Sheils, Philip Singer, and Sheila Womack. 1982. "Magic: A Theoretical Reassessment [and Comments and Replies]." *Current Anthropology* 23(1): 37–66.

Zusne, Leonard, and Warren H. Jones. 1989. *Anomalistic Psychology: A Study of Magical Thinking*. 2nd ed. Hillsdale: Lawrence Erlbaum Associates.

GENERAL SOURCES

Baxter, Jane Eva. 2005. *The Archaeology of Childhood: Children, Gender, and Material Culture*. Walnut Creek: Alta Mira Press.

Briggs, Katharine. 1953. "Some Seventeenth-Century Books of Magic." *Folklore* 64(4): 445–62.

Burne, Charlotte. 1913. *The Handbook of Folklore: Traditional Beliefs, Practices, Customs, Stories and Sayings*. London: Senate.

Calvert, Karin. 1992. *Children in the House: The Material Culture of Early Childhood, 1600–1900*. Boston: Northeastern University Press.

Clodd, Edward. 1921. *Magic in Names and Other Things*. New York: E. P. Dutton and Company.

Davies, Owen. 2009. *Grimoires: A History of Magic Books*. Oxford: Oxford University Press.

Drury, Nevill. 2005. *The Watkins Dictionary of Magic*. London: Watkins Publishing.

Duffy, Eamon. 1992. *The Stripping of the Altars: Traditional Religion in England 1400–1580*. New Haven: Yale University Press.

Gilmore, David D. 2003. *Monsters: Evil Beings, Mythical Beasts, and All Manner of Imaginary Terrors*. Philadelphia: University of Pennsylvania Press.

González-Wippler, Migene. 2003. *The Complete Book of Amulets & Talismans*. St. Paul: Llewellyn Publications.

Hand, Wayland D. 1980. *Magical Medicine: The Folkloric Component of Medicine in the Folk Belief, Custom, and Ritual of the Peoples of Europe and America*. Berkeley: University of California Press.

Hazlitt, W. C. 1905. *Dictionary of Faiths & Folklore: Beliefs, Superstitions and Popular Customs*. London: Senate.

Joyce, Rosemary A. 2008. *Ancient Bodes, Ancient Lives: Sex, Gender, and Archaeology*. New York: Thames and Hudson.

Leach, Edmund. 1976. *Culture and Communication: The Logic by which Symbols Are Connected*. Cambridge: Cambridge University Press.

Lecouteux, Claude. 2005. *The High Magic of Talismans & Amulets: Tradition and Craft*. Rochester, VT: Inner Traditions.

McLaren, Angus. 1984. *Reproductive Rituals*. New York: Methuen & Co.

Morgan, David, ed. 2010. *Religion and Material Culture: The Matter of Belief*. London: Routledge.

Nelson, Felicitas H. 1998. *Talismans & Amulets of the World*. New York: Sterling Publishing.

Paine, Sheila. 2004. *Amulets: Sacred Charms of Power and Protection*. Rochester, VT: Inner Traditions.

Pettegrew, David K., William R. Caraher, and Thomas W. Davis, eds. 2019. *The Oxford Handbook of Early Christian Archaeology*. New York: Oxford University Press.

Puhvel, Martin. 1976. "The Mystery of the Cross-roads." *Folklore* 87(2): 167–77.

Purkiss, Diane. 2003. *At the Bottom of the Garden: A Dark History of Fairies, Hobgoblins, Nymphs, and Other Troublesome Things*. New York: New York University Press.

Rappoport, Angelo S. (1928) 2007. *Superstitions of Sailors*. Mineola: Dover Publications.

Rose, Mark, ed. 2005. *The Archaeology of War*. New York: Hatherleigh Press.

Stein, Rebecca L., and Philip L. Stein. 2005. *The Anthropology of Religion, Magic, and Witchcraft*. Boston: Pearson.

Wileman, Julie. 2005. *Hide and Seek: The Archaeology of Childhood*. Stroud, UK: Tempus.

Wilson, Stephen. 2001. *The Magical Universe: Everyday Ritual and Magic in Pre-Modern Europe*. London: Hambledon.

Index